Families
as Nurturing Systems:
Support Across
the Life Span

The *Prevention in Human Services* series:

Families
as Nurturing Systems:
Support Across
the Life Span

Donald G. Unger
Douglas R. Powell
Editors

The Haworth Press
New York • London

Families as Nurturing Systems: Support Across the Life Span has also been published as *Prevention in Human Services*, Volume 9, Number 1 1990.

The Haworth Press, Inc. 10 Alice Street, Binghamton, NY 13904-1580
EUROSPAN/Haworth, 3 Henrietta Street, London WC2E 8LU England

Library of Congress Cataloging-in-Publication Data

Families as nurturing systems : support across the life span / Donald G. Unger, Douglas R.
  Powell, editors.
      p. cm.
    "Has also been published as Prevention in human services series, volume 9, number 1,
1990" — T.p. verso.
    Includes bibliographical references.
    ISBN 1-56024-078-4 (alk. paper)
    1. Family — United States — Psychological aspects. 2. Problem families — Counseling of —
United States. 3. Life cycle, Human. 4. Social networks — United States. I. Unger, Donald G.
II. Powell, Douglas R.
    [DNLM: 1. Family. 2. Interpersonal Relations. 3. Social Environment. W1 PR497 v. 9,
no. 1 / HQ 728 F1984]
HQ536.F33353   1990
306.85'0973 — dc20
DLC
for Library of Congress   90-5298
                                                                                              CIP

Families as Nurturing Systems: Support Across the Life Span

CONTENTS

FAMILY SUPPORT ACROSS THE LIFE SPAN AND WITHIN DIFFERENT SETTINGS

ABOUT THE EDITORS

Donald G. Unger, PhD, is Assistant Professor in the Department of Individual and Family Studies at the University of Delaware at Newark. Dr. Unger has published articles on social support and resource programs for teen parents, neighborhood support systems, and services for families of children with special needs. He serves on the Board of Directors of the Delaware Children's Trust Fund, and is a member of the American Psychological Association, the National Council on Family Relations, and the Society for Research in Child Development. He co-edited a volume with Marvin B. Sussman entitled *Families in Community Settings: Interdisciplinary Perspectives* (The Haworth Press, 1990), and serves on the editorial board for *Marriage and Family Review*.

Douglas R. Powell, PhD, is Professor in the Department of Child Development and Family Studies at Purdue University, West Lafayette, Indiana. Prior to joining the Purdue faculty, Professor Powell served on the faculties of the Merrill-Palmer Institute and Wayne State University in Detroit, Michigan. While at the Merrill-Palmer Institute, he founded and directed an innovative parent-child educational support program in a low-income neighborhood. Professor Powell has conducted major investigations on relations between families and child care programs, patterns of participation in family resource programs, and the effects of peer discussion groups during the transition to parenthood. He has published extensively in scholarly journals and authored or edited three volumes, including the book *Parent Education as Early Childhood Intervention.* Professor Powell, a founding member of the Board of Directors of the Family Resource Coalition, serves on the editorial boards of six scholarly journals.

Acknowledgements

We thank the authors for their help in making this volume a reality and for their commitment to the welfare of children and families. Thanks to Rob Hess for his interest and enthusiasm in the topic of families and without whose support this volume would never have happened. Appreciation is expressed to Kay Pietras, Ellen Squires, and Valerie Sugg for their help with the final preparation of the volume. We thank our wives, Sharon Jacobs and Barbara Powell, for their nurturance throughout the editing process.

List of Contributors

Richard P. Barth, PhD, Family Welfare Research Group and School of Social Welfare, 120 Haviland Hall, University of California, Berkeley, Berkeley, CA 94720.

Marianne Berry, School of Social Welfare, University of California, Berkeley, Berkeley, CA 94720.

Richard Birkel, PhD, Washington Business Group on Health, 229 1/2 Pennsylvania Ave., S.E., Washington, DC 20003.

Sally Bould, PhD, Department of Sociology, Univeristy of Delaware, Newark, DE 19716.

Moncrieff Cochran, PhD, Department of Human Development and Family Studies, Cornell University, MVR Hall, Ithaca, NY 14853.

Vanella Crawford, MSW, Congress of National Black Churches, 600 New Hampshire Avenue, N.W., Suite 650, Washington, DC 20037-2403.

Stephen F. Duncan, PhD, Department of Family and Child Development, Auburn University, Auburn, AL 36849-5604.

Carl Dunst, PhD, Center for Family Studies, Western Carolina Center, Morganton, NC 28655.

Christoph Heinicke, PhD, Department of Psychiatry and the Biobehavioral Sciences, University of California, Los Angeles, Los Angeles, CA 90024.

Sharon Lynn Kagan, EdD, Bush Center in Child Development and Social Policy, Box 11-A, Yale Station, New Haven, CT 06520-7447.

Robert A. Lewis, PhD, Department of Child Development and Family Studies, and The Family Research Institute, Purdue University, 525 Russell St., West Lafayette, IN 47907.

Deborah Lonow, Department of Residential Life, Fordham University, Bronx, NY 10458.

Harriette McAdoo, PhD, School of Social Work, Howard University, 6th and Howard Place, Washington, DC 20059.

Janet E. O'Keeffe, DrPH, Office of Public Interest Legislation, American Psychological Association, 1200 17th Street, N.W., Washington, DC 20036.

Angela Barron McBride, PhD, RN, Indiana University School of Nursing, 610 Barnhill Drive, Indianapolis, IN 46202; Department of Psychology (Purdue University School of Science at Indianapolis); Department of Psychiatry (Indiana University School of Medicine) and Women's Studies (Indiana University-Purdue University at Indianapolis).

Douglas R. Powell, PhD, Department of Child Development and Family Studies, Purdue University, West Lafayette, IN 47907.

Richard Price, PhD, Department of Psychology and Institute for Social Research, University of Michigan, Ann Arbor, MI 48106.

Eleanor Stokes Szanton, PhD, National Center for Clinical Infant Programs, 2000 14th Street, North, Suite 380, Arlington, VA 22201.

Rebekah B. Thompson, Center for Family Studies, Western Carolina Center, Morganton, NC 28655.

Elizabeth Tracy, PhD, Mandel School of Applied Social Sciences, Case Western Reserve University, 2035 Abington Road, Cleveland, OH 44106.

Carol M. Trivette, MA, Western Carolina Center, Morganton, NC 28655.

Donald G. Unger, PhD, Department of Individual and Family Studies, University of Delaware, Newark, DE 19716.

Bernice Weissbourd, MA, Family Focus, Inc., 2300 Green Bay Road, Evanston, IL 60201.

James K. Whittaker, PhD, School of Social Work, University of Washington, 4101 15th Ave. N.E., Seattle, WA 98195.

Brian Wilcox, PhD, Office of Public Interest Legislation, American Psychological Association, 1200 17th Street, N.W., Washington, DC 20036.

Preface

Tolstoy was probably wrong when he wrote, "Happy families are all alike; every unhappy family is unhappy in its own way." Even if he was right when he wrote that observation in *Anna Karenina*, the formulation is unlikely to hold in our current era. Today strikingly different views of what is good for families are advocated by both ends of the political spectrum. One set of voices glorifies the traditional family and argues for noninterference. On the opposite end of the spectrum, advocates of the welfare state have proposed massive interventions, many of which now are recognized to be insensitive to family and community needs.

Despite cries of deteriorating family structures and clear indications of major changes in family demography and interaction patterns, the family still remains the most potent source of support and nurturance for most people throughout their life span. Unger and Powell recognize this power when they characterize families as nurturing systems. The notion that families serve a nurturing function acknowledges the potent role that families play in human development. And Unger and Powell's recognition of the system character of families emerges both in their recognition of the interdependence of roles and functions of family members within the family itself and the interdependence of the family as a unit within the community environment.

The chapters in this volume recognize an emergent view of the relationship between families and their environment. The new view is neither advocacy for nonintervention (and in some cases neglect) on the one hand, or massive infusions of bureaucratic intervention on the other. On the contrary, most of the authors in this volume advocate a set of approaches collectively described as "family resource programs" that are aimed as much at family self determination as they are of the recognition of the real needs of many families, particularly the poor and the disadvantaged.

It is probably fair to say that the idea of family resource programs represents a general perspective about families and the role that social and material support can play in their lives. It does not seem to be a particular set of policies and programs. Indeed, in her chapter on the family resource movement, Bernice Weissbourd acknowledges that this perspective is better thought of as a social movement. It is a social movement based on the idea that families need to have power to determine what their own needs actually are and how their needs are best met. This theme is echoed by the rest of the chapters in this volume in a variety of different ways. The family resource perspective argues that family self determination is at least as important as efforts aimed at removing or preventing harmful policies or practices. While the goals of family self determination and prevention are probably complementary in most cases, most of the contributors to this volume argue that efforts to promote family self determination should lead the way. Indeed, Dunst argues explicitly that preventive and promotion oriented efforts are quite different in their intent and consequences and that efforts aimed at promotion and support mobilization should be the first priority.

These sentiments are echoed by other authors concerned with specific aspects of family relationships to the larger community. In her chapter Kagan argues that the current "restructuring" movement in the schools provides an opportunity for new forms of family-school collaboration. Szanton strikes a similar chord in advocating changes in the way practitioners relate to parents of small children with special needs. Bould offers us a provocative look at the danger of intrusive intervention with the "oldest old," advocating instead for efforts to create a new interdependence between supporters and older citizens. Still other chapters recognize already existing strengths in our communities and strive to draw on those strengths to enrich family life. McAdoo and Crawford provide an inspiring example in their description of Project Spirit, an example of how the church can be a part of the family support effort in African-American communities.

In addition to contributions already mentioned, several contributions in this volume prescribe new more collaboratively oriented ways for practitioners to work with families, including Heinicke's discussion of the importance of collaborative relationships between interveners and mothers, Whittaker and Tracy's strategies for mapping the networks of families, Barth and Berry's description of strategies for preventing adoption disruption, and Lewis et al.'s discussion of father response to youths leaving and returning home. It appears that a new more collaboratively oriented view of professional work with families is emerging, one that credits the family with its own wisdom about family needs.

Finally, several authors in this volume recognize that we are badly in need of new conceptions of emerging family roles and relationships and how these roles are related to the larger policy environment. Cochran shows us how policies on housing discrimination or post-secondary education may affect the personal social networks and social support of families. Birkel offers a conceptualization of caregiving across the life span, an issue once thought to concern only children but now equally salient for our care of the elderly. McBride documents the burden of multiple roles and the struggle to balance them in various work-family configurations, and finally, Wilcox and O'Keeffe argue convincingly that a family policy is indeed emerging. That policy is *ad hoc*, multiply determined, and emergent. Nevertheless, Wilcox and O'Keeffe's discussion of respite care and family leave policies provide examples of the ways in which neglected needs and new and emergent needs of families are becoming part of the policy debate.

Perhaps the only thing that is certain is that families will continue to be at the center of the scientific and political debate. In its many forms the family represents the institution that embodies and reflects our most cherished values about childhood and parenthood, about caring and giving, and about human connections and well-being. The debate about the balance between the provision of support and the need for self determination will not soon disappear. But, volumes such as this will help to articulate the role that professional and scientific knowledge can play in supporting the many kinds of families that will be part of our future.

Richard H. Price

Families as Nurturing Systems:
An Introduction

Donald G. Unger
Douglas R. Powell

In America today, there is growing recognition of the need to help families carry out their nurturing function. It has been long and widely assumed that family members depend upon each other for support, from the transition to parenthood, throughout child rearing, to providing help to elderly parents. However, the roles, structures, and support systems of families in the United States have changed over time, most abruptly with increased urbanization and industrialization (Keniston, 1977). Many functions such as the education of children previously performed by the family have been assumed by institutions such as the schools. Family life has become more complex as family functions intertwine with other institutions. While the nostalgic view of the family with its extended family members living happily together and solely relying upon each other for support is historically a mythical representation of the family (Hareven, 1989), kin have always been important to each other as sources of nurturance and support (Sussman & Burchinal, 1962; Wellman, 1990). The patterns of support and the ability of family members to care for each other, though, have changed along with the problems which challenge the health and functioning of families.

In recent years, it has become increasingly clear that families cannot fulfill their nurturing role without assistance. Families require environments which support and strengthen their ability to serve as healthy, caregiving systems. The need for support cuts across a wide spectrum of families, including intact or "mainstream" families, nontraditional families such as adoptive families, and families facing special difficulties because of biological, economic, or structural factors. A family's needs for support also change across the family life cycle.

A diverse set of program and policy initiatives has emerged in response to escalating public and private sector interest in helping families strengthen their caregiving capacities. Schools, child care centers, mental health and medical services, and churches have launched family resource and support programs (Kagan, Powell, Weissbourd & Zigler, 1987). Policymakers at local, state and federal levels have shown growing interest in legislative directions aimed at supporting families. To date most program and policy responses have been small-scale, experimental, and/or limited to targeted populations. Nonetheless, a movement toward better understanding and supporting the nurturing functions of families is well underway.

The purpose of this volume is to refine and extend existing knowledge about approaches to supporting the caregiving roles of families across the life span. The contributions offer a description and critical appraisal of new directions in supporting families. The appearance of this volume coincides with an important shift in concerns about the quality of family life. The realization that families need support has led many practitioners, researchers and policymakers to explore difficult questions about how best to bolster the strengths of families. The volume will have served its purpose if it helps inform and shape ongoing and forthcoming journeys in support of families.

CHANGING FAMILIES, CHANGING RESPONSES

Today's families face numerous stressors. Over half of the women with children under age six are working (O'Connell & Bloom, 1987). This poses a tremendous new responsibility on young families to balance jobs, family, and child care (Powell, 1987). More and more children are being reared in single parent households, making issues of child care and family support even more critical (Levitan, Belous, & Gallo, 1988). The highest poverty rates are for single parent households; 51% for those with children under six and 44% for school-age children (Bronfenbrenner, 1986). The incidence of divorce continues at high rates, with one in three children spending a portion of their lives in a single parent household (Teachman, Polonki, & Scanzoni, 1987). The problems of mother-only families are frequently complicated by conditions of poverty and economic instability (Garfinkel & McLanahan, 1986).

Adolescence continues to represent a challenging time for many families. The increased presence of drug usage, high rates of teenage pregnancy, problems of school dropouts and family violence are but a few of the factors affecting today's youth and their families (Schorr, 1988). Black youth are particularly vulnerable. Nearly half live in families that are below the poverty line, with approximately 40% reared in single-mother households (Gibbs, 1988). Youth in families under extreme stress are at risk of entering the child welfare system and experiencing out-of-home placements. Youth who become eligible to be placed in adoptive homes face a long wait for a new family and many difficult adjustments once the adoption occurs (Barth & Berry, 1988; Unger, Deiner, & Wilson, 1988).

Family responsibilities do not stop with child rearing. Young adults are living longer at home and frequently returning to live with their families for brief periods after college. More and more adult children are involved in the care of their parents. With new medical technology, the elderly are living longer and they present new challenges to families (Riley, 1989). The elderly are the fastest growing age group in the United States, especially those 85 years and over. The majority of the elderly do not live in nursing homes but reside in the community. Of the frail elderly who are not in institutions, over 90% depend on support from family and friends (Soldo & Agree, 1988).

Programmatic and policy responses to the "new" family demographics and lifestyles have been inspired by a growing recognition of the family as a microsystem which nurtures its members within a broader context of larger supportive as well as undermining influences. Bronfenbrenner's (1979) ecological approach to development has provided an important framework to guide supportive interventions with families. Members of a family are viewed as nested within larger systems within which they interact and which have indirect influences on the course of human development.

An ecological perspective on development leads to many new avenues of understanding and working with families. Within these systems there are risks, opportunities, and constraints on development which occur at individual and systemic levels (Garbarino, 1982). Supporting families and developing preventive interventions require that the complexity of family life be taken into account. The family is but one system in which family members interact. Work, school, church, agency, and community settings all potentially influence and are shaped by families (Unger & Sussman, 1990). Within these settings are the potential to support or hinder healthy family development.

Programmatic and policy responses also have been influenced by an interest in identifying and building family strengths rather than emphasizing deficits and approaching families as pathological or helpless entities. Increasingly descriptions of programs acknowledge the participant as an active contributor to the substance and structure of program operations. Families are encouraged to serve as collaborators with program staff who recognize the strengths of families and actively expect their contributions. Families are not viewed as if they have "failed" when they have problems because all families in today's society are assumed to need support.

A program from this perspective is not something one "does" to a family. Rather, the program respects the family's strengths and current resources, intervening in a way that supports the family's integrity and fosters a sense of competence to grow and change in healthy, nurturant ways. The family is seen as a partner in the change process. With the elderly and their families, for example, a collaborative empowering process can occur between the elderly, family members, and formal support services in determining the appropriateness and type of supportive intervention with the oldest old (Bould, this volume).

NEW DIRECTIONS IN SUPPORTING FAMILIES

The first section of this volume examines new and emerging directions in the design and implementation of family resource and support programs. Attention is given to the conceptual frameworks that guide program goals and methods, the roles of personal social networks and relationships between family members and professionals in supportive interventions, the need for a life span perspective on family caregiving, and the potential for policies aimed at supporting families.

It is common for programs designed to support families to organize their rationales on the basis of a prevention framework. Typically the goal is to help families before problems develop. Whether a prevention strategy is the most useful or appropriate conceptualization for family resource programs is questioned by Dunst, Trivette and Thompson. They argue that prevention operates from a "weakness" perspective, assuming people are generally vulnerable and need protection from events which will otherwise result in negative outcomes. This guides the choice of preventive objectives and desired outcomes. A distinct alternative intervention strategy is guided by a promotion or empowerment perspective (e.g., Bond, 1982; Rappaport, 1981). In this model, the focus is on enhancing family strengths and capabilities, and providing opportunities for families to develop their competencies and sense of self-efficacy. Preventive interventions are concerned with reducing the incidence or prevalence of negative outcomes. Preventing problems does not assure the strengthening of family functioning. Promotion interventions, on the other hand, focus on competence building and strengthening adaptive functioning. Dunst and his colleagues argue that a promotion approach is more consistent with enhancing a sense of community, protecting family integrity, shared responsibility and collaboration, and strengthening family functioning than a prevention orientation.

Many family preventive interventions have been influenced by the "discovery" of social support and kin helpers (Cobb, 1976; Stack, 1974). Numerous studies have shown how social support can facilitate parenting and child development by reducing the number of stressful events confronting the family as well as by serving as a buffer between the family and the stressor (Crockenberg, 1988; Unger & Wandersman, 1988a; Vondra, 1990). Social support has been cited as a key factor in preventing emotional and behavioral problems (Albee, 1982; Elias & Branden, 1988). To date there has been little theoretical or research guidance on how to promote the development of naturally occurring, supportive social networks (Gottlieb, 1988). Recent advances toward this end have been made by Cochran, whose paper suggests that an empowerment approach to support is a useful perspective in guiding the process of building natural helping networks. Empowerment is viewed as "an intentional, ongoing process centered in the local community, involving mutual respect, critical reflection, caring, and group participation, through which people lacking an equal share of valued resources gain greater access to and control over those resources." He presents a model which describes how the social networks of parents develop and the consequences of these networks. The interface of environmental and individual factors is emphasized. Identifying the constraints and enablers of social networks are key to understanding how to empower families by enhancing their support networks.

Because of the recent growth of family resource and support programs, it is important to assess the status of and challenges facing these community-based initiatives. Weissbourd offers such an assessment in a paper on family resource programs as an innovation in the human services. She notes that these programs have their foundation in parent education, settlement house and self-help movements, social work, and research on Head Start which emphasized the importance of early childhood and the family's influence on development. Weissbourd observes that a shift in perspective in working with families does not come without challenges in implementation. She describes the numerous tasks which lie ahead to ensure the viability of family resource programs, including the creation of stable funding sources and decisions about requisite competencies and training of personnel.

The relationship between program staff and family members is a major component of family-oriented services that warrants thoughtful attention in the design and implementation of programs. Szanton identifies the challenges which families face as they interact with professionals in health and social service settings as a result of the special needs of their young children. The "professional culture" is often inconsistent with the needs of parents. The emotional distancing and diagnostic categorizing, for instance, place a strain on parent-professional relations. Parent-to-parent counseling, political activism, and professional education have been useful strategies to forge partnerships between parents and practitioners.

Birkel suggests that care-giving is a lifespan responsibility which must be understood within the larger context of other interpersonal and family behaviors. Care-giving involves complex issues involving costs to the caregiver which must be weighed against the benefits received by a family member. Further, Birkel shows how individual developmental influences on the caregiver, the life-stage of the caregiver, caregiving as one of several types of interpersonal interaction, and the experience of both caregiver and receiver must all be taken into consideration in understanding how and whether the family can serve the role of "care-giver."

In the last paper in this section, Wilcox and O'Keeffe discuss the importance of family policy as a preventive strategy. Comprehensive family policy has had a difficult and rather unsuccessful history. They suggest that family policies which have a specific focus with relatively modest, concrete goals are much more likely to be successful. The issues of parental leave and respite care which are of vital importance to supporting families are carefully examined by Wilcox and O'Keeffe. Their analysis of family policy issues highlights the many barriers and solutions facing policy advocates.

FAMILY SUPPORT ACROSS THE LIFE SPAN AND WITHIN DIFFERENT SETTINGS

Papers in the second section of this volume examine approaches to supporting families at various stages in the family life cycle and in different settings. The intent is to increase our understanding of the unique and normative issues facing families at different developmental points and as they interact with major institutions and settings.

Heinicke offers a perspective on interventions aimed at families with very young children that identifies the relationship between the parent and intervenor as extremely important to the success of the intervention. Through this relationship, a parent can enhance his or her capacity for having a mutually satisfying relationship and developing effective coping strategies. The parent's partnership capacity and adaptation-competence are viewed as critical influences on family development.

Two major institutional settings that dramatically affect family life — the work place and schools — are examined in this section. McBride highlights the difficulties of combining work and family roles for women. The challenges to women presented by both work and family roles require a complex, systems analysis to address solutions at multiple levels. McBride describes individual and structural change strategies which can help women achieve a balance between these roles.

Kagan and Lonow review how family-school relations have changed over time and outline a continuum of family-school interactions. Family resource programs are described as the newest and most broad based approach to improving family-school relations. While these programs are very exciting, there are many challenges concerning implementation brought about by differing values and organizational structures which remain to be addressed. Kagan and Lonow suggest that for school-based family resource programs to thrive, there needs to be more evaluation research, greater funding, and support from schools and policies.

Efforts to strengthen the interface between informal social support resources and formal intervention programs hold promise of enhancing the efficacy of work with families. Whittaker and Tracy describe strategies which have been developed to assess and enhance social support resources which help prevent out-of-home child placement and maintain positive family changes as a result of family preservation services. Family preservation programs provide intensive in-home services for families at risk of disruption through the unnecessary placement of a child. An equally important goal of Whittaker and Tracy's approach to support is to improve the fit between professionally delivered family preservation services and the client's social network. Individualized, culturally sensitive social network approaches which are consistent with the professional's intervention framework are critical to this process.

The supportive role that churches play in the African American community is described in a paper by McAdoo and Crawford. The rich history of the black church points to its instrumental role in affecting human rights and social services, and its constant source of support and positive influence on mental health. The paper describes project SPIRIT as one example of a comprehensive family support program offered by churches to assist families with after-school child care and other support services.

Changes in family structures bring about new demands on families and their support systems. Three structural challenges to the family as a nurturing system — adopting a child, a young adult child leaving home, and an elderly parent who lives independently yet is interdependent upon family support — are explored in three separate papers.

Barth and Berry describe the special needs of older children who are adopted into a nurturing family system. Many of the older children available for adoption have been abused and neglected, and subsequently developing a new family is often quite problematic. The many strains involved in older adoptions which are experienced by the child and family can be ameliorated through informal and formal supportive services for the family with the goal of preventing disruption.

Lewis and Duncan report an investigation of the stress that fathers experience when their adult children leave home. The fathers' evaluation of the event as disturbing was associated with paternal distress. Lewis and Duncan's findings have significant implications for family life education and for recognizing the needs of fathers in family support intervention.

In regard to the oldest old who live in the community, those elderly aged 85 or older, Bould discusses the importance of adult children providing support without prematurely assuming a caregiving role. For many elderly family members, nurturing as support will have more positive consequences for their emotional well-being compared to nurturing which is expressed by adult children assuming caregiving responsibilities. For many of the oldest old, with a combination of informal and formal support they can maintain an "interdependent" lifestyle. Such a living arrangement involves reciprocal support and self-determination rather than a dependent relationship.

FROM PARADIGMS TO PRACTICE:
FUTURE DIRECTIONS

Since the early 1970s there have been important advances in our understanding of how to strengthen the resources of families for supporting individual growth and development. The papers in this volume contribute to the accumulating research and practice knowledge on approaches to working with families, and point to needed directions in refining the conceptualizations and methods of how to enhance family functioning.

Operationalizing an Ecological Perspective

As noted earlier in this paper, an ecological perspective on individual-family-community-society interactions has provided a framework for much of the recent program development activity focused on strengthening families. While this conceptualization has opened new avenues for the design of family support programs, attempts to operationalize an ecological paradigm have proved to be exceedingly difficult in the design and implementation of programs and institutional practices. Calls for considering the social contexts of individual behavior and development have not been fully realized in policies and programs aimed at families. A cursory review of the diverse range of contemporary programs aimed at families suggests that most initiatives have attended to primarily one segment of an ecological perspective: individual-family relations. Less programmatic attention has been given to family-environment relations or to the interconnections among systems in which families and their members are involved. Moreover, the bidirectionality of individual-family-environment influences largely has been ignored. One-way chains of influence—from program to family and from family to target individual—prevail in the conceptualization and operations of many initiatives. As McBride demonstrates, most policies and interventions have yet to employ a truly systems approach that moves beyond linear models of cause-and-effect to consider the multiple transactions among individual, family, and other societal institutions.

To do so will require dramatic changes in the ethos of professions and institutions serving families (Tyler, Pargament, & Gatz, 1982). Consider family-oriented programs offered by schools (see Kagan & Lonow). The expertise of schools—knowledge dissemination and skill development—provides an extensive technical repertoire for working with families via parent education, especially when focused on strategies for improving a child's academic skills. At the same time, this expertise places content boundaries on the institutional windows through which families are viewed and served. For schools to operationalize a families-in-context paradigm, it is necessary to recognize the limits of the institutional lens and to form cooperative ties with formal and informal institutions involved with families (see also Whittaker, 1983).

The problem is not the uniqueness of technical expertise per se. All institutions bring an ideology and tradition to their work with families. McAdoo and Crawford note the reluctance of the African-American churches to attend to family problems surrounding sex and drugs, for instance. Institutional expertise and ideologies are problematic when they create blinders in relations with families and foster institutional isolation. It is unlikely that any one institution or program can garner the material resources and multiple perspectives required to be responsive to the growing diversity of families and their contexts. The future of fully operationalizing an ecological view in family-oriented programs and practices, then, rests in part with the development of mutually supportive linkages within and across the formal and informal institutions that touch the lives of families.

How these settings and institutions work together *from the family's eye view* warrants careful program design, implementation and evaluation work. Typically the concept of inter-agency cooperation translates into a multidisciplinary team of professionals, each connecting to a different domain of family functioning. Such strategies may be less than optimal if Heinicke is correct that work with high-risk families proceeds from a stable, intensive relationship between intervenor and family.

There are many structural, systemic features of the socio-economic environments of families which make it difficult or possible to mobilize, access, and/or acquire support resources. Cochran, for instance, cogently argues that living in a neighborhood with more resources and a sense of community makes it more likely that a family can acquire support. Social structures which promote opportunities for positive social relations are a necessary but not a sufficient condition for persons to experience support from others and to be a provider of supportive resources (Heller, Price, & Hogg, in press). Interventions on a policy as well as an individual project level are necessary to meet the needs of many families under distress. Education, employment, and training issues must be addressed in order to provide opportunities for the support and empowerment process to work for children and families (Chilman, 1990; Edelman, 1987).

While larger systems influence the success of interventions, serious efforts to implement ecologically-driven interventions also require a recognition of person variables. A critical challenge is to develop and refine program initiatives that recognize the contributions of both person and environment to individual functioning. One of the problems encountered by programs attempting to respond to the ecology of family functioning is that the target individual can get lost in the press to address the myriad of relationships and influences impinging on families (Powell, 1988b; Halpern & Larner, 1988). Heinicke's argument that early intervention programs should foster adaptive-competence in individuals serves to remind us that personal skills and dispositions are important ingredients in the development of supportive social ties and optimal well-being. Yet exclusive focus on skill development is likely to offer a partial solution given that major life circumstances serve to enhance or limit the development of personal social networks (Cochran, this volume).

Advances in the design and fine-tuning of family resource programs require a stronger empirical base than presently exists. Especially needed are investigations that uncover the processes by which supportive interpersonal ties are initiated and sustained, the ways in which naturally-occurring support networks can be stimulated and strengthened, and the mechanisms through which formal and informal support systems can be connected. A number of chapters in this volume offer promising directions for future investigations in these areas.

Context-sensitive research carried out within an intervention program is fraught with methodological and conceptual problems. Prevention and family support programs bring to the researcher a unique set of evaluation issues (cf. Olds, 1988; Halpern & Larner, 1988). There are several field research frameworks available which provide guidelines that are useful for the evaluation of preventive and supportive interventions with families (Jacobs, 1988; Kelly, 1988a; Price, 1985; and Whittaker & Tracy, this volume). What they share in common is that program evaluations must involve a progressive, knowledge building, and collaborative step-wise approach. Such a strategy can lead to an understanding of how a program functions, whether the program format is effective, and what aspects of the program work best for which families in which cultural groups.

Just as the philosophy of family support programs encourages the active involvement of parents and collaboration between parents and staff, Whittaker and Tracy suggest that research on family programs must involve practitioners in all phases of research (see also Zigler & Weiss, 1985). Staff need to feel a sense of control and input into the research. In fact, documenting the "process" of family support programs, a critical need in understanding the effective components of these programs (Powell, 1988a), requires the active collaboration with program staff. Putting such a research philosophy into practice, however, continues to be a major challenge (Florin & Wandersman, in press).

How to define the outcome of family interventions is also a difficult problem and its solution will largely depend upon the theoretical framework guiding the program. As Dunst et al. point out, the outcomes of interest will be quite different depending upon whether the program is "preventing" problems or "empowering" parents. Assessment may need to occur on a child, family, social network, and/or community-wide level. Competencies and strengths which are needed to interact within the environment change at different developmental levels and within different life courses of families (L'Abate, 1990). Programs which work with families over time must be able to develop evaluation approaches which are sensitive to the matching process which frequently occurs between the unique needs of the family and the components which are available in the program (Unger & Wandersman, 1988b).

Intervening with families involves entering a very complex set of systems, each with their own unique processes. If one assumes that a family is one system which is nested within many other systems, there is a clear potential for unexpected side and potentially negative effects (Kelly, 1988b; Lorion, 1983). The limits to the power of an intervention, particularly for specific types of families and those with contextual constraints, need to be carefully addressed in research. Longitudinal models will be required to assess long term expected and unforeseen consequences of family support interventions. Our research knowledge of working with ethnic families is particularly limited and generalizing the effectiveness of interventions for a majority population poses significant uneasiness.

Developing supportive programs for families will require a better understanding of the relation between families and their communities (Goodnow, 1988; Unger & Sussman, 1990). The diversity in family forms and communities makes this a difficult task. Community settings may undermine or support a family intervention. The community's linkages to outside resources and openness to change, along with currently existing support systems are but a few factors which may be critical to the success of a family program (Powell, 1989; Warren, 1980).

Operationalizing an Active Participant Perspective

Collaborative ties between professionals and program participants represent a radically different way of doing business in the helping professions and therefore require innovative, empirically-based program development work. Szanton's identification of the factors influencing partnerships between parents and professionals interested in children with special needs illustrates the typically inherent tensions in the relationship. Szanton's juxtaposition of the standard professional demeanor and parental emotional responses to a disabled child reminds us of disparate world views as well as the power imbalance due to differing levels of expertise. Some of the proposed remedies are orthogonal to the tenets of professionalism, e.g., workshops for professionals conducted by parents, and accommodating parents' perspectives in decisions about intervention plans.

The task here is to generate strategies of tailoring program services to the specific needs and situations of families. Rhetorical nods in this direction long have prevailed. Actual program development work is seriously limited. Contributions to this volume suggest that a promising starting point is at the level of the individual. The research of Lewis and Duncan, for instance, indicates that how fathers define the departure of an offspring is a strong predictor of fathers' responses to the actual departure.

It is a major challenge to tap and build upon *individual cognitions* in the design of programs. Most interventions are organized with *group charac-teristics* in mind. Assumptions and sometimes empirical data about the needs and characteristics of a given population, such as adolescent moth-ers, are the basis of decisions about program format and content. The problem is when individuals vary from the anticipated characteristics of the larger pool of participants, e.g., stereotypic images of a particular ethnic minority group may fail to generalize to all participants in a pro-gram aimed at said minority group. Especially needed are strategies of securing useful information on participant's perspectives. The social net-work map developed by Whittaker and Tracy is a particularly exciting development in this regard. Also needed are mechanisms of fine-tuning program services to the characteristics of individuals within a group-based delivery mode. While there are obvious limits to a group's ability to ac-commodate individual needs, it is not clear that family-based programs have experimented sufficiently with the modest range of individualization that can occur within a group format.

Garnering Program Resources

The lack of an existing, stable funding stream for family resource pro-grams is indicative of the innovative nature of these initiatives as well as the societal value that families are to be protected from government intru-sion and various forms of professional meddling (Wilcox & O'Keeffe). However, growing concern about the quality of life in American families as well as the costs to society when families are unable to provide support-ive environments may soften traditional stances toward the provision of public resources to support families. Advocates of increased societal sup-port walk a tightrope. Extreme caution must be used so family-oriented initiatives are not oversold or underfunded in terms of expected outcomes; at the same time, there is a need to promote the potential benefits of helping families develop and foster competencies. Strengthening the ratio-nale to include *actual* rather than the potential benefits of working with families is the superordinate challenge facing both researchers and practi-tioners. As shown in this volume, significant progress is already being made. Much exciting and difficult work remains to be done in the critically important service of supporting the healthy functioning of children, youth, the elderly and their families.

REFERENCES

Albee, G. W. (1982). Preventing psychopathology and promoting human potential. *American Psychologist, 37*, 1043-1050.
Barth, R. P. & Berry, M. (1988). *Adoption and disruption: Risks, rates and responses.* NY: Aldine.
Bond, L. A. (1982). From prevention to promotion: Optimizing infant development. In L. A. Bond & J. M. Joffe (Eds.), *Facilitating infant and early childhood development* (pp. 5-39). Hanover, NH: University Press of New England.
Bronfenbrenner, U. (1979). *The ecology of human development: Experiments by nature and design.* Cambridge, MA: Harvard University Press.
Bronfenbrenner, U. (1986). The war on poverty: won or lost? America's children in poverty: 1959-1985. *Division of child, youth, and family services newsletter, 9*, 2-3.
Chilman, C. S. (1990). Low-income families and public welfare organizations. In D. G. Unger & M. B. Sussman (Eds.), *Families in community settings: Interdisciplinary settings.* NY: Haworth.
Cobb, S. (1976). Social support as a moderator of life stress. *Psychosomatic Medicine, 38*, 300-314.
Crockenberg, S. B. (1988). Social support and parenting. In H. E. Fitzgerald, B. M. Lester, & M. W. Yogman (Eds.), *Theory and research in behavioral pediatrics, v. 4* (pp. 141-174). NY: Plenum Press.
Edelman, M. W. (1987). *Families in peril.* Cambridge: Harvard University Press.
Elias, M. S. & Branden, L. R. (1988). Primary prevention of behavioral and emotional problems in school-aged populations. *School Psychology Review, 17*, 581-592.
Florin, P. & Wandersman, A. (in press). An introduction to citizen participation, voluntary community organizations and community development: Insights for empowerment through research. *American Journal of Community Psychology.*
Garbarino, J. (1982). *Children and families in the social environment.*
Garfinkel, I. & McLanahan, S. S. (1986). *Single mothers and their children: A new American dilemma.* Washington, D.C.: The Urban Institute Press.
Garfinkel, I. & McLanahan, S. (1986). *Single mothers and their children.* Washington, D.C.: The Urban Press.
Gibbs, J. T. (1988). Young, black males in America: Endangered, embittered, and embattled. In J. T. Gibbs (Eds.) *Young, black, and male in America* (pp. 1-36). Dover, MA: Auburn Publishing.
Goodnow, J. J. (1988). Children, families, and communities: Ways of viewing their relationships to each other. In N. Bolger, A. Caspi, G. Downey, M.

Moorehouse (Eds.). *Persons in context: Developmental processes* (pp. 50-76). Cambridge: Cambridge University Press.

Gottlieb, B. H. (Ed.) (1988). *Marshalling social support*. Beverly Hills: Sage.

Halpern, R. & Larner, M. (1988). The design of family support programs in high risk communities: Lessons from the Child Survival/Fair Start Initiative. In D. R. Powell (Ed.), *Parent education as early childhood intervention* (pp. 181-208). NJ: Ablex.

Hareven, T. K. (1989). Historical changes in children's networks in the family and community. In D. Belle (Ed.), *Children's social networks and social supports* (pp. 15-36). NY: Wiley.

Heller, K., Price, R. H., & Hogg, J. R. (in press). The role of social support in community and clinical intervention. In I. G. Sarason, B. R. Sarason, & F. R. Pierce (Eds.) *Social support: An interactional view*. NY: Wiley.

Jacobs, F. H. (1988). The five-tiered approach to evaluation: Context and implementation. In H. Weiss & F. Jacobs (Eds.), *Evaluating family programs* (pp. 37-68). Hawthorne, N.Y.: Aldine.

Kagan, S. L. & Powell, D. R., Weissbourd, B., & Zigler, E. F. (1987). *America's family support programs: Perspectives and prospects*. New Haven: Yale University Press.

Keniston, K. (1977). *All our children*. NY: Harcourt Brace Jovanovich.

Kelly, J. (1988a). *A guide to conducting prevention research in the community: First Steps*. NY: Haworth.

Kelly, J. (1988b). Side effects. *Prevention in Human Services*, *6*, 141-158.

L'Abate, L. (1990). A theory of competencies X settings interactions. In Unger, D. G. & Sussman, M. B. (Eds.), *Families in community settings: Interdisciplinary perspectives*. NY: Haworth.

Levitan, S. A., Belous, R. S., and Gallo, F. (1988). *What's happening to the American family? Tensions, hopes, realities*. Baltimore, MD: Johns Hopkins University Press.

Lorion, R. P. (1983). Evaluating preventive interventions: Guidelines for the serious social agent. In R. D. Felner, L. A. Jason, J. N. Moritsugu, & S. S. Farber (Eds.), *Preventive psychology* (pp. 251-272). NY: Pergamon.

O'Connell, M. & Bloom, D. E. (1987). Juggling jobs and babies: America's child care challenge. *Population Reference Bureau*, *12*.

Olds, D. (1988). Common design and methodological problems encountered in evaluating family support services: Illustrations from the parental/early infancy project. In H. B. Weiss & F. H. Jacobs (Eds.), *Evaluating family programs* (pp. 239-265). NY: Aldine de Gruyter.

Powell, D. R. (1987). Day care as a family support system. In S. L. Kagan, D. R. Powell, B. Weissbourd, E. F. Zigler (Eds.), *America's family support programs* (pp. 115-132). New Haven: Yale University Press.

Powell, D. R. (1988a). Client characteristics and the design of community-based intervention programs. In A. R. Pence (Ed.), *Ecological research with children and families* (pp. 122-142). NY: Teachers College Press.

Powell, D. R. (1988b). Emerging directions in parent-child intervention. In D. R. Powell (Ed.), *Parent education as early childhood intervention* (pp. 1-22). Norwood, NJ: Ablex.

Powell, D. R. (1989). *Families and early childhood programs*. Washington, D.C.: NAEYC.

Price, R. H. (1985). *A guide to evaluating prevention programs in mental health*. Rockville, MD: NIMH.

Rappaport, J. (1981). In praise of paradox: A social policy of empowerment over prevention. *American Journal of Community Psychology, 9*, 1-25.

Riley, M. W. (1989). The family in an aging society: A matrix of latent relationships. In A. S. Skolnick & F. H. Skolnick (Eds.), *Family in transition* (pp. 521-533). Boston: Scott, Foresman, & Co.

Schorr, L. B. (1988). *Within our reach*. NY: Doubleday.

Soldo, B.J. & Agree, E. M. (1988). America's elderly. *Population Bulletin, 43* (3).

Stack, C. (1974). *All our kin: Strategies for survival in a black community*. NY: Harper & Row.

Sussman, M. B. & Burchinal, L. (1962). Kin family network: Unheralded structure in current conceptualizations of family functioning. *Marriage and Family Living, 24*, 231-240.

Teachman, J. D., Polonki, K. A., & Scanzoni, J. (1987). Demography of the family. In M. B. Sussman & S. K. Steinmetz (Eds.), *Handbook of marriage and the family* (pp. 3-36). NY: Plenum.

Tyler, F. B., Pargament, K. I., & Gatz, M. (1982). The resource collaborator role: A model for interactions involving psychologists. *American Psychologist, 38*, 388-398.

Unger, D. G., Deiner, P., & Wilson, N. (1988). Families who adopt children with special needs. *Children and Youth Services Review, 10*, 317-328.

Unger, D. G. & Sussman, M. B. (1990). A community perspective on families. In D. G. Unger & M. B. Sussman (Eds.), *Families in community settings: Interdisciplinary perspectives*. NY: Haworth.

Unger, D. G. & Wandersman, L. P. (1988a). The relation of family and partner support to the adjustment of adolescent mothers. *Child Development, 59*, 1056-1060.

Unger, D. G. & Wandersman, L. P. (1988b). A support program for adolescent mothers: Predictors of participation. In D. R. Powell (Eds), *Parent education and support programs* (pp. 105-130). NJ: Ablex.

Vondra, J. (1990). The community context of child abuse and neglect. In D. G. Unger & M. B. Sussman (Eds.), *Families in community settings: Interdisciplinary perspectives*. NY: Haworth.

Warren, D. (1980). Support systems in different types of neighborhoods. In J. Garbarino, S. Stocking & Associates (Eds.), *Protecting children from abuse and neglect* (pp. 61-93). San Francisco: Jossey-Bass.

Wellman, B. (1990). The place of kinfolk in personal community networks. In

Unger, D. G. & Sussman, M. B. (Eds.), *Families in community settings: Interdisciplinary settings*. NY: Haworth.

Whittaker, J. K. (1983). Mutual helping in human service practice. In J. K. Whittaker & J. Garbarino (1983). *Social support networks: informal helping in the human services* (pp. 29-67). NY: Aldine.

Zigler, E. & Weiss, H. (1985). Family support systems: an ecological approach to child development. In R. N. Rapoport (Ed.), *Children, youth, and families: the action-research relationship*. Cambridge: Cambridge University Press.

NEW DIRECTIONS FOR FAMILY RESOURCE AND SUPPORT PROGRAMS

Supporting and Strengthening Family Functioning: Toward a Congruence Between Principles and Practice

Carl J. Dunst
Carol M. Trivette
Rebekah B. Thompson

SUMMARY. The thesis of this article is that family resource programs which employ prevention models fail to recognize that the prevention of poor outcomes cannot be equated with the strengthen-

The preparation of this paper and the work reported herein was supported, in part, by grants from the National Institute of Mental Health, Center for Prevention Research (#MH38862); the National Institute of Child Health and Human Development, Mental Retardation and Developmental Disabilities Branch (#HD23038); the U.S. Department of Health and Human Services, Administration on Developmental Disabilities (#90DD0144); and Children's Trust Fund, North Carolina State Board of Education (#C-1912). Appreciation is extended to Carol Nelson and Lauren Starnes for assistance with compilation of the background materials for this article, Deborah Hamby and Barbara Pollock for data analysis, and Pat Condrey and Norma Hunter for assistance in preparation of the manuscript. The authors would like to extend special thanks to Julian Rappaport, Ted Bowman, and Edward Zigler for their comments and criticisms on an earlier draft of this paper.

ing of family functioning. Evidence from divergent but conceptually coherent lines of research is presented which indicates that the absence of problems does not necessarily mean the presence of positive functioning. The use of promotion models which are more consistent with the aims and principles of family resource programs is advanced as a way of bridging the gap between intervention models, family support principles, and family resource program practices.

The emerging interest in family resource programs as the context for supporting and strengthening family functioning represents a significant departure from the ways in which human service practitioners have traditionally rendered services and resources. In contrast to traditional human service practices where interventions are typically provided following the onset of some problem or difficulty, family resource programs are "oriented toward preventing families' and children's problems rather than toward treatment" (Weissbourd & Kagan, 1989, p. 21). Family resource programs are to a large degree based upon the presupposition that the prevention of parent and child problems will result in the strengthening of family functioning. But is this a valid assumption?

The two major theses of this article are as follows: (1) the *absence* of psychological or physical problems does not necessarily mean the *presence* of positive functioning, and (2) the *prevention of problems* by family resource programs does not necessarily guarantee the *strengthening of family functioning*. It is our contention that the use of prevention models for guiding the practices of family resource programs is inconsistent with the aim of strengthening family functioning. We argue that the use of promotion and enhancement models increase the likelihood that people will become more capable and competent as a result of intervention efforts. Evidence to support this contention is aggregated and presented in this article.

The paper is divided into four sections. In the first section we examine the aims of family resource programs and the major principles upon which these programs are based. In the second section we describe the major characteristics and features of treatment, prevention, and promotion models, and describe the limited, problem reduction perspective of both treatment and prevention models, and the expanded, growth-enhancing perspective of promotion models. In the third section we integrate available evidence which indicates that the absence of poor functioning cannot be equated with the presence of positive functioning. This evidence is used to support the two theses presented above. In the last section we conclude by integrating the material on family support principles, human development models, and the empirical evidence regarding the absence-presence of negative and positive aspects of functioning. We argue that there is a greater congruence between the aims of family resource programs and the characteristics of promotion models, than there is between the goals of family resource programs and prevention models. We conclude this final section with a discussion of the implications of the material presented in the article for refining and "fine-tuning" practices in family resource programs.

CHARACTERISTICS
OF FAMILY RESOURCE PROGRAMS

It is generally recognized that the aims and assumptions of family resource programs are different from those of other types of family-oriented service-delivery programs (e.g., Kagan, Powell, Weissbourd, & Zigler, 1987; Zigler & Black, 1989). These differences are derived from a number of distinctive characteristics that make family resource programs unique in both their aims and guiding principles.

Aims of Family Resource Programs

Although there is no single accepted definition delineating the aims and goals of family resource programs, several descriptions can be found which share common elements. According to Kagan and Shelley (1987),

> Family support efforts are directed at reforming existing policies and practices so that major institutions will improve family functioning by their support . . . (and) . . . empower (people) to act for their own good and the good of their immediate community. (p. 8)

Similarly, Zigler and Berman (1983) stated that the aim of family resource programs is "not to provide families with direct services, but to enhance parent empowerment—to enable families to help themselves and their children" (p. 904). Dunst (1989) defined family resource programs as "efforts designed to promote the flow of resources and supports to families in ways that strengthen the functioning and enhance the growth and development of individual family members and the family unit" (p. 1). He also noted that family resource programs conduct interventions in ways that have empowering consequences, and therefore aid families and their members in becoming more capable and competent. Yet another definition has been offered by Weissbourd and Kagan (1989): "family support programs provide services to families that empower and strengthen adults in their roles as parents, nurturers, and providers" (p. 21).

Each of the above definitions as well as others found in the family resource program literature (see Kagan et al., 1987; Powell, 1988; Weiss & Jacobs, 1988a) share a common theme; namely, family resource programs place primary emphasis on the *strengthening* of individual and family functioning. This emphasis is reflected in the careful selection of terms like improve, enhance, promote, nurture, enable, and empower to describe the *processes* and *outcomes* of intervention efforts. Stated differently, the aims of family resource programs are to enable and empower people by enhancing and promoting individual and family capabilities that support and strengthen family functioning.

At first glance, this definition may not seem new or novel. Upon reflection, however, it is quite radical. It suggests a significant change and shift in the ways in which we both conceptualize and operationalize intervention practices (Rappaport, 1981; Seeman, 1989). This shift is reflected to a large degree in the guiding principles of family resource programs.

Family Support Principles

Over a dozen sets of family support principles can now be found in the literature (Center on Human Policy, 1986; Dokecki, 1983; Family Resource Coalition, 1987; Hobbs, Dokecki, Hoover-Dempsey, Moroney, Shayne, & Weeks, 1984; Musick & Weissbourd, 1988; Nelkin, 1987; Roberts, 1988; Shelton, Jeppson, & Johnson, 1987; Smith, 1987; Weiss & Jacobs, 1988b; Weissbourd, 1987; Weissbourd & Kagan, 1989; Zigler, 1986; Zigler & Black, 1989). According to Weissbourd (1987), these principles make family resource programs unique, and distinguish these programs from other human service initiatives. Many of these principles share common features that make clear the presuppositions of efforts to support and strengthen family functioning.

An aggregation and categorization of the different family support principles finds that they can be conveniently organized into six major categories (Dunst, 1989). These include: Enhancing a sense of community, mobilizing resources and supports, shared responsibility and collaboration, protecting family integrity, strengthening family functioning, and human service practices. Table 1 includes examples of principles that fall into each of the six categories.

Enhancing a sense of community. Principles in this category emphasize efforts that "promote the coming together of people around shared values and the pursuit of common cause . . . where people concern themselves with the well-being" of all people and not just those who are most needy

TABLE 1. Examples of Family Support Principles Divided According to Six Major Categories

Category/Principles	Sources[a]
Sense of Community	
Interventions should focus on the building of interdependencies between members of the community and the family unit	2,3,5,8,11,12, 13,15
Interventions should emphasize the common needs and supports of all people and base intervention actions on those commonalities	2,3,4,12,13,14
Resources and Support	
Interventions should focus on building and strengthening informal support networks for families rather than depend solely on professional support systems	1,2,3,4,5,9,11, 12,13,15
Resources and supports should be made available to families in ways that are flexible, individualized, and responsive to the needs of the entire family unit	1,5,6,8,9,10
Shared Responsibility	
Interventions should employ partnerships between parents and professionals as a primary mechanism for supporting and strengthening family functioning	2,4,5,6,10
Resources and support mobilization interactions between families and service providers should be based upon mutual respect and sharing of unbiased information	9,10,14

TABLE 1 (continued)

Category/Principles	Sources[a]
Protecting Family Integrity	
Resources and support should be provided to families in ways that encourage, develop, and maintain healthy, stable relationships among all family members	1,2,4,5
Interventions should be conducted in ways that accept, value, and protect a family's personal and cultural values and beliefs	2,4,8,10,14,15
Strengthening Functioning	
Interventions should build upon family strengths rather than correct weaknesses or deficits as a primary way of supporting and strengthening family functioning	2,3,4,5,8,12,13, 14,15
Resources and supports should be made available to families in ways that maximize the family's control over decision-making power regarding services they receive	1,2,3,4,5,6,9,12
Human Services Practices	
Service-delivery programs should employ prevention/ promotion rather than treatment approaches as the framework for strengthening family functioning	3,5,11,12,13,14, 15
Resource and support mobilization should be consumer-driven rather than service provider-driven or professionally prescribed	1,2,4,5,8,9,11

[a]1=Center on Human Policy (1986), 2=Dokecki (1983), 3=Family Resource Coalition (1987), 4=Hobbs et al. (1984), 5=Musick & Wlessbourd (1988), 6=Nelkin (1987), 8=Roberts (1987), 9=Smith (1987), 10=Shelton et al. (1987), 11=Weiss & Jacobs (1988b), 12=Weissbourd (1987), 13=Weissbourd & Kagan (1989), 14=Zigler (1986), and 15=Zigler & Black (1989).

or hold some special status (Hobbs et al., 1984, p. 46). Weiss and Jacobs (1988b), for example, noted that family resource programs are grass-roots, community-based efforts that are sensitive to the local needs and resources of all people. Similarly, Weissbourd (1987) stated that family resource programs "recognize a need for interaction and support, and understand that the ability to relate to others" (p. 49) enhances interdependencies and mutually beneficial exchanges among community members. Family resource programs recognize that in a strong community there is both reciprocity and mutual support among its members and that family resource programs aim to enhance a *sense of community* that reflect strong, interdependent ties among people (Moroney, 1987). As noted by Zigler (1986), family resource programs are "valuable in fostering communication, exchanging information, and giving individuals a *sense that they are members of a caring unit*" (p. 10, emphasis added).

Mobilizing resources and supports. This category includes principles that describe the bases for creating opportunities for building and mobilizing social support networks in ways that enhance the flow of resources necessary so families have the time, energy, knowledge, and skills to carry out family functions, particularly parenting responsibilities (Hobbs et al., 1984). These principles emphasize the building and strengthening of informal support systems, and the provision of resources and supports in ways that are flexible, individualized, and responsive to the changing needs of families. Scholars and practitioners almost uniformly agree that building and strengthening informal support systems is at the heart of the family resource movement (e.g., Center on Human Policy, 1986; Smith, 1987; Weissbourd, 1987; Zigler & Black, 1989). On the one hand, those who endorse this principle recognize the wealth of resources that already exist within personal social networks. On the other hand, the principle recognizes the fact that mobilizing and utilizing informal support systems as sources of resources decreases the likelihood of dependency on professional and formal human service systems as sources of all or most of a family's resources.

Shared responsibility and collaboration. Principles in this category emphasize the sharing of ideas, knowledge, and skills between families and program staff in ways that encourage partnerships and collaboration, rather than traditional client-professional relationships, as the mechanism for resource mobilization and community building. A call for a breakdown in the traditional role relationships between service providers and community people has been voiced on a number of fronts (Dunst & Paget, in preparation; Rappaport, 1981; Weissbourd & Kagan, 1989). According to Musick and Weissbourd (1988), service providers who "view themselves as partners with parents . . . reduce dependence on professionals and re-emphasize the capability of individuals and the power of peer support, mutual aid, and social networks" (p. 5). The use of mutually agreed upon roles in pursuit of a common goal creates not only the types of collaborative relationships between parents and professionals that are the essence of partnership arrangements, but are also the conditions that will likely have mutually empowering consequences in both partners (Dunst & Paget, in preparation).

Protecting family integrity. This category includes principles that emphasize efforts to protect the integrity of the family unit from (a) intrusion upon the family's personal and cultural values and beliefs by "outsiders," (b) enhancing healthy, stable relationships among family members (Musick & Weissbourd, 1988), and (c) protecting the family and individual family members from abuse and neglect by provision of supports and resources that reduce the likelihood of risk factors functioning as precipitators of maltreatment (Hobbs et al., 1984). Protecting family integrity is seen as one important way of laying the groundwork necessary to alleviate the need for taking remedial measures (Weissbourd & Kagan, 1989).

Strengthening family functioning. Principles in this category emphasize opportunities and experiences that permit the family and its members to become capable of mastering a wide range of developmental tasks and functions. Family support scholars and practitioners universally advocate that family resource programs should identify and build on family strengths rather than correct weaknesses or cure deficiencies (e.g., Family Resource Coalition, 1987; Musick & Weissbourd, 1988; Weissbourd, 1987; Zigler, 1986; Zigler & Black, 1989). This principle attempts to reverse previous human service practices based upon deficit and "cultural difference" approaches to addressing human concerns. Additionally, there is near universal acceptance that primacy be given to promotion and enhancement of family competencies and capabilities as the way to support and strengthen families (Zigler & Berman, 1983; Zigler & Black, 1989). The foci of principles that emphasize the strengthening of family functioning are considered by many the cornerstone of family resource programs. Enabling experiences are seen as the processes and empowerment as the outcome derived from the operationalization of principles that aim to strengthen family functioning (Hobbs et al., 1984; Zigler & Berman, 1983).

Human service practices. This category, somewhat different from the others, includes principles that specify human service models and practices that are most likely to produce outcomes consistent with the aims of family resource programs. By far, most scholars and practitioners have called for the use of prevention rather than treatment models for guiding human service practices (Family Resource Coalition, 1987; Musick & Weissbourd, 1988; Weiss & Jacobs, 1988b; Weissbourd, 1987; Weissbourd & Kagan, 1989; Zigler, 1986; Zigler & Black, 1989). Such models emphasize the prevention of family problems and negative outcomes as opposed to treatment following the onset of pathology or crisis. A prevention approach is viewed as *the* alternative to human service practices where interventions almost always occur following a hardship or difficulty, which only increases the likelihood of a paternalistic solution to the problem (Rappaport, 1981, 1987; Swift, 1984). By intervening before problems manifest themselves, it is argued, the need for professional assistance with many of life's difficulties are eliminated or at least significantly reduced.

There is little doubt that family support principles not only differentiate family resource programs from traditional human service programs, but also suggest new and novel ways of addressing human development concerns and rendering resources to meet family needs. Close inspection of the principles, however, shows some to be contradictory and inconsistent in their assumptions, methods, and outcomes.

The contradiction that is the focus of this paper is the incongruence between the emphasis on the enhancement of the positive aspects of family functioning and adoption of prevention models as the interventive approach for achieving the aims of family resource programs. The implicit assumption that a preventive approach will result in the strengthening of functioning, as we shall see, cannot be supported either conceptually or empirically. It is this evidence that we use as a basis for arguing that promotion rather than prevention models be employed by family resource programs as the framework for guiding interventive actions to strengthen family functioning.

HUMAN SERVICE INTERVENTION MODELS

In this section we describe both the limited, problem reduction perspective of different prevention models as well as the expanded, growth-enhancing perspective of promotion models. We begin by contrasting two systems for classifying human service intervention models — illustrating the pitfalls of one and the strengths of the other — for intervention practices in general and those specific to family resource programs.

The classification system of disease prevention advanced by the Commission on Chronic Illness (1957) — categorizing prevention as either primary or secondary — has been used widely for categorizing interventive efforts based on the onset and timing of preventive actions. Primary prevention refers to actions taken *prior to* the onset of a disease or problem aimed specifically at reducing or eliminating the likelihood of a disorder. Secondary prevention refers to actions taken *after* a disease or problem has been identified but *before* it has caused disability or suffering. Subsequent to the development of this classification scheme, the term tertiary prevention was added and applied widely to describe intervention efforts designed to reduce the negative consequences of a disease and disability *following their onset*. Tertiary prevention is most commonly used to describe actions that are considered treatment in nature.

Discussions abound regarding the utility of a prevention scheme for structuring human service intervention practices (e.g., Cowen, 1980; Lamb & Zusman, 1979). An analysis of the pros and cons of this framework is beyond the scope of this paper. We point out, however, that all three types of prevention, by definition, aim to avert or forestall negative outcomes or their consequences, and again by definition, do not necessarily have anything to do with the enhancement of positive aspects of functioning. Herein lies the potential pitfall of the tripartite classification scheme, and the danger of its use by family resource programs.

About a decade after the tripartite prevention scheme had been developed, Hoke (1968) proposed an alternative framework for categorizing interventive aims and methods that is derived from a completely different orientation and perspective. This framework provides a basis for conceptually and operationally distinguishing between problem oriented and competency enhancement models of intervention. It also provides a framework for empirically testing the validity of the argument that absence of poor functioning does not necessarily mean the presence of positive functioning. According to Hoke, both prevention and treatment models have disease buffering underpinnings, whereas promotion models have health enhancement orientations. He noted:

> (T)he philosophy of promotive medicine goes beyond the goal of protecting people's health and preventing harm or disease. . . . (M)edicine has had two primary orientations: *curing disease and preventing disease*. Actually these are but two aspects of a single orientation — disease orientation. . . . Health and disease have been regarded as polar opposites with health being the absence of disease. . . . Promotive medicine views health . . . as a developmental process involving multi-level responses to a total environment (where)

healthy responses are *life enhancing*. Promotive medicine seeks to promote healthy, positive, adaptive responses. (pp. 269-270)

A similar distinction between treatment, prevention, and promotion models is presented in the Surgeon General's (1979) report *Healthy People*. Others as well have noted the underlying differences between, and implications of, differing models of intervention (e.g., Bond, 1982; Danish & D'Augelli, 1980). This is especially true regarding the differences between prevention and promotion. Klein and Goldston (1977), for example, noted that "Prevention is directed toward reducing the incidence of a highly predictable undesirable consequence. The term should not be used interchangeably with 'promotion of mental health' or 'improving the quality of life'" (p. vii). According to Bond (1982), "(Prevention) presumes that disaster is impending in our lives and that our efforts should be focused upon its diversion. . . . Protecting ourselves from negative influences is, at most, a narrow perspective on the course of growth and well-being" (p. 5). Although there are clear differences between prevention and promotion models, there is controversy over whether these are in fact different approaches to intervention.

The introduction of promotion as a procedurally and methodologically distinct intervention model posed a dilemma for prevention enthusiasts. Proponents of the tripartite prevention scheme were quick to argue that promotion is a special case of primary prevention (e.g., ADAMHA, 1981; Edelman & Mandle, 1986; Jason & Bogat, 1983; L'Abate & Young, 1988) but such a leap of reasoning seems faulty. There is considerable evidence indicating that prevention and promotion approaches differ considerably in their assumptions, presuppositions, and processes so as to make them conceptually and procedurally distinct. Rappaport (1981), for example, argued persuasively that enhancement of competence and a sense of personal control is derived from a set of assumptions and beliefs at variance with the prevention of poor functioning. Similarly, Zautra and Sandler (1983) contrasted and illustrated the differences between intervention models that focus on the prevention of distress compared to models that emphasize optimization of functioning. They noted that adoption of either model would be expected to produce quite different outcomes. Others as well have noted the fundamental differences in the underlying assumptions of promotion and prevention models and their implications for practice (e.g., Bond, 1982; Danish & D'Augelli, 1980; Hoke, 1968; Sanford, 1972; Seeman, 1989).

Three Models of Intervention

Available material indicates the existence of three contrasting models of intervention — treatment, prevention, and promotion — each of which has distinctive characteristics and differential features (Cowen, 1985; Dunst, 1987; Dunst & Trivette, 1987, 1988; Hoke, 1968; Rappaport, 1981, 1987; Rappaport, Swift, & Hess, 1984; Stanley & Maddux, 1986; Zautra & Sandler, 1983). The term intervention is used broadly to mean a planned effort to alter or influence the course of development in an anticipated direction. The unique characteristics of the three models are shown in Table 2, and are described next.

Each of the models defines intervention quite differently. *Treatment* is defined as the management and provision of care (assistance, help, etc.) in order to eliminate or minimize the negative effects of a disorder, problem, or disease. Interventions focus on the remediation or amelioration of an aberration or its consequences. *Prevention* is defined as the deterrence or hindrance of a problem, disorder, or disease. Interventions occur prior to the onset of negative functioning in order to reduce the incidence or prevalence of negative outcomes. *Promotion* is defined as the enhancement and optimization of positive functioning. Interventions focus on the acquisition of competence and capabilities that strengthen functioning and adaptive capacities.

Table 2 also shows the major features of the three intervention models and some of the outcomes that would be expected using each model. The three models are characterized by features that collectively represent the major emphasis and underlying assumptions of the interventive approach. Either implicit or explicit adoption of the differential characteristics would in turn be expected to produce differing outcomes that manifest themselves in the cognitive, behavior, and social-affective domains (Bond, 1982; Seeman, 1989).

Treatment model. The treatment model is perhaps best characterized as *corrective* in its orientation. Primary emphasis is typically placed on the *reduction* of negative effects associated with an identifiable problem or disability. The treatment model is *counteractive* in the sense that interventive actions attempt to overcome or at least neutralize the effects of the presenting disorder or disability. This approach is *deficit-based* since it specifically targets the reduction or elimination of the actual or inferred deficiencies of a person. This would be expected to result in *fragility appraisals* by the "patient" who must be treated for his or her condition or problem. That is, a person receiving treatment would likely see him or herself as handicapped or weakened by the condition even if the disability or its consequences are minimized or subdued. Other types of outcomes one would expect using treatment models include problem reduction, elimination of dysfunctional behaviors, correction of aberrations, and the minimization of complications and deterioration in functioning.

Prevention model. The primary orientation of the prevention model is *protection* against either actual or perceived events that are likely to result in negative reactions or outcomes. Major emphasis is placed on the *deterrence* or forestalling of otherwise negative consequences (Cowen, 1985). This is accomplished by "reducing and/or coping with harmful or otherwise threatening events . . . (using) . . . *defense* as the primary orientation" (Zautra & Sandler, 1983, p. 39, emphasis added). Cowen (1985) characterized interventive actions that assume this stance as *reactive* because they attempt to avert problems and "short-circuit otherwise probably negative psychological effects" (p. 34). This approach is *weakness-based* since it presumes that people are basically vulnerable, and need to be protected or buffered from potentially damaging situations. Preventive actions based upon these characteristics communicate, sometimes implicitly and sometimes explicitly, that life is full of troubles, and life events constitute threats to one's health. Consequently, one would expect to see people make *life-threatening appraisals* in response to interventive actions that are preventive in orientation (Zautra & Sandler, 1983). That is, a person participating in an intervention that takes this orientation will likely come to believe that he or she has a need to protect oneself from potentially or presently unnerving threats. Interventions that aim to deter negative outcomes would be expected to produce results like stress and anxiety circumvention, avoidance of maladaptive functioning, thwarting of distress or disease, and the warding off of other harmful reactions.

Promotion model. In contrast to treatment and prevention models that are both problem-oriented, the promotion model is best characterized as having a *mastery and optimization* orientation. Major emphasis is placed on the development, enhancement, and elaboration of a person's *competencies and capabilities* (Bond, 1982), particularly those that increase a sense of control over important aspects of one's life (Rappaport, 1981). Cowen (1985) called this approach *proactive* because it gives primacy to actions that support and strengthen functioning. Promotion efforts are *strengths-based* because they assume all people have strengths or the capacity to become competent (Rappaport, 1981). Moreover, by building on strengths rather than rectifying deficits, people become more adaptive in not only dealing with difficult life events but in setting growth-oriented goals and achieving personal aspirations. Operationalization of these char-

TABLE 2. The Major Characteristics of Treatment, Prevention and Promotion Models

Characteristics	Treatment
Definition	Management and provision of care following the onset of a disorder, disease, disability, or problem
Intervention Focus	Remediation or amelioration of a disorder or disease or the consequences of associated problems
Differential Features	"Corrective" orientation Reduction of negative effects Counteractive Deficit-based
Examples of Outcomes	"Fragility" appraisals Stress reduction Elimination of dysfunctional behavior Minimization of disability complications

acteristics conveys the message that people, *all* people, have the capacity to better themselves. Therefore, promotive interventions are likely to evoke *self-efficacy appraisals* (Rappaport, 1981; Zautra & Sandler, 1983; Stanley & Maddux, 1986). That is, a person participating in promotion interventions will likely come to believe that he or she has the capacity to master a wide range of developmental tasks and functions if afforded certain opportunities to learn. Other types of outcomes one would expect as a result of promotive interventions include enhanced well-being and health, better adaptive functioning and social competence, and other positive indicators of personal and family growth and development.

The classificatory framework of intervention practices proposed by Hoke (1968) and elaborated upon in this paper represents an alternative to

Prevention	Promotion
Deter, hinder, or forestall the occurrence of problems or negative functioning	Enhance, bring about, and optimize positive growth and functioning
Avoidance or reduction in the prevalence or incidence of negative outcomes	Facilitate competence by enhancing capabilities that strengthen functioning
"Protection" orientation Deter occurrence of negative outcomes Reactive Weakness-based	"Mastery" orientation Develop adaptive capabilities/competencies Proactive Strengths-based
"Life-threatening" appraisals Stress prevention Avoidance of maladaptive functioning Averting disease	"Self-efficacy" appraisals Enhanced psychological well-being Enhancement of adaptive functioning Sense of self-efficacy

the tripartite prevention scheme that has dominated thinking in the human services arena. This alternative framework considers prevention and treatment models more alike than different, and considers promotion and prevention models more different than alike. This contention is similar to positions advanced by Bond (1982), Danish and D'Augelli (1980), Rappaport (1981, 1987), Seeman (1989), and Zautra and Sandler (1983), but is different than that of Cowen (1985) who considered both prevention and promotion approaches alternative pathways to the same outcomes. Corroborative evidence from diverse but conceptually coherent lines of research converges to support our argument that the absence (prevention) of problems cannot be taken to mean the presence (promotion) of positive aspects of functioning. Relevant research studies are examined next.

RELATIONSHIP BETWEEN POSITIVE
AND NEGATIVE ASPECTS OF FUNCTIONING

An implicit assumption underlying preventive interventions is that the absence of problems (negative functioning, stress, etc.) may be taken as evidence for the presence of positive functioning. This position is derived, in part, from yet another assumption in which health is considered a continuous variable with the absence of disease at one end of the continuum and the presence of healthy functioning at the other end of the continuum (see Antonovsky, 1981). This notion of health has been historically associated with Western thought (Seeman, 1989), and is a view that has been implicitly woven into the fabric of both treatment and preventive interventions. This perspective differs considerably from the definition of health formulated by the World Health Organization (WHO, 1964) in which health is not considered merely the absence of disease but the presence of complete physical, mental, and social well-being.

Empirically, if the position that health is a continuous variable is correct, one would expect to find evidence demonstrating strong *interdependencies* (covariation) between the absence of poor functioning and the presence of positive functioning (or vice versa), whereas the position advanced in this paper with regard to the relationship between prevention and promotion models posits *independence* between negative and positive functioning. Investigative interest in the interdependence-independence relationships between psychological phenomena has more than a 100-year history (see e.g., Beebe-Center, 1932). In recent years there has been renewed interest in the relationships between positive and negative aspects of functioning by investigators using instruments and measurement procedures that include specific sets of negative functioning items and specific sets of positive functioning items (Bradburn, 1969; Dunst, Trivette, Jodry, Morrow, & Hamer, 1988; Kammann & Fleet, 1983; Kanner, Coyne, Schaefer, & Lazarus, 1981; Orden & Bradburn, 1968; Reich & Zautra, 1983; Trivette, Dunst, Morrow, Jodry, & Hamer, 1988). Data from such scales allow direct tests of the interdependence-independence hypothesis. The findings from studies that have used these instruments yield corroborative evidence demonstrating that the positive and negative aspects of functioning are much more independent than they are interdependent, and that positive and negative aspects of functioning are differentially related to other aspects of functioning in a predictable manner.

Independence-Interdependence Relationships

The most extensive evidence supporting the independence hypothesis comes from studies of well-being in which measures of both positive and negative affect are obtained from the same individuals and the nature of the relationship between the two types of affect discerned (e.g., Beiser, 1974; Harding, 1982). The results of these investigations were extensively reviewed by Diener (1984) who concluded that the *"absence of negative affect is not the same as the presence of positive affect"* (p. 547, emphasis added). In those studies in which negative and positive affect have been statistically correlated, a shared variance interpretation of the findings also supports the independence position. If the absence of problems is not associated with the presence of positive functioning, one would expect a very small amount of shared variance between the two functioning measures. Examination of the correlations between positive and negative affect show that only about 30% of the variability in one dimension of affect is related to variability in the other dimension (e.g., Brenner, 1975; Kammann, Christie, Irwin, & Dixon, 1979).

In our own research we have obtained positive and negative well-being measures (Bradburn, 1969; Bradburn & Caplovitz, 1965) on quite different samples of parents and prospective parents (pregnant women, parents of preschoolers with handicaps, and parents of young children without developmental delays), and consistently find very little covariation between negative and positive affect.[1] The average amount of shared variance between these two well-being indices in five separate studies is only 7% (range = 3 to 12%), indicating that positive and negative affect are mostly independent aspects of psychological functioning.

Besides well-being, the independence between the negative and positive aspects of functioning has been studied in other behavioral areas as well. Orden and Bradburn (1968), for example, found only 20% shared variance between marital happiness and marital tensions. Similarly, Beiser (1974) found only 2% shared variance between negative affect and pleasurable feelings, and Watson and Pennebaker (1989) found that the absence of health complaints was only minimally related to positive health status. As noted by Rappaport (in press), "in studies of health, when high scores on indicators of wellness may indicate health, low scores do not necessarily indicate illness" and vice versa.

An interesting line of research by Kanner and his colleagues (Kanner et al., 1981; Kanner, Feldman, Weinberger, & Ford, 1987), studying the relationship between daily hassles and daily uplifts, provides evidence that the presence of irritating and frustrating day-to-day demands is only minimally related to their counterparts—uplifts, (i.e., day-to-day experiences that are positive and desirable). In our own research using the Personal Assessment of Life Experiences Scale (Trivette et al., 1988) with expectant mothers, data similar to that obtained by Kanner et al., (1981) on hassles and uplifts were gathered in which judgments were made by respondents regarding whether different life events represented either positive or negative experiences. An analysis of the frequency of occurrence of positive and negative events showed less than 1% shared variance between the two measures. This finding indicated that the absence of negative life experiences did not necessarily mean that a person was experiencing positive life experiences.

Finally, in yet another part of our own research, the relationship between the use of *reactive* and *proactive* coping strategies has been examined using the Personal Assessment of Coping Experiences Scale (Dunst et al., 1988) with a sample of pregnant women. Reactive strategies are ones used in response to difficult or stressful life events, and proactive strategies are ones used to evoke or prolong pleasurable or desirable life experiences. The shared variance between the total number of proactive and reactive coping techniques used by the subjects is only 9%, and the shared variance between the use of a range of different proactive and reactive techniques across different life events is only 14%.

Collectively, available evidence strongly demonstrates that positive and negative aspects of behavior are relatively independent, and that the absence of negative or unpleasant functioning does not mean the presence of positive or pleasurable behaviors.

Differential Relationships in Behavior Functioning

There is also a rich database showing that positive aspects of functioning tend to be related to other aspects of positive but not negative functioning, and that negative aspects of functioning tend to be related to other negative but not positive aspects of functioning (see Diener, 1984). Warr, Barter, and Brownbridge (1983), for example, found positive affect significantly correlated with desirable but not undesirable life events, and found negative affect significantly correlated with undesirable but not desirable life events. Similarly, Kanner et al. (1981) found daily hassles significantly related to negative but not positive affect, and daily uplifts significantly related to positive but not negative affect. In another relevant study, Harding (1982) reported significant correlations between physical and psychological indices of symptomatology and negative affect, but found no relationship between the absence of symptomatology and positive affect.

In our own research examining the differential relationships between positive and negative aspects of functioning, we have found similar results. In a study of pregnant women, for example, we found that use of proactive coping techniques was significantly correlated with positive but not negative affect, and use of reactive coping techniques was more highly correlated with negative compared to positive affect. In addition, we found that negative life experiences were highly related to use of reactive coping strategies but were unrelated to positive coping techniques, and that positive life experiences were highly related to use of proactive coping strategies but were unrelated to negative coping techniques.

Taken together, data regarding the differential relationships between sets of positive and negative functioning measures bolster the contention that absence of problems cannot be considered an index for the presence of positive aspects of functioning.

Independent Contributions of Negative and Positive Functioning

Yet another set of findings provide further evidence that positive and negative aspects of functioning operate relatively independently, and make separate, incremental contributions to the relationship between positive and negative functioning as predictor variables, and other behavioral measures, as dependent variables. In the studies described next, hierarchical multiple regression techniques were used in which negative functioning was entered into the analysis first followed by the positive functioning measure. This strategy provides a way of assessing the extent to which negative aspects of functioning make contributions to the variability in other aspects of functioning. It also provides a way of discerning the contributions that positive aspects of functioning make to enhanced functioning beyond that accounted for by negative behavior functioning.

Kanner et al. (1987), using hassles and uplifts as independent measures and a set of seven adaptational measures as outcomes (e.g., depression, self-worth), found that in nearly every analysis, hassles accounted for a significant amount of variance in the outcomes, and uplifts accounted for additional significant amounts of variance in the outcome measures. In a similar study, Reich and Zautra (1983) used demands and desires as predictor variables and quality of life, positive and negative mood, and symptomatology as outcome measures. They found, for two separate samples of subjects, that demands accounted for significant amounts of variance in all eight sets of analyses, and desires accounted for additional significant amounts of variance in 6 of the 8 analyses.

In several investigations conducted in our own laboratory in which we had positive and negative functioning measures that could be used as independent measures, we conducted the same analyses as performed by Kanner et al. (1987) and Reich and Zautra (1983). In a study of parents of preschool aged children without handicaps, we found that both negative and positive affect made significant, incremental contributions to both anxiety and depression. As we expected, negative affect was associated with higher levels of anxiety and depression, whereas the opposite was true for the relationship between positive affect and the two dependent measures. In a study of pregnant women also conducted in our laboratory, negative affect was associated with less intimacy in personal relationships, whereas positive affect was significantly related to the enhanced intimacy.

In this same study of pregnant women, a particularly compelling set of findings was produced in the regression analyses of the relationship between reactive and proactive coping techniques and five dimensions of social support (frequency of contacts with personal network members, dependability of network members, frequency of use of social support, emotional ties with network members, and satisfaction with support; Dunst & Trivette, 1988). In none of the analyses were reactive coping techniques related to any of the support measures, but in all of the analyses proactive techniques were significantly related to greater levels and amounts of social support.

SUMMARY

In summary, available evidence indicates that the absence of negative functioning or problems cannot be considered a necessary condition for arguing that a person's behavior will reflect positive functioning. Extrapolating from this evidence, a strong case can be made for the argument that the prevention of poor outcomes will not necessarily result in enhancement and strengthening of positive functioning. Certainly, comparative studies of the differential effects of promotion versus prevention interventions would provide a more direct test of the two major tenets presented in the introductory section of this paper. But also certainly, the evidence argues against the position that strengthening of functioning has necessarily taken place when one prevents negative outcomes.

CONCLUSION

In the first section of the paper, we described the major aims and principles of family resource programs. We pointed out that family resource programs aim to support and strengthen functioning in ways that have empowering consequences. We noted, however, an apparent contradiction with the implied relationship between this aim and the call for use of prevention models as the interventive strategy for achieving the goals of such programs.

In the second section of the paper, we described the differences in the assumptions and presupposition of treatment, prevention, and promotion models. In the third section, we reviewed evidence to support the argument that the absence (prevention) of negative outcomes could not be equated with the presence (promotion) of positive aspects of functioning.

When one considers the information presented in the first section of this paper in relationship to the information presented in the second and third sections, one begins to see that there is a greater congruence between the aims of family resource programs and the goals of promotion models than there is between the respective goals of family resource programs and prevention models. Both theoretically and empirically, evidence indicates a need to *rethink* at least some of the assumptions of family resource programs.

There is one major implication from the material presented in this paper. If one aim of family support programs is to support and strengthen family functioning, this is more likely to occur if interventionists adopt promotion models for structuring interventive actions. Our rationale is simple. The evidence points to the differentially produced positive effects that are likely to accrue from use of promotion and enhancement actions.

As the family resource movement continues to grow and break new ground, it is incumbent upon scholars and practitioners to critically examine and scrutinize their efforts to be sure what they believe is congruent with what they do. In this paper we have taken a first step in that direction.

NOTE

1. Throughout this section we present data from our own but yet to be published research analyzed specifically to yield evidence to either support or refute the independence-dependence hypothesis.

REFERENCES

ADAMHA. (1981). *Alcohol, Drug Abuse, and Mental Health Administration prevention policy and programs: 1979-1982.* Rockville, MD: U.S. Department of Health and Human Services.

Antonovsky, A. (1981). *Health, stress, and coping.* San Francisco: Jossey-Bass.

Beebe-Center, J. G. (1932). *The psychology of pleasantness and unpleasantness.* (Reprinted by Russell & Russell, 1965.) New York: New York Public Library.

Beiser, M. (1974). Components and correlates of mental well-being. *Journal of Health and Social Behavior, 15*, 320-327.

Bond, L. (1982). From prevention to promotion: Optimizing infant development. In L. Bond & J. Joffe (Eds.), *Facilitating infant and early childhood development* (pp. 5-39). Hanover, NH: University Press of New England.

Bradburn, N. (1969). *The structure of psychological well-being.* Chicago: Aldine.

Bradburn, N., & Caplovitz, D. (1965). *Reports on happiness.* Chicago: Aldine.

Brenner, B. (1975). Enjoyment as a preventive of depressive affect. *Journal of Community Psychology, 3*, 346-357.

Center on Human Policy. (1986). *A statement in support of families and their children.* Syracuse: Division of Special Education and Rehabilitation, School of Education, Syracuse University.

Commission on Chronic Illness. (1957). *Chronic illness in the United States* (Vol. 1). Cambridge, MA: Harvard University Press.

Cowen, E. (1980) The wooing of primary prevention. *American Journal of Community Psychology, 8*, 258-284.

Cowen, E. L., (1985). Person-centered approaches to primary prevention in mental health: Situation-focused and competence-enhancement. *American Journal of Community Psychology, 13*, 31-48.

Danish, S. J., & D'Augelli, A. R. (1980). Promoting competence and enhancing development through life development intervention. In L. A. Bond & J. C. Rosen (Eds.), *Primary prevention of psychopathology* (Vol. 4). Hanover, NH: University Press of New England.

Diener, E. (1984). Subjective well-being. *Psychological Bulletin, 94*, 542-575.

Dokecki, P. (1983). The place of values in the world of psychology and public policy. *Peabody Journal of Education, 60*(3), 108-125.

Dunst, C. J. (1987). *What is effective helping?* Paper presented at the biennial meeting of the National Clinical Infants Program Conference, Washington, DC.

Dunst, C. J. (1989). *Development and implementation of family support initiatives: A framework for analysis of policies and practice.* Unpublished paper, Center for Family Studies, Social Policy Laboratory, Western Carolina Center, Morganton, NC.

Dunst, C. J., & Paget, K. D. (in preparation). Parent-professional partnership and family empowerment. In M. Fine (Ed.), *Collaborative involvement with parents of exceptional children.*

Dunst, C. J., & Trivette, C. M. (1987). Enabling and empowering families: Conceptual and intervention issues. *School Psychology Review, 16*, 443-456.

Dunst, C. J., & Trivette, C. M. (1988). *Personal Assessment of Social Support Scale.* Unpublished scale, Center for Family Studies, Family Ecology Laboratory, Western Carolina Center, Morganton, NC.

Dunst, C. J., Trivette, C. M., Jodry, W. L., Morrow, J. B., & Hamer, A. W. (1988). *Personal Assessment of Coping Experiences Scale.* Unpublished scale, Center for Family Studies, Family Ecology Laboratory, Western Carolina Center, Morganton, NC.

Edelman, C., & Mandle, C. L. (Eds.). (1986). *Health promotion: Throughout the life span*. St. Louis, MO: C. V. Mosby.

Family Resource Coalition. (1987). *What are the assumptions of the Family Resource Movement?* Chicago: Family Resource Coalition.

Harding, S. D. (1982). Psychological well-being in Great Britain: An evaluation of the Bradburn Affect Balance Scale. *Personality and Individual Differences*, *3*, 167-175.

Hobbs, N., Dokecki, P., Hoover-Dempsey, K., Moroney, R., Shayne, M., & Weeks, K. (1984). *Strengthening families*. San Francisco: Jossey-Bass.

Hoke, B. (1968). Promotive medicine and the phenomenon of health. *Archives of Environmental Health*, *16*, 269-278.

Jason, L., & Bogat, G. A. (1983). Preventive behavioral interventions. In R. Felner, L. Jason, J. Moritsugu, & S. Farber (Eds.), *Preventive psychology* (pp. 128-143). New York: Pergamon Press.

Kagan, S., Powell, D., Weissbourd, B., & Zigler, E. (Eds.). (1987). *America's family support programs*. New Haven: Yale University Press.

Kagan, S. L., & Shelley, A. (1987). The promise and problems of family support programs. In S. L. Kagan, D. R. Powell, B. Weissbourd, & E. F. Zigler (Eds.), *America's family support programs* (pp. 3-18). New Haven, CT: Yale University Press.

Kammann, R., Christie, D., Irwin, R., & Dixon, G. (1979). Properties of an inventory to measure happiness (and psychological health). *New Zealand Psychologist*, *8*, 1-9.

Kammann, R., & Fleet, R. (1983). Affectometer 2: A scale to measure current level of general happiness. *Australian Journal of Psychology*, *35*, 257-265.

Kanner, A., Coyne, J., Schaefer, C., & Lazarus, R. S. (1981). Comparison of two modes of stress measurement: Daily hassles and uplifts versus major life events. *Journal of Behavioral Medicine*, *4*, 1-39.

Kanner, A., Feldman, S., Weinberger, D., & Ford, M. (1987). Uplifts, hassles, and adaptational outcomes in early adolescence. *Journal of Early Adolescence*, *7*, 371-394.

Klein, D. C., & Goldston, S. E. (Eds.). (1977). *Primary prevention: An idea whose time has come* (DHEW Publication No. ADM77-447). Rockville, MD: Alcohol, Drug Abuse, and Mental Health Administration.

L'Abate, L., & Young, L. (1988). *Casebook: Structured enrichment programs for couples and families*. New York: Brunner/Mazel.

Lamb, H. R., & Zusman, J. (1979). Primary prevention in perspective. *American Journal of Psychiatry*, *136*, 12-17.

Moroney, R. M. (1987). Social support systems: Families and social policy. In S. L. Kagan, D. Powell, B. Weissbourd, & E. Zigler (Eds.), *America's family support programs* (pp. 21-37). New Haven, CT: Yale University Press.

Musick, J., & Weissbourd, B. (1988). *Guidelines for establishing family support programs*. Chicago: National Committee for Prevention of Child Abuse.

Nelkin, V. (1987). *Family-centered health care for medically fragile children:*

Principles and practice. Washington, DC: National Center for Networking Community Based Services.

Orden, S., & Bradburn, N. M. (1968). Dimensions of marriage happiness. *American Journal of Sociology*, *73*, 715-731.

Powell, D. (Ed.). (1988). *Parent education as early childhood intervention*. Norwood, NJ: Ablex.

Rappaport, J. (1981). In praise of paradox: A social policy of empowerment over prevention. *American Journal of Community Psychology*, *9*, 1-25.

Rappaport, J. (1987). Terms of empowerment/exemplars of prevention: Toward a theory for community psychology. *American Journal of Community Psychology*, *15*, 121-148.

Rappaport, J. (in press). Research methods and the empowerment social agenda. In P. Tolan, C. Keys, F. Chertok, & L. Jason (Eds.), *Researching community psychology*. Washington, DC: American Psychological Association.

Rappaport, J., Swift, C., & Hess, R. (Eds.). (1984). *Studies in empowerment: Steps toward understanding and action*. New York: Haworth Press.

Reich, J., & Zautra, A. (1983). Demands and desires in daily life: Some influences on well-being. *American Journal of Community Psychology*, *11*, 41-59.

Roberts, R. N. (1988). *Family support in the home*. Washington, DC: Association for the Care of Children's Health.

Sanford, N. (1972). Is the concept of prevention necessary or useful? In S. E. Golamn & C. Eisdorfer (Eds.), *Handbook of community mental health* (pp. 269-278). New York: Appleton-Century-Crofts.

Seeman, J. (1989). Toward a model of positive health. *American Psychologist*, *44*, 1099-1109.

Shelton, T. L., Jeppson, E. S., & Johnson, B. (1987). *Family-centered care for children with special health care needs*. Washington, DC: Association for the Care of Children's Health.

Smith, F. (1987). UCPA "Think Tank" identifies essential, components of family support. *Family Support Bulletin*, *1*(1), 4.

Stanley, M. A., & Maddux, J. E. (1986). Cognitive processes in health enhancement: Investigation of a combined protection motivation and self-efficacy model. *Basic and Applied Social Psychology*, *7*, 101-113.

Surgeon General. (1979). *Healthy people: The Surgeon General's report on health promotion and disease prevention*. Washington, DC: U.S. Department of Health, Education, and Welfare.

Swift, C. (1984). Empowerment: An antidote for folly. In J. Rappaport & R. Hess (Eds.), *Studies in empowerment: Steps toward understanding and action* (pp. XI-XV). New York: Haworth Press.

Trivette, C. M., Dunst, C. J., Morrow, J. B., Jodry, W. L., & Hamer, A. W. (1988). *Personal Assessment of Life Events Scale*. Unpublished scale, Center for Family Studies, Family Ecology Laboratory, Western Carolina Center, Morganton, NC.

Warr, P., Barter, J., & Brownbridge, G. (1983). On the independence of positive and negative affect. *Journal of Personality and Social Psychology, 44*, 644-651.

Watson, D., & Pennebaker, J. W. (1989). Health complaints, stress, and distress: Exploring the central role of negative affectivity. *Psychological Review, 96*, 234-254.

Weiss, H., & Jacobs, F. (Eds.). (1988a). *Evaluating family support programs*. Hawthorne, NY: Aldine de Gruyter.

Weiss, H., & Jacobs, F. (1988b). Introduction: Family support and education programs—Challenges and opportunities. In H. Weiss & F. Jacobs (Eds.), *Evaluating family support programs* (pp. XIX-XXIX). Hawthorne, NJ: Aldine de Gruyter.

Weissbourd, B. (1987). A brief history of family support programs. In S. L. Kagan, D. R. Powell, B. Weissbourd, & E. Zigler (Eds.), *America's family support programs* (pp. 38-56). New Haven, CT: Yale University Press.

Weissbourd, B., & Kagan, S. L. (1989). Family support programs: Catalysts for change. *American Journal of Orthopsychiatry, 59*, 20-31.

World Health Organization. (1964). *Basic documents* (15th ed.). Geneva, Switzerland: WHO.

Zautra, A., & Sandler, I. (1983). Life event needs assessment: Two models for measuring preventable mental health problems. In A. Zautra, K. Bachrach, & R. Hess (Eds.), *Strategies for needs assessment in prevention* (pp. 35-58). New York: Haworth Press.

Zigler, E. (1986). The family resource movement: No longer the country's best kept secret. *Family Resource Coalition, 3*, 9-12.

Zigler, E., & Berman, W. (1983). Discerning the future of early childhood intervention. *American Psychologist, 38*, 894-906.

Zigler, E., & Black, K. B. (1989). America's family support movement: Strengths and limitations. *American Journal of Orthopsychiatry, 59*, 6-19.

Personal Social Networks
as a Focus of Support

Moncrieff Cochran

SUMMARY. This chapter begins with a definition and comparison of the concepts "personal social network" and "social support." Then a model is introduced to articulate what is known about how personal networks are developed. The transition from concepts to practices is accomplished in the chapter through a discussion of networks and the empowerment process. This discussion is followed by examination of an experimental family support program designed with personal networks in mind. The chapter ends with an articulation of links between the healthy network development and public policy.

The traditional approach to the relationship between personal social networks and support has been to focus on the supportive aspects of network ties. This orientation has generated a good deal of interest during the past 15 years, especially among psychologists interested in stress and coping. Far less attention has been paid, however, to a more encompassing and policy-related connection between support and networks. I am referring to consideration of the ways that personal networks can be supported and enhanced by public policies. Both this perspective and the more traditional orientation are brought to bear in this chapter. I begin by defining and comparing the concepts "personal social network" and "social support." Then a model is introduced to articulate what we know about how personal networks are developed. The transition from concepts to practices is accomplished in the chapter through a discussion of networks and the empowerment process. This is followed by examination of an experimental family support program designed with personal networks in mind. I end the chapter by linking what we know about factors stimulating and constraining network development to existing and potential public policies.

WHAT ARE PERSONAL SOCIAL NETWORKS?

Social networks are a specific set of linkages between defined sets of people (Mitchell, 1969). One type of social network of particular interest in the context of this chapter is "personal"; that is, anchored to a specific person or family. In this case our focus is on the personal networks of parents or children, or the whole family. These networks consist of those relatives, neighbors, co-workers, and other friends who are directly linked to a family member, and who may be linked to one another as well.

In an article linking child development with personal social networks, Jane Brassard and I (1979) defined the network of interest to us as consisting of "those people outside the household who engage in activities and exchanges of an affective and/or material nature with the members of the immediate family" (pg. 601). Reaching agreement on definitions is never easy, and this one has been no exception. In our original formulation we specifically excluded spouse and children from the parent's personal network, and siblings from the child's, as long as they lived together with the parent or child anchoring the network. More recently Brenda Bryant (1985), examining sources of support in middle childhood, defined the network as including the family members in the child's household, and explicitly rejected our earlier definition.

From a conceptual standpoint the important distinction here is between the nuclear family and the personal network. Elizabeth Bott (1957), in her classic networks study *Family and Social Networks*, emphasized the distinction in her attempt to show that the definition of roles in a marital relationship is a function in part of the structure of the personal networks that each person brings to the new family. In so doing she carefully distinguished membership in the nuclear family from membership in the networks of husband and wife.

Study of nuclear families has a long tradition in sociology and anthropology, and the sub-discipline of family sociology has become well established during the past half-century. Family historians and others conceive of the family as an emotional entity resting on sentimental ties between husband and wife and parents and children, and as a social unit with economic significance (Hareven, 1984).[1]

The nuclear family is a concept that has meaning in the real world and significance for the development of the individual, separate from the impacts of other kin, associates and friends.[2] I am convinced that spousal and parent-child relations are qualitatively different from those relationships maintained by parents or children with people living outside the household. More recently Brassard (1982) applied the in- versus outside the family distinction in the design of her own study of mother-child interaction and personal social networks, by comparing stress and support in one- and two-parent families and measuring the contributions of the father separately from those of other kin and non-kin. She found that the effects of a supportive father on mother-child relations were quite different from the effects of a supportive network. Her research indicates the value of making a distinction between members of the nuclear family and the rest of the personal network, both in theory and in practice.

WHAT IS SUPPORT?

Another definitional issue central to this chapter involves the distinction between social support and social networks. Most of those using the concept of social support refer to support as information that leads an individual to believe that he or she is cared for and loved, valued, and a member of a network of mutual obligation (Cobb, 1976; Eckenrode and Gore, 1981; Gore, 1980). As noted earlier, the personal social network is defined most generally as a specific set of linkages among a defined set of persons, with the content of those linkages ranging from information of various kinds (where to find work, how to rear your child, which day care arrangement to choose) to emotional and material assistance and access to role models (Cochran and Brassard, 1979; Mitchell, 1969). Thus the social support concept focuses primarily on the psychological state of the receiving individual ("cared for and loved, valued"), while with the personal network the emphasis is both on the characteristics of the "set of linkages" (structure) and on a broader range of types of exchanges between the anchoring individual and members of the network (content).

Researchers interested only in support have tended to map the networks of their respondents with the use of probes which are oriented explicitly to support, like "Please give me the names of all the people who provide you with emotional support." These particular defining characteristics lead to identification of a partial network, excluding all of those people in a person's life who are not thought of primarily in terms of support. Such other people are more likely to be included in response to an orienting question like "Please give me the names of all the people who make a difference to you in one way or another." This more inclusive approach is the one my colleagues and I have adopted (Cochran and Riley, 1988; Riley and Cochran, 1988; Cochran, Larner, Riley, Gunnarsson, and Henderson, 1990).

Both the personal networks and social support concepts are valuable. The distinction between the two concepts is important. This distinction can be underscored, in part, by acknowledging that network relations are stressful as well as supportive and that network members can influence development in ways that extend well beyond those included in the "support" concept.[3] In her study of low-income mothers with young children, Deborah Belle (1982) was interested in the costs as well as the benefits of social ties, and concluded that "one cannot receive support without also risking the costs of rejection, betrayal, burdensome dependence, and vicarious pain" (pg. 143). Barry Wellman (1981) distinguishes the two concepts in a provocative way in this statement of how the social support concept has, in his view, been used to oversimplify the nature of social networks:

> Its focus on a simple "support/nonsupport" dichotomy de-emphasizes the multifaceted, often contradictory nature of social ties. Its assumption that supportive ties form a separate system isolates them from a person's overall network of interpersonal ties. Its assumption that all of these supportive ties are connected to each other in one integrated system goes against empirical reality and creates the dubious expectation that solidary systems are invariably more desirable. Its assumption that there are no conflicts of interest between "supporters" invokes the false premise of a common good. (pg. 173)

Personal social networks are clearly much more than social supports. From a developmental perspective, networks provide both stress and support, and opportunity as well as security.

DEVELOPMENT OF THE PERSONAL NETWORK: A MODEL

What forces and factors influence how personal networks develop? What determines their size and shape, and how do they change over time? These questions are much too complicated to answer in part of a single chapter, but a summarizing model, using parents as the social reference-point, is provided in Figure 1. A detailed presentation of the model and the empirical evidence upon which the framework is based are presented elsewhere (Cochran, Larner, Riley, Gunnarsson, and Henderson, 1990). The model incorporates the forces constraining or shaping network development, the factors stimulating individual initiatives at network-building, the parent's network itself, and reference to the resultant developmental processes and outcomes for both parent and child.

It is very important to project the dynamic qualities of the processes

FIGURE 1
DEVELOPMENT OF THE PERSONAL NETWORK: A MODEL

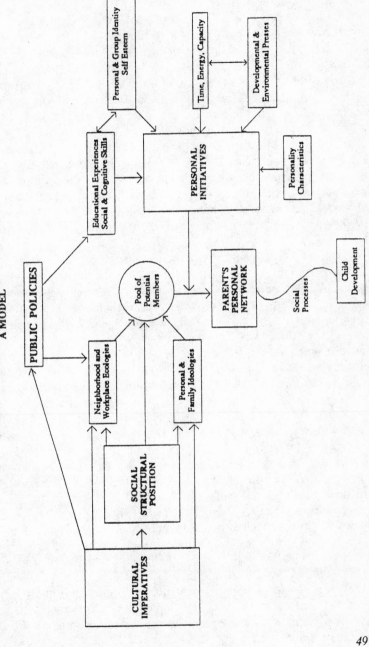

49

driving this model. Most of the potential for network change comes from the forces and factors shown on the right side of the figure; shifts in developmental stage, level of knowledge and skill, and personal identity all affect the amount and direction of social initiatives taken by the parent. Initiatives themselves can take two forms; (a) the selection of network members from the pool of individuals available to the parent, and (b) maintenance activities undertaken within the existing network.

A "pool of eligibles" distinguishes between the people actually available to the parent for inclusion in the network and those selected as members. The pool of eligibles consists of those people to whom the parent has access for *potential* inclusion in the network. Use of this concept permits me to define the constraints on the left side of the model as establishing the boundaries for the size and content of the pool, while at the same time providing the individual parent with a role in building a network from that pool.

A more stable set of factors on the left side of the model plays a large part in determining who is available in the pool of potential network members. Cultural imperatives are the values and beliefs guiding a society. For instance, our cross-national networks research indicates that Swedish and American mothers have networks made up of a much higher proportion of non-relatives than do mothers in Wales and West Germany. We attribute this difference to the greater value placed on women's roles outside the home in Sweden and the United States, and the opportunities for network-building that these additional roles provide these women. Social structural position is defined in a given society by how resources like education, work, and income are allocated according to race, gender, ethnic background and type of family. In general, network size increases with increases in the educational level of parents and in family income (Fischer, 1982; Cochran et al., 1990). Here in the U.S., African-American parents report networks that are smaller than those of their white counterparts with the same amounts of education and income. Again, these differences are primarily found in the non-kin part of the network (Cross, 1990). In many societies status hierarchies based on race, gender and other personal and social characteristics are deeply rooted in the culture and rather rigidly maintained. Our own findings indicate that in the United States the only malleability on the constraints side of this model involves the interrelations among educational attainment, job type and residential neighborhood; for instance, more education can provide access to a job more suited to network-building, and greater income that can permit a move to a neighborhood in which neighboring is more feasible.

In selecting the term "constraints" to characterize the factors included on the left side of the model we have chosen the terminology of Claude Fischer and other sociologists doing network research (Fischer, 1982; Wellman, 1979). To us this term connotes restraint on individual action. While the emphasis here is on the ways in which individuals and families are restrained from establishing social relations that are crucial to their development, we also recognize that many of the constraints by societies placed on individual behavior are constructive. Limits placed on violence against children and spouses, for example, and on the right of parents to relinquish responsibility for financial support of their children are positive constraints.

It is also important to note our use of the word "initiatives," rather than Fischer's (1982) "choices," to characterize the behavioral contribution of the individual parent to the construction of his or her network. We prefer "initiatives" to "choices" because it conveys action without necessarily assuming that alternatives exist. That is, a parent can initiate the act of including or excluding a person available in the "pool of eligibles" without necessarily choosing among alternatives available in the pool.

Our evidence indicates that a substantial number of parents experience severe constraints on free choice because of the structural forces arrayed on the left hand side of the figure. Fischer (1982) says early in *To Dwell Among Friends* that "In general, we each construct our own networks" (pg. 4). Our findings, taken as a whole, indicate (1) that it is inappropriate to generalize across ecological niches, and (2) that the networks of poor and undereducated parents—who make up 20-25% of all parents in the United States—are largely constructed for them by their life circumstances. Our model conveys the power struggle between cultural and social structural forces on the one hand and the individual on the other for control over the content of the personal social network. For any given adult the tilt in the power balance is determined by that person's location in the social structure of the society to which he or she belongs. In the United States an unemployed, poor, Black, single mother has far less potential for control over who is included in her personal network than does a White, married, middle income mother working outside the home.

NETWORKS AND THE EMPOWERMENT PROCESS

Are there community-level interventions that can enhance the supportive aspects of the network resources available to parents and other family members? Personal networks are not themselves interventions, they are naturally occurring social systems established and maintained by individuals — in this case parents — within the constraints imposed by the larger society. The beliefs and "laws" governing establishment and maintenance of network ties are not the same as those directing formal provision of social services by the local community or the state. This means that any intervention by the community aimed at enhancing "natural" network resources must be based on values and norms that are compatible with natural provision of network supports.

What are the rules governing network relations? The "first law" framing relationships might be called the "reciprocity principle." This is the idea that, other factors being equal, there should be a reasonable balance between how much is given and how much is received in a given network relationship. Of course, often other things are not equal. For instance, I might provide more support to my brother than he provides me, simply because he is my brother. Thus, another rule may give special weight to kinship, or common ethnicity, or racial background, maintaining that a certain amount of support will be provided even in the absence of reciprocal behavior. A third "unwritten" rule has to do with what might be called "mutual respect"; the idea that the parent respects each member of her network at some basic level, and that they in turn respect her. This mutuality of respect also operates indirectly, to some extent. That is, when I learn that James is a friend of my brother's, then I may automatically accord him respect, even though we have never met, because of the respect I have for my brother. To the extent that these indirect influences operate within networks, they can be thought of as maintaining a collective consciousness, even though all the members of a person's network probably never come together as a group. If community-level interventions aimed at parents are to be *contrived* to facilitate the growth or enhancement of supportive network ties, then the ideology and practices characterized by that intervention must be compatible with those driving the *natural* establishment and maintenance of personal networks.

Human services in the United States are not designed with special priority given to reciprocity and mutual respect between consumer and provider. In fact, since World War Two, human services in this country have in general become increasingly dominated by the deficit perspective (Cochran and Woolever, 1983; Cochran, 1985; Grubb and Lazerson, 1982). In brief, the deficit perspective is an orientation toward community support for family life based on the idea that the isolated nuclear family must be fully responsible for the support and nurturance of its members. The most basic belief is that each family is a competitor in our free enterprise economic system, and as such should be able to bring in enough money to buy the necessary services in the marketplace. When families are unable to purchase the needed resources, it is they who have failed — they have lost the competition. William Ryan (1971) called this *blaming the victim*; an economic system is created that requires unemployment and a low minimum wage to generate profit, and then blame is assigned to those who cannot support their children for giving in to forces over which they have little or no control.

This combination of beliefs, or assumptions, has led to a "deficit model" of intervention, in which the "client" must *demonstrate inadequacy* before being defined as "eligible" for assistance. In income supplement, food supplement, housing assistance and job training programs participants must prove that their income falls below the poverty line, thereby showing conclusive evidence that they cannot support their family without assistance.

The final irony is that this whole system of beliefs requires that human services be designed to move families toward independence and away from public support or assistance. We require parents and others to become totally dependent, through demonstrated inadequacy, in order to become eligible for services designed to make them independent and self-supporting.

The deficit model of intervention is built not on reciprocity, but on dependence by the powerless on those with the power to grant or withhold basic subsistence resources. Complete lack of respect, based on admission of inadequacy, is fundamental to the deficit model. This ideology is in direct opposition to the values underlying natural network relations. Given the value contradictions in the two systems, it is likely that involvement with traditional human service programs would be more likely to interfere with than to facilitate the development of natural social supports.

The empowerment approach to family support has been developed explicitly as an alternative to the deficit model (Cochran and Woolever, 1983; Rappoport, Swift, and Hess, 1984; Cochran, 1985; The Cornell Empowerment Group, 1989). The Cornell Empowerment Group defines empowerment as "an intentional, ongoing process centered in the local community, involving mutual respect, critical reflection, caring, and group participation, through which people lacking an equal share of valued resources gain greater access to and control over those resources." A few points can be emphasized to underscore the potential in the approach for complementing natural network-building processes. First, the empowerment process is built on an ecological understanding of the environment, which includes personal social networks as one of a number of key environmental systems. Second, mutual respect is considered central to the process, and must be embodied in practices designed on the basis of a key set of beliefs. These include the belief that all people have strengths, that diversity (race, gender, family form, age, sexual preference) is positively valued, that people without power have as much capacity as the powerful to assess their own needs, that relations between groups in the local community should be organized to provide an equal balance of power, and that the people disadvantaged by the way that society is currently structured must play the primary role in developing the strategies by which they gain increased control over valued resources (Cornell Empowerment Group, 1989).

Mutual respect is a commitment to be striven for in the practice of family support, rather than a prerequisite to that practice. A part of the empowerment process is the growth in respect for one another that occurs when people are able to work together under circumstances that provide participants with relatively equal power over the allocation of roles and resources. This process has its parallel in the workings of well-functioning social networks, where each network member has enough resources to be helpful to others, and the reciprocity principle provides members with the opportunity to maintain respect through active contribution to the support of others.

Several other aspects of the empowerment process also have analogues in natural helping networks. This process, if carried forward successfully, must generate increased investment in caring and mutual support among participants in the process, and in the community as a whole. Another essential part of the empowerment process is the positive validation, by others in the group living in similar circumstances, of feelings, ideas and beliefs negatively experienced by the isolated individual.

The empowerment process provides a model for family support that is much more compatible with the facilitation of network supports than is the traditional deficit model. The values and assumptions underlying empowerment as we define it correspond with and complement, rather than compete with, those underlying natural network-building and maintenance. This does not mean, however, that natural network-building processes necessarily contribute to community-wide empowerment processes. For instance, highly intense, exclusionary networks may not contribute at all to development of mutual respect, but rather actively foster discrimination and power inequity (Suttles, 1970). The vulnerability of individuals who depend upon natural helping systems is also heightened because these systems are not usually organized to manipulate the larger social system in order to gain power in the form of access to additional resources.[4]

Three lessons can be drawn from what we know about social networks that can be applied to family and community-level resource programs. First, there is a great deal of evidence to indicate that the "interventions" which most powerfully affect families in positive ways, at least in Western, industrialized societies, are higher education and work outside the home (National Academy of Sciences, 1976). What our own research into natural networks tells us is that their capacity to be supportive is dependent on those very same resources — schooling and jobs that pay decently. As such, education and work have powerful potential for contributing to the empowerment process in a community *because* of the security and opportunity they can lead to through the building of network ties.

A second lesson is that interventions carried out without an understanding of personal and family networks will meet great resistance, even if they are designed *in the interest of* producing greater opportunity for disenfranchised people. This is because they threaten to destroy the security provided by core network ties. Policies designed to provide valued resources through network-building must recognize and validate existing networks in the process of expanding opportunity-related linkages.

A third lesson learned from networks research is that networks are very efficient ways of gathering and communicating information. Networks needn't be thought of as attached to individuals or families, but can instead have groups as their anchor. For instance, a group of parents wishing to find space to house a child care cooperative can carry out a systematic analysis of the people they know outside the group who might have access to space. This strategy uses personal networks to develop resources on behalf of a group that extends beyond family membership. At the same time, such a strategy is built on personal ties, and so must be sensitive to the dangers of upsetting the equilibrium maintaining those ties by making demands without providing reciprocal services.

THE NETWORK IMPACTS
OF A FAMILY SUPPORT PROGRAM:
A CASE STUDY

Is there any evidence that community-level interventions, if properly designed and implemented, can have positive effects on the natural helping networks of parents? In 1979, when several Cornell University colleagues set out through the Family Matters Project to use change in personal networks as one measure for assessing the impacts of a family support program, there were virtually no previous findings to guide the inquiry. We could uncover no reports of explicit attempts to assess the impacts of social interventions on informal social ties. However, there were one or two accidental findings that piqued our interest. Especially striking was the report of an experimental intervention carried out by Robert Hess, Virginia Shipman, and their colleagues, in which the focus was on helping mothers more effectively to stimulate the cognitive capacities of their young children (Hess, Shipman, Brophy, and Bear, 1968). The authors noted in passing that the mothers receiving the intervention were more likely than those in a control group to have become involved in social activities outside the home (clubs, courses, etc.). This finding suggested the possibility of a relationship between increased interest in parenting and involvement with social activities outside the household.

In the decade since we began the Family Matters Project, knowledge about how social interventions might affect and be affected by personal networks has increased surprisingly little, given the burgeoning interest in social supports that has developed during the same period. A significant exception in this regard has been the work of Douglas Powell (Eisenstadt and Powell, 1987; Powell, 1979; Powell, 1987; Powell, 1988). The goal of the Child and Family Neighborhood Program (CFNP) Powell designed was to strengthen family supports through improvement in the ways families used social networks and neighborhood resources in support of their childrearing efforts. Peer participants were seen as potential providers of informal support to parents in the program. The strategy of choice was neighborhood group meetings, supported by home visits and health and social services. Participating families were those in the neighborhood with children six months old or younger.

Powell reports that parents' social networks first came into play during the recruitment phase of the program, and that these impacts were of several different kinds.

> There were instances where mothers routinely and frequently congregated with family and friends. One individual, for example, socialized with her own mother and sisters several times a week. The program, she reported, would be duplicative of these gatherings. It also seemed that significant members of one's social network had an influence on the decision about joining. It was not uncommon to learn that a person's husband or mother did not approve of the program. There were also cases of a mother's relatives (especially her own mother) encouraging program participation but the mother not wanting to join. (Powell, 1988, pg. 130)

Powell and his colleagues also found a relationship between parents' social networks and termination of program participation. Those mothers who terminated involvement early had less extensive social networks than the mothers who stayed with the program longer.

In the course of the Child and Family Neighborhood Program, parents began to develop interpersonal ties at about the same point that they started to become verbally active in the parent group meetings. The rate at which this involvement came about depended on how much stress the mothers were experiencing, with the more stressed parents becoming actively involved more slowly (Eisenstadt and Powell, 1987).

The Nature and Impacts of the Family Matters Intervention

The Family Matters support program that we developed evolved during the same time period as Powell's Child and Family Neighborhood Program, and had a number of features in common with that intervention. The program was sponsored by the larger community, represented by the state land grant university (Cornell) through the county Cooperative Extension Service and as such provides an example of how a formally established, institutionally provided social program can affect the informal relationships maintained by parents. A description of the workings and outcomes of that program is provided here to illustrate the ways that an empowerment-oriented intervention can have a positive impact on natural networks, and in turn affect other aspects of parent and child development.

The Program

The Family Matters program had five major goals, all related broadly to the parenting role. First, we wanted to find ways to recognize parents as experts. Second, we wished to exchange information with family members about children, the neighborhood, community services, schools, and work. A third goal was to reinforce and encourage parent-child activities. The fourth goal was more explicitly network-related, and involved social exchange beyond rather than within the immediate family: the exchange of informal resources such as babysitting, child-rearing advice, and emotional support with neighbors and other friends. Finally, we wished to facilitate concerted action by program participants on behalf of their children, where those parents deemed such action appropriate. A neighborhood-based community development process was envisioned, in which needs assessments carried out by the parents of young children would lead to the identification of issues of common concern and to a change in efforts related to those issues.

The Sample

The program was offered to 160 families, each containing a three-year-old child, in 10 different urban neighborhoods. Two processes were used to involve families in activities related to their children: (a) a home-visiting approach aimed at individual families, and (b) a cluster-building approach aimed at linking together all the Family Matters families in a given neighborhood. Child care was provided at all cluster-group gatherings, and the content of these sessions included socializing as well as group activities aimed at finding solutions to neighborhood problems of common concern (Cochran, 1988a; Cochran, 1988b).

Families were involved with program activities for an average of 24 months, and the program itself came to a close early in the summer prior to first-grade entry for most of the target children included in the study.

A comparison group of 128 families, living in eight other neighborhoods in the same city, was also included in the study. The parents in these families provided baseline and follow-up information about stresses and supports, social networks, parent-child activities, and child performance in school, but did not participate in the family support program.

About 20% of the program and comparison families dropped out of the study during its three year duration, leaving 126 program and 99 comparison families. Twenty-eight percent of these 225 families were African-American, and 35% were headed by a single parent.

Guiding Questions

Two general questions guided our analysis of networks-related impact. First, has participation in the program altered social supports? If the answer to the first question proved to be yes, then are those network changes reflected in parents' attitudes, parent-child activities, or child performance in school? We started by focusing only on the networks themselves, comparing changes in the networks of mothers participating in the program with changes in the networks of the comparison group mothers. Then those changes in the networks over time were examined in relation to mothers' perceptions of themselves, parent-child activities, and child performance in school, to see whether program-related alterations in networks might have contributed to, or been the consequence of, changes in these other arenas.

Network Effects

Our analyses indicate that participation in the family support program did change the networks of parents. But the findings are not that simple. Mothers in some circumstances were affected more than those in others, and those circumstances also influenced the aspects of network structure manifesting change.

Unmarried mothers were especially responsive in network terms to program involvement, and this responsivity was more evident with unmarried Caucasian women than with their African-American counterparts. At the end of the study White, unmarried program mothers reported more nonrelatives in their networks, typically involving borrowing, work-related, and emotional support. Black unmarried mothers who participated in the program also added a significant amount of new nonkin membership to the primary portion of the network, but these increases were almost as likely to involve relatives as nonrelatives. This reflected a more general tendency by Black than by White women to rely upon kinship ties.

Program effects for *married mothers* were much less pervasive than had been the case for single mothers, and what effects could be discerned were confined to relations with kin. White married mothers reported an overall decrease in network size, balanced at the primary level by an increase in kin. These kin were primarily people already present in the network three years earlier, but not defined as especially important at that time. In the case of married Black women there was also an increase at follow-up in the number of relatives reported in the primary network, but most of these kin had not been in the network at all three years before.

Effects on Parents and Children

The impacts of the empowerment program upon children's school performance were heavily mediated by changes occurring within and around their parents. In the case of the *Black one-parent family*, increases in the number of relatives included in the mother's primary support network were associated with reports of more joint activity with the child. Joint activity involving household chores was linked in turn with higher performance in school. Expansion of nonkin membership in the primary networks of those mothers was also linked with their children's school outcomes, especially when those outcomes involved school readiness (personal adjustment, interpersonal relations, relations with the teacher).

With *White single mothers* it was their perceptions of themselves as parents that emerged as a key determinant in whether successful performance was reported for their children in school. More positive parental perceptions were also associated, with expansion of their primary networks and an increase in the activities they reported engaging in with the child. There is evidence that the nonkin sector of the primary network played a positive role in its own right, with increase in nonkin linked to higher school outcomes, again primarily in the area of school readiness.

The pictures for two-parent families proved more ambiguous than those for one-parent families. For *Black married mothers*, increased involvement with kin was related to greater amounts of mother-child activity. However, neither network change nor changes in parent-child activity level could be linked to performance of the child in school, despite the fact that better school performance was positively associated with program involvement. However, one set of possible mediating links did emerge for *White married mothers*, if those mothers had schooling beyond high school. The proposed sequence involved higher perception of self as parent, related to more mother-child activities, and in turn to better performance by the child in school.[5]

Are These Network Changes Necessarily Good?

It is important to ask whether a program of social support like Family Matters makes a positive contribution by speeding the movement of mothers and their families toward patterns of informal social relations that they might otherwise realize more slowly, and perhaps less fully. We have addressed that question by examining links between program-related network increases and other process and outcome variables. The answer can be given more or less definitively, depending upon the subgroup of interest.

The network appears to be a key transmission center for White unmarried mothers, primarily through the nonkin sector, the growth of which is positively associated with perception of self as parent and the child's performance in school. Black unmarried mothers involved in the program also showed substantial growth in the network, with kin linked to increases in parent-child activities and nonkin to improved performance by the child in school.

Less can be said about the impact of expanded primary kin networks for program mothers in the married subgroups, where the only link was with parent-child activities for the African American portion of the sample. On balance, however, there is little in our data to indicate that the expansion of the primary network associated with participation in the Family Matters program had deleterious consequences, and considerable indication of positive contribution, especially for unmarried mothers. A different set of outcome measures might have led to an alternative conclusion, of course, but our data leave us cautiously optimistic about the consequences for mothers and children of facilitating network-building activities.

Networks as Convoy

One of the exciting aspects of social supports as program outcomes is their potential for the development of the individual in the future as well as the present. The *convoy* analogy is appropriate here (House, 1980; Kahn and Antonucci, 1980; Larner, 1990). Such an analogy clearly implies that network-related changes associated with the program might be as strongly linked to subsequent developments in the child as they are to more immediate ones. The findings from the Family Matters Project begin to provide outlines for the forms of transport making up such convoys. One vehicle is likely to be composed of close friends and relatives committed to the welfare of both parent and child. This is the conveyance that has been the central focus of this chapter. Another vehicle is parental self-confidence, which I believe comes in part from the support of key network members, but is also an ingredient needed to stimulate network-building or modification. A third vehicle, and perhaps the one to be heading the convoy, is the parent's level of formal education. As has been pointed out earlier, schooling provides both network-building skills and access to people outside the kinship circle. Contained in the vehicles making up this convoy are the resources essential to sustaining the child throughout the developmental journey: human energy, time, material goods, information, skills, and emotional support.

Some environments are more likely than others to produce and maintain social supports in transaction with parents. Our evaluation of the Family Matters program indicates that affirmative steps can be taken by agencies operating at the community level to activate such informal supports on behalf of healthy family functioning.

Social Networks, Social Support, and Public Policy

There is an unspoken assumption in the United States, and indeed in most industrialized societies, that personal networks are private affairs; that they spring from the privacy of the extended family and from individual friendships, freely sought and built on individual initiative. From a policy perspective the implication of this assumption is that public bodies should not invade our privacy; they should not be involved in determining whether we have friendships, or who those friends are, and have no role to play in relationships among relatives.

At the same time, the public role in education is well established in American society, and that role may increase in the future. In the area of employment, while there has been resistance in the United States to direct creation of jobs by the public sector, certainly there is clear recognition that governments have an indirect role to play in job creation and employment stability.

The network studies we have carried out in the Family Matters Project, taken as a whole, provide compelling evidence for the argument that 40-50% of the support we receive from our personal networks — our ties with nonkin — is strongly affected by how much schooling we have received, the extent and nature of our employment, and the kind of neighborhood in which we live. This means that, to the extent that educational opportunity, employment opportunity and the quality of neighborhood life can be traced to public policies, the quantity and quality of support received from our network membership is affected by those same policies.

The connections between network resources and socioeconomic resources are well established. These links clearly refute the myth, popular in some political circles, that the lack of economic resources experienced by poor people is compensated for by richer and more authentic social relations. In reality the reverse is true; network resources become richer as economic resources increase (Cochran et al., 1990; Riley and Eckenrode, 1986).

Network resources in turn reduce the probability of occurrence of certain mental and physical illnesses (Alcalay, 1983; Antonovsky, 1979; Berkman and Syme, 1979; Cohen and Syme, 1985).[6] Health is generally considered a public issue, because illness is usually costly to society, in productivity terms. If public policies in the areas of education and employment have a significant impact — positive or negative — on the health-sustaining capacities of personal networks, then surely those policies should be encouraged that will enhance rather than retard those capacities.

Our model indicates that many of the policies likely to contribute to the expansion and enrichment of personal networks involve freeing the developing individual from social structural constraints. Policies that increase the availability of post secondary education would appear to deserve highest priority, because those parents who had acquired such schooling were much richer in network resources than those who had not. College scholarships, student loans and programs providing incentives to adolescents and young adults for continuation of schooling through high school and beyond would seem to be an especially good investment to society from this standpoint.

Policies that stimulate job creation and continuation would also deserve high priority from a "networks in context" perspective. The workplace has been seen in our studies to be an important context for network-building, and the economic returns associated with working provide the resources needed to sustain network relations.

The neighborhood represents another point of public policy access to personal networks, especially through assistance in home ownership, but also through basic safety and maintenance efforts like lighting, street repairs and active police and fire services. At least as important, particularly to African-Americans and other minority groups, are government policies that reduce or eliminate discrimination in the sale of private housing. The impact of public policies that encourage families to invest in their neighborhoods of residence is to increase the probability that neighboring will in fact take place, and that through such neighboring, adults will be healthier and children will be reared with greater sensitivity.

In discussing networks and public policies I have concentrated so far on the constraint side of our model, because the greatest pay-off would seem to come from loosening the restrictions experienced by the disadvantaged individuals and families in our society. Does this mean that the individual network-building initiatives of developing human beings are unaffected by public policies? Our findings suggest otherwise. Higher education seems to have such a powerful effect on networks because it contributes to individual initiative *as well as* to the reduction of constraints on access to potential network members. Thus when young people are able, because of public programs, to continue their education, their social skills and their perceptions of themselves change in ways that are likely to stimulate the building and maintenance of network ties.

The self-esteem needed to take social risks in the building of network ties may be enhanced indirectly, through educational achievement. Evidence from our Family Matters support program indicates that it can also be increased directly, by helping parents appreciate the important contributions they make to community and society through their childrearing efforts. Those of us now working with the empowerment approach to family support are convinced that any agency or organization in direct contact with parents can operate in ways that increase parental self esteem, and through that process increase the potential in those parents for network-building and maintenance. Workplaces, schools, social service agencies, health facilities and other institutions are all in a position to implement policies that contribute to an empowerment process which includes as one aspect the strengthening of personal networks.

The most important lesson to be learned for policy from our research is that—if parents are to be supported on behalf of their own development and that of their children—it is not nearly enough simply to make them more willing to help themselves, and convinced that social ties are important. Public policies must give first priority to freeing parents, and those who will become parents, from the constraints of inequality and oppression, by insuring the provision of adequate and sufficient education, employment and humane housing conditions. Our findings suggest that freedom to grow, through schooling, work, and leisure activities, will lead in turn to the social network connections that form the basis of healthy, productive communities.

NOTES

1. See also the chapter by G. Elder in the same volume (Review of Child Development Research, Vol. 7, *The Family*). Within the body of literature addressing family dynamics and structure, Douglas Poweli (1979) is one of very few developmentally oriented social scientists who has distinguished between the nuclear family and the personal social network in an overall system of family-environment relations.

2. I recognize that the distinction between nuclear and extended families may not be valid beyond societies in North America and Europe.

3. Perhaps the most powerful articulation of network influences that are distinct from social support can be found in Granovetter's article "The strengths of weak ties." (1973)

4. My thinking about the disadvantages of relying on natural helping systems has benefited from discussions with Dr. Josephine Allen.

5. For more elaborated presentations of the Family Matters program and its effects on parents and children, see Cochran, 1985, 1988a, 1988b.

6. This is especially true for people with high and middle socioeconomic status (Turner and Noh, 1981; Sandler and Lakey, 1982).

REFERENCES

Alcalay, R. (1983). Health and social support networks: a case for improving interpersonal communication. *Social Networks*, 5, 71-88.

Antonovsky, A. (1979). *Health, Stress and Coping* San Fransisco: Jossey Bass.

Belle, D. (1982). Social ties and social support. Chapter 10 in D. Belle (Ed.) *Lives in Stress: Women and Depression*. Beverly Hills, Calif.: Sage Publications.

Berkman, L. and Syme, S. (1979). Social networks, host resistance and mortality; a nine year follow-up study of Alameda County residents. *Am. J. of Epidemiology*, 109(2), 196-204.

Bott, E. (1957). *Family and social networks*. London: Havistock.

Brassard, J. (1982). *Beyond family structure: mother-child interaction and personal social networks*. Unpublished doctoral dissertation, Cornell University, Ithaca, N.Y.

Bryant, B. (1985). The neighborhood walk: sources of support in middle childhood. *Monographs of the Society for Research in Child Development*, Serial No. 210, *50*, No. 3.

Cobb, S. (1976). Social support as a moderator of life stress. *Psychosomatic Medicine*, *38*, 300-314.

Cochran, M. (1985). The parental empowerment process: Building upon family strengths. In John Harris (Ed.) *Child psychology in action: Linking research and practice*. London: Croom Helm. Reprinted in *Equity and Choice, 4, #1*, Fall, 1987.

Cochran, M. (1988a). Parental empowerment in Family Matters: lessons learned from a research program. In D. Powell (Ed.) *Parent education as early childhood intervention: Emerging directions in theory, research, and practice*. New York: Ablex.

Cochran, M. (1988b). Between cause and effect: the ecology of program impacts. In A. Pence (Ed.) *Ecological research with children and families*. New York: Teacher's College Press.

Cochran, M.& Brassard, J. (1979). Child development and personal social networks, *Child Development*, *50*, 601-616.

Cochran, M., Larner, M., Riley, D., Gunnarsson, L. and Henderson, C., Jr. (1990) *Extending Families: the Social Networks of Parents and their Children*. Cambridge, Eng./New York: Cambridge University Press.

Cochran, M. & Riley, R.(1988). Mother reports of children's personal networks: Antecedents, concomitants and consequences. In S. Salzinger, J. Antrobus & M. Hammer (Eds.) *Social networks of children, adolescents, and college students*. Hillsdale, N.J.: Lawrence Erlbaum.

Cochran, M.& Woolever, F.(1983). Beyond the deficit model: The empowerment of parents with information and informal supports. In I.Siegel and L. Laosa (Eds.), *Changing Families*, New York: Plenum Publishing, pp.225-246.

Cohen, S. and Syme, S. (Eds.) (1985). *Social support and health*. Orlando, Fla.: Academic Press.

Cornell Empowerment Group. (1989). *Empowerment and family support*. Department of Human Development and Family Studies, Cornell University, unpublished manuscript.

Cross, W. (1990). Social networks, race, and ethnicity. Chapter 5 in: M. Cochran, M. Larner, D. Riley, L. Gunnarsson, and C. Henderson, Jr. (1990) *Extending Families: the Social Networks of Parents and their Children*. Cambridge, Eng./New York: Cambridge University Press.

Eckenrode, J. and Gore, S. (1981). Stressful events and social support: The significance of context. In B. Gottlieb (Ed.), *Social networks and social support*. Beverly Hills: Sage Publications.

Eisenstadt, J. and Powell, D. (1987). Processes of participation in a mother-infant program as modified by stress and impulse control. *J. of Applied Developmental Psychology*, *8*, 17-37.

Elder, G. (1984). Families, kin, and the life course: a sociological perspective. In R.D.Parke (ed.) *Review of Child Development Research. Vol. 7* Chicago: University of Chicago Press.

Fischer, C. (1982). *To Dwell among Friends: Personal Networks in Town and City*. Chicago: University of Chicago Press.

Gore, S. (1980). Stress-buffering functions of social supports: an appraisal and clarification of research models. In B.S. Dohrenwend and B.P. Dohrenwend (Eds.) *Life Stress and Illness*. New York: Neal Watson.

Granovetter, M. (1973). The strength of weak ties. *Am. J. of Sociology*, *78*, (May), 1360-80.

Grubb, W. & Lazerson, M. (1982). *Broken Promises.* New York: Basic Books.

Hareven, T. (1984). Themes in the historical development of the family. In R.D. Parke (Ed.) *Review of Child Development Research. Vol. 7* Chicago: University of Chicago Press.

Hess, R., Shipman, V., Brophy, J., and Bear, R. (1968). *The cognitive environments of urban preschool children*. Graduate School of Education, University of Chicago, unpublished.

House, J. (1980). *Work, stress, and social support*. Reading, Mass: Addison-Wesley.

Kahn, R. and Antonucci, T. (1980). Convoys over the life course: Attachment, roles, and social support. In P. Baltes and O. Brim (Eds.), *Life-span development and behavior, Vol. 3*. New York: Academic Press.

Larner, M. (1990). Changes in network resources and relationships over time. Chapter 11 in: M. Cochran, M. Larner, D. Riley, L. Gunnarsson, and C. Henderson, Jr. (1990). *Extending Families: the Social Networks of Parents and their Children*. Cambridge, Eng./New York: Cambridge University Press.

National Academy of Sciences. (1976). *Toward a National Policy for Children and Families*. Washington, D.C.: National Academy of Sciences Printing Office.

Powell, D. (1979). Family environment relations and early childrearing: The role of social networks and neighborhood. *J. of Research and Development in Education*, *13*, 1-11.

Powell, D. (1987). A neighborhood approach to parent support groups. *J. of Community Psychology*, *15*, 51-62.

Powell, D. (1988). Client characteristics and the design of community-based intervention programs. In A. Pence (Ed.) *Ecological Research with Children and Families*. New York: Teachers College Press.

Mitchell, J.C. (1969). The concept and use of social networks. In J.C. Mitchell (Ed.) *Social networks in urban situations*. Manchester, Eng.: Manchester University Press.

Rappoport, J., Swift, C., and Hess, R. (Eds.) (1984). *Studies in Empowerment*. New York: The Haworth Press.

Riley, D. and Cochran, M. (1988). Children's relationships with non-parental adults: sex-specific connections to early school success. *Journal of Sex Roles*, *17*, 637-655.

Riley, D. and Eckenrode, J. (1986). Social ties: Subgroup differences in costs and benefits. *Journal of Personality and Social Psychology*, *51*(4).

Ryan, W. *Blaming the victim*. NY: Pantheon, 1971.

Sandler, I. and Lakey, B. (1982). Locus of control and stress moderator: the role of control perceptions and social support. *Am. J. of Community Psychology*, *10*, 65-80.

Suttles, G. (1970). *The Social Order of the Slums*. Chicago: University of Chicago Press.

Turner, R. and Noh, S. (1981). *Class and psychological vulnerability among women: the significance of social support and personal control*. Paper presented at the annual meetings of the Society for the Study of Social Problems, Toronto, Ontario.

Wellman, B. (1979). The community question: The intimate networks of East Yorkers. *American Journal of Sociology*, *84*, 1201-1231.

Wellman, B. (1981). Applying network analysis to the study of support. In: B. H. Gottlieb, (Ed.) *Social Networks and Social Support*. Beverly Hills, Calif: Sage Publications. Chapter 7.

Family Resource and Support Programs: Changes and Challenges in Human Services

Bernice Weissbourd

SUMMARY. Family resource programs are a set of principles and a compendium of program characteristics that respond to today's urgent need to reorient policies and services for families. Premises underlying program development and the origins from which program concepts are defined are discussed, as are applications of family resource principles and programs at the state level, in child-focused programs, and in conjunction with medical and mental health services. Current challenges faced by program developers and policymakers are presented, with a perpective that those issues will be pivotal in shaping the future of both the family resource movement and the field of human services at large.

INTRODUCTION

In the span of less than two decades, the field of family resource programs has drawn the interest of many who are reevaluating the American system of delivering human services: a system whose demands are increasingly great and whose inadequacies are increasingly evident. A growing body of information supports the viewpoint of scholars, policy analysts, researchers, legislators, and social service professionals, that the concept and practices of family resource programs present a promising solution to the dilemma of how to provide effective services for families. This is a significant step forward from the 1970s when, unknown to one another, grassroots family resource programs began to emerge in communities throughout the country.

Margaret Mead observed that Americans seem capable of organizing to deal with a crisis, but never utilize those same resources to prevent it. Her analysis offers an interesting context within which to consider the fact that the family resource program concept has, of late, been eagerly embraced.

Increased documentation and media coverage of the state of children and families has brought the crisis we face into sharp focus. The number of children who live in poverty, in two-parent working families, and single-parent households is striking. The problems that result from teenage parenthood (Children's Defense Fund, 1988) and cocaine addiction among pregnant women have drawn considerable attention (Griffin, 1989). The impact of these realities, reflected in skyrocketing rates of illiteracy, school drop-out, and delinquency has been noted by every sector of our society, including corporate executives and those who claim not to involve themselves in issues of the family (Committee for Economic Development, 1987).

As the search for solutions to and preventions for this crisis has broadened and intensified, family resource programs have been hailed as a new movement, generating the kind of pioneering spirit that is associated with all new frontiers. Noting the newness of the programs, however, should not obscure the fact that they are also well-rooted in the past. Lessons learned through experience have been applied both to adapt programs to current social needs and to formulate principles that are based upon recently acquired knowledge. Furthermore, the ecological approach upon which the movement is based has drawn, by necessity, from the many fields that interface with family concerns, including the disciplines of child development, mental health, social work, education, and community development.

Beyond promise, the family resource movement carries with it the destructive potential of *over*-promise and its corresponding danger of diminishing the impact of programs. Programs should not be saddled with the unrealistic expectation that they will solve the macro-level ills that contribute to family crises such as poverty, inadequate housing, and unemployment. What they *can* do is enhance the competency of parents and enable participants to build skills, utilize resources, and develop the confidence necessary to advocate on their own behalf. Attracted by their prevention focus and holistic orientation, a variety of sectors, most notably state social service delivery systems, schools, childcare centers, and medical and mental health agencies are examining family resource principles and integrating them into their programs and services. Systems that have incorporated the principles have grown more family-oriented, less bureaucratic, and more community-conscious (Bruner, 1989).

This chapter will delineate family resource programs as a set of principles and a compendium of program characteristics that address current social conditions and respond to the urgent need to reorient policies and services for families. It will define the premises underlying program development and the origins from which program concepts emerged. The chapter also will suggest that because the field of family resource programs is relatively new and continually expanding, the process by which it merges into existing human service systems raises a number of challenging issues and questions for program developers and policymakers. The manner in which these issues and questions are addressed may well determine the future direction of human services.

PREMISES

Representing a point of departure in thinking about families and society, the premises that underlie family resource programs are values that most people share regardless of political preference. These premises erase the barriers between liberal and conservative approaches and between families and states. By focusing on the promise of self-sufficiency in families, they allay conservative fears that public programs will create dependency. Likewise, by providing support to families to enhance effective functioning, they allay liberal concerns over the lack of public efforts to benefit families. "These programs create a middle ground where conservatives and liberals can join together to support programs designed to strengthen families and communities" (Weiss, 1989b, p. 36). Five premises which underlie family resource programs follow:

1. *Primary responsibility for the development and well-being of children lies within the family.* During the 1970s, there was concern that if families were given support through institutions, nonfamilial agencies would assume too much responsibility for childrearing. Today there is non-partisan recognition that families want to retain their childrearing responsibilities in full, and want access to necessary resources and support.

2. *The cornerstone of a healthy society is the well-being of its families.* Dysfunctional families jeopardize the development of future generations of adults, ultimately placing our society at risk.

3. *Families exist as part of an ecological system.* Children cannot be seen as separate from their families, nor families separate from their communities or from the greater society. Decisions made on behalf of children must integrate and acknowledge their interconnectedness to the social-ecological system in which they live, making the concept of "saving" a child from his or her environment appropriate only in extreme circumstances.

4. *Our society, its communities, institutions, and government at all*

levels must assist, not hinder, the capacity of families to raise children. The systems and institutions upon which families rely must effectively respond to their needs if families are to establish and maintain environments that promote growth and development. Systems must be continually evaluated, modified, and coordinated to increase and insure their effectiveness (Garbarino, 1982).

5. *Families who receive adequate support are more capable of supporting themselves.* It is a myth that any family can "do it alone." Rather, it is through the *inter*-dependence of people and between people and institutions such as schools, hospitals, and social services that family independence is fostered (Keniston & The Carnegie Council on Children, 1977).

PRINCIPLES

The above premises propel the principles upon which family resource programs are based. These principles, which are described below, serve as guidelines for program development and as a blueprint for reorienting more traditional services for families:

1. *The most effective approach to families emanates from a perspective of health and well-being.* An approach that builds upon strengths and solutions instead of dwelling upon deficits and problems preserves one's integrity and increases opportunities for growth and change (McCubbin & Patterson, 1981).

2. *The capacity of parents to raise their children effectively is influenced by their own development.* A distinct, evolving, ever-changing stage of life, parenthood is shaped by relationships, life experiences, and knowledge (Benedek, 1970). Parents' sense of confidence and competence emerges out of these dynamics, influencing who they are as people and how they parent their children (Unger & Wandersman cited in Littell, 1985).

3. *Childrearing techniques and values are influenced by cultural and community values and mores.* Effective involvement with families demands an understanding of and appropriate responsiveness to cultural, individual, and community traditions and values (Spiegel, 1982).

4. *Social support networks are essential to family well-being.* Social support networks provide parents with the concrete and psychological resources that are essential if they are not to become overwhelmed by their responsibilities (Gottlieb, 1983, 1988).

5. *Information about child development enhances parents' capacity to respond appropriately to their children.* Informed parents are better

equipped to problem-solve, more confident of their decisions, and more likely to respond sensitively to their children's developmental needs (Wandersman, 1987).

6. *Families who receive support are empowered to advocate on their own behalf.* As an outgrowth of their increased sense of confidence and capability, parents who receive support begin to view themselves as able to act on their own behalf as individuals and as members of a constituency (Pizzo, 1987).

7. *Programs for families are most effective when participation is voluntary.* Parents who are voluntarily involved in programs are more likely to feel in control of their lives and to be more receptive to change (Zigler & Berman; Valentine & Stark; Fein cited in Powell, 1988).

PRACTICES

As program principles are implemented, the characteristics that distinguish one program from another become evident. Programs vary in terms of the populations they target, the settings in which they exist, and the range of services they provide. Though their diversity makes defining programs more difficult, within that diversity lies their responsiveness and, therefore, their strength. Programs share these practices:

1. Relationships between professionals and parents are characterized by collaboration and shared decisionmaking.
2. Program services are designed with parents to meet their expressed needs and to enhance individual and family strengths.
3. Programs are planned to assure their relevance and sensitivity to the culture and values of the families served.
4. Linkages and cooperative relationships are established with community organizations and institutions.
5. Peer support networks are nurtured and facilitated.

As family resource program practices are implemented, core services may include any or all of the following: informal and structured groups providing information on child development, personal growth, and family relationships; peer support groups, parent-child activities, home visits, drop-in programs, early developmental screening, outreach, community referral and follow-up, job skills training, and/or literacy training.

ORIGIN AND EVOLUTION

Family resource programs and principles represent a convergence of concepts from various sources. Historically, they have grown out of the principles which underlie the parent education, settlement house, and self-help movements and the tenets basic to Head Start.

The parent education movement, which promoted the concept that parents should have access to pertinent information about child development and parent-child interaction, is strongly represented in family resource programs; as is the settlement house movement's commitment to advocacy and the belief that families are integrally interrelated to their communities. The self-help movement, whose central concept involves the provision of mutual support and guidance through peer relationships, lies at the root of programs' orientation toward fostering independence through interdependence, and the assumptions underlying programs such as Head Start which consider the family to be the major influence upon a child's development serve as the foundation of family resource principles and programs (Weissbourd & Kagan, 1989).

In addition, programs were influenced by early social work practices, exemplified by the work of Charlotte Towle, who emphasized the importance of the formulation of policies and practices that reflect an "understanding of the common needs of the individual and of the decisive import of individual well-being for the good of society" (Towle, 1965, p. xvii), and by research evidence that pointed to the importance of early childhood. The burgeoning information on the capacities of children in the first three years of life reinforced a growing orientation toward prevention.

The first family resource programs emerged in the 1970s. Until that time, with the exception of services for parents of disabled children, programs for families with very young children (birth through three years) were virtually nonexistent. As programs for this population were established, a number of grassroots groups representing parents with children of all ages, including adolescents, voiced their strong desire for programs that would respond to their needs as well. Those requests, validated by research literature that documented both the importance and lack of intergenerational family support, led to an acknowledgment that family resource programs were needed for all parents, not only those with very young children. Although programs for children in the early years remains the focus, the intergenerational approach is reflected in one of the several current program definitions: "Family resource programs are community-based service agencies that offer sustained assistance to families at various stages of their development" (Farrow, 1989).

The majority of the initial programs were the outgrowth of grassroots efforts and others were initiated in universities or established by professionals in cooperation with parents. With the exception of a few that were based in universities, the early programs were not evaluated. In an effort to rectify this situation, considerable effort is being made today to conduct program evaluations and to design research tools that can be effectively applied to a variety of program models.

The progress of the movement since the 1970s might be charted in relation to four important milestones. The first, which dates to 1981, was driven by a desire to share information among the many programs that had been established by that time. Family Focus, a Chicago-based family resource program, organized an informal conference which was funded in part by the Administration for Children Youth and Families. On the final day of this event, conferees established a national organization of family resource programs, naming it the Family Resource Coalition.

Two years later, the Yale Bush Center in Child Development and Social Policy sponsored a conference that was to become the movement's second major milestone. Fully funded by the Administration for Children Youth and Families, academicians, researchers, policymakers, and program directors from across the United States and Canada gathered to discuss family resource and support. In doing so, they awarded the movement official recognition.

The third milestone occurred in the spring of 1989, when state legislators who were interested in family support officially gathered for the first time at a colloquium sponsored jointly by The Center for the Study of Social Policy, the Harvard Family Research Project and the Family Resource Coalition. Together, invitees explored the potential impact that family resource principles and policies might have upon public policy: its opportunities and its challenges.

Current plans to initiate legislation on the national and state levels that would include family resource programs in essential services for children and families might be considered the movement's fourth, and most recent milestone. The provision of family resource services as a component of both the federal Comprehensive Child Development Centers Act of 1988, and the original Act for Better Child Care, indicate a recognition of the importance of including services for families in programs that serve children. Legislation that relates specifically to developing and evaluating family resource programs was introduced by Senator Barbara Mikulski (Democrat, MA) in the 101st Session of Congress, and plans are underway to initiate legislation establishing family resource programs as the prevention component in a continuum of child welfare services.

At the state level, significant developments have grown out of the interest of policymakers and administrators to utilize family resource programs and principles to reorient educational and social service delivery systems. As a result, family resource principles and programs are now represented at the state level, in child-focused institutions such as schools and child-care centers, and in mental health and medical services.

State-level Service Delivery Systems

Acknowledging the failure of traditional approaches to reduce rates of child abuse, delinquency, and school drop-out, increasing numbers of state legislators have begun to examine the merits of family resource principles and programs. Many have found the comprehensive, non-categorical nature of the programs, with their emphasis upon prevention and well-being, family and community concerns, and self-sufficiency and competency well-suited to their state's service delivery needs.

A number of models for state-wide family resource programs exist, each evolving out of the political climate, foci of leadership, and social conditions particular to its region. Some programs are seated in departments of education (Kentucky, Minnesota, Missouri), others in departments of human services (Connecticut, Iowa, Illinois, Maryland, Oregon, Vermont). The programmatic focus may be upon teenage pregnancy and the multitude of problems of teenaged youth (Maryland, Illinois), families at risk of long-term welfare dependency (Iowa), or the entire birth-to-three population (Minnesota, Missouri) (Weiss, 1989). They may be home-based, center-based, school-based, or, very often, a combination of the three. In spite of their many variations, the elements that state-level programs hold in common are precisely those that individual programs share with one another: direct service personnel develop partnerships with program participants or clients, minimize bureaucratic paperwork, promote feelings of personal strength and competence, and view families in the context of the culture and traditions of their communities (Bruner, 1989). Not only their similarities, but the differences among programs highlight how essential it is that family resource programs remain flexible and responsive to the communities they serve.

The recently enacted federal welfare reform law known as the Family Support Act (Public Law 100-485) represents a major initiative to implement change in the delivery of social services in state-level public welfare systems. It requires that there be family assessments in addition to client assessments, a process for families to establish goals, linkages between state agencies and community-based organizations, and interagency cooperation and coordination at the state and local level. These provisions in the law provide a unique opportunity for changing welfare practices from a "client maintenance" focus to an approach based on promoting self-sufficiency and competency. The results of evaluations conducted after such changes were instituted in Delaware and Virginia suggest that both self-sufficiency in clients and job satisfaction in caseworkers increase when public welfare services are delivered through a positive relationship that supports personal strengths (Mumma, 1989). The integration of family resource principles into the welfare system may very well become the turning point for positive change in all state social service delivery systems.

Child-focused Programs

It is a widely accepted notion that parents should maintain close ties with their child's childcare center or school; the rationale being that a child's capacity to function is increased when such supportive linkages exist (Bronfenbrenner, 1979; Weiss, 1989b).

In traditional child-focused programs, the above concept translates into the involvement of parents primarily in routine parent-teacher conferences and as classroom volunteers. In these settings, the major focus is upon the child who is enrolled in the program; the secondary focus is upon that child's relationship with his or her parents.

When family resource principles are integrated into a child-focused program, the program's impact is broadened. The overall focus becomes the *family*, and teachers and staff members are as concerned with the child's parents as individuals and with the parent-child relationship as they are with the child himself.

This broadened perspective often dictates that school-based programs become involved with families long before their children are enrolled as students (Kagan, 1987). Among these programs are Missouri's birth-to-three school-based program which utilizes the Parents as Teachers (PAT) curriculum, Minnesota's birth-to-three program which includes a variety of program services that offer both a parent and a parent-child component, and the Parent and Child Education programs (PACE) of Kentucky, which combines parent-child programming with adult literacy training (Weiss, 1989a). All such programs are unified by two overall goals: to reduce the number of children who enter school unable to learn and to address parents' need to receive guidance on issues relating to child development and parenting.

Family resource principles have also reshaped many childcare services. In addition to programming for children, programs that operate with the family resource perspective also give considerable attention to providing programming for parents and families. Beyond being involved in the more traditional venues discussed earlier, parents in these programs play a role in determining program policies and practices and planning center activities. The relationships that parents develop with staff members and other parents as a by-product of their involvement become vehicles through which they receive support personally and as parents.

Cost is a major barrier to the proliferation of such comprehensive programs in both school and childcare settings, but in light of the benefits these services hold for families, it is understandable that an increasing number of teachers and childcare professionals have become advocates for family-centered programming and seek funding policies that will enable them to integrate these components into their programs.

Mental Health and Medical Services

Traditionally, relationships between mental health agencies and family resource programs have been reciprocal referral linkages; the accepted paradigm being that each required the other in order to adequately meet the needs of families in stress. Recently, mental health professionals have begun to examine and emphasize their role in not only the treatment, but in the prevention of mental health problems and, as a result, have begun to revisit the concept and practice of providing community-based services to families. Some agencies have added a family resource program as a service component, others have integrated their services into existing community-based family resource programs.

In Little Rock, Arkansas, for example, SCAN Volunteer Service, Inc., was founded to provide additional support to traditional child protection services. Serving families who are already receiving treatment for documented cases of child abuse, the program includes home visits to families two to three times per week to provide general information about parenting and child development and assist families in solving problems and decisionmaking (Levine, 1988).

Developed as a joint program of the Departments of Pediatrics and Obstetrics, the Infant Care Program at Evanston Hospital in Evanston, Illinois, makes available to all their new parents sibling preparation activities, neonatal assessment, follow-up telephone contact following discharge, fathers' classes, post-discharge family-infant groups (in conjunction with a community-based family resource program), and referrals to community services with follow-up by an Infant Care Developmental Specialist (Levine, 1988).

Indications are that, on the basis of shared principles, family resource and mental health personnel will continue to explore possibilities for combined programmatic efforts, resulting in a considerable increase in the effectiveness of all programs, but particularly in those serving at-risk populations (Mumma, 1989).

CHALLENGES

The rapid rate at which programs and principles are being integrated into state level human service systems, schools, childcare centers, and medical and mental health agencies hastens the need to address the movement's most challenging issues. Six challenges are discussed below:

Challenge #1

To maintain the salient characteristics of family resource programs as they are integrated into larger systems and human services programs.

In order to incorporate the unique characteristics of family resource programs into more traditional systems, considerable adjustments must be made in staff orientation and approach, personnel management and training, monitoring, and recordkeeping. Such transitions may be difficult for personnel who have related to their constituencies in more distant and formal ways, and whom are accustomed to complex and time-consuming monitoring and reporting systems.

State administrators report that the transition is apt to proceed more smoothly, and the resulting programs to be more effective when the lead agency believes in and is committed to family resource principles. To facilitate a decisionmaking process, some agencies have found it worthwhile to establish and utilize an area-wide advisory committee whose membership is representative of both the professional community and the population being served. In addition, it is considered advisable to select staff and administrators whose orientation and experiences are compatible with the collaborative relationships that are the hallmark of family resource programs and to insure that those individuals receive relevant support and training both before the program opens and throughout its lifetime (Bruner, 1989). Ultimately, each state's challenge is to develop strategies that will assure that the requirements of successful programs are understood and adhered to at every level.

Challenge #2

To professionalize the family resource field by defining its role in the human services.

Some of the steps necessary to establish family resource as an area of professional expertise are known and others are yet to be determined. One of the most obvious needs is to identify the characteristics of high-quality programs (Powell, 1988), define standards for staff qualifications and program operation, and formulate curricula for training. Whether family support will become a discrete professional field of study with workers certified as such, perhaps in the way social workers and teachers are currently certified, is not yet known and remains an issue to be explored.

Achieving professional status further requires the existence of a national organization that represents those working in the field, advocates for their interests, and acts as an information resource.

The Family Resource Coalition has assumed a leadership role in this effort and the challenge continues to work with others to assure that the critical issues are addressed and that the movement receives essential recognition.

Challenge #3

To prepare professionals and paraprofessionals to assume positions in family resource programs and in existing systems that adopt family resource principles.

There is a danger that the impetus to start programs may exceed the capacity to operate them effectively, for if program personnel are not appropriately prepared to implement programs, positive outcomes will be jeopardized. Addressing these training needs requires examination on two levels: in-service and pre-service.

A multitude of in-service training programs have been developed by local programs and states, each designed to meet a particular program and as different from one another as the programs they support. Yet, the prevailing opinion is that an effective family resource training curriculum is based upon the principles of family resource programs it is intended to teach, elucidating and modeling them through the training process itself. Equally critical is the need to provide high quality pre-service training to those most likely to work in family resource programs.

Although progress has been made, many training questions remain unanswered, including: what constitutes the requisite content and pedagogy for training people to work in family resource programs? What do practitioners, policymakers, and social service personnel need to know to be effective in their respective roles? What are the best methods for communicating family resource concepts?

Giving due recognition to the primary importance of training will require allocation of training funds in all legislation and planning for family resource initiatives and expansion.

Challenge #4

To understand the dynamics of communities; how they function and inter-relate with programs.

Although the concept of "community-based" is dominant in both practice and policymaking and the term "culturally sensitive" is heard often, there is surprisingly little known about the meaning of these terms, or how to implement them.

As discussed earlier, all too often, traditional social services are discrete and categorical in relation to the communities they serve, making linkages with other community services only for referral purposes. In contrast, family resource programs are integrated into the community at many levels and in many dimensions, acting as a central resource through which a wide range of interests and needs are addressed, and minimizing the tendency toward the delivery of piecemeal, disconnected services. This approach requires an understanding at every level, both in theory and practice, of how communities function, how cultural values and norms influence family life and childrearing, how to coordinate efforts among community agencies to assure that families are well cared for, and how to deal with competing interests among service providers, factions among community groups, and situations in which political ambitions seem to take priority over meeting the needs of families. Legislators, administrators, and providers who are not knowledgeable in these areas cannot steer programs to be integral to the community or to properly support parents in their roles as community advocates. The challenge, therefore, is to increase understanding of the dynamics of communities and to utilize that knowledge as a basis to guide the establishment and operation of programs.

Challenge #5

To refine and expand the research and evaluation of family resource programs.

In *Within Our Reach*, Lisbeth Schorr (1988) documented successful family resource programs in broad strokes, validating the principles and practices of family resource and support. Further analysis, detailing exactly "what works" for whom, under what circumstances, and through what program elements is imperative as programs and principles become part of the public policy agenda. Results of evaluations conducted to date have been promising and have validated that providing social support to parents is associated with positive parent-child interaction, increased education and employability, and more positive views of and behavior toward their children (Littell, 1985). But there is much more to know: How can programs be individualized to suit a specific family's needs? What are the qualities and qualifications necessary for staff? What program structures best accommodate a population of families whose needs range from "every day" issues to serious maladjustment? What are the essential components that every family resource program must have? How can high-risk families be reached and adequately served? What program elements are most essential for different target populations?

Although evaluation results are essential to guide planning and practice and to determine "what works for whom," the establishment of programs should depend not only upon evaluation results, but upon a belief in society's commitment to supporting and strengthening families. Anecdotal evidence from parents overwhelmingly conveys that they think that their involvement in family resource programs has been instrumental in changing their lives for the better (Florin & Dokecki, 1983). Optimally, a public consciousness based on the premises of family resource and support can be developed which will ultimately be translated into suitable public policy.

It remains necessary to increase evaluation efforts in order to maintain and sustain the support of those who initiate programs and to garner the support of those wary of instituting less traditional services.

Challenge #6

To secure a stable funding base for the establishment, maintenance and expansion of programs.

Given budgetary constraints on public funds, the voluntary nature of community programs has wide appeal among policymakers. Unfortunately, however, far too many good programs have closed their doors because they have lost the struggle for overcommitted individual, local, and community trust funding. The fact is that the private sector alone cannot adequately maintain a system of community-based family resource programs.

The notion of government funding of these programs is no longer foreign to our public policy. As states have initiated programs and reoriented systems to include family resource principles, they have assumed a corresponding responsibility for funding, often spurred by the expectation that the provision of family resource programs is a prevention service which ultimately will decrease expenditures for treatment.

Levels and sources of funding vary from state to state depending on program goals and objectives, populations served, and the availability of funds. In some states, public and private partnerships have been established, reflecting the current national priority of encouraging voluntary participation and commitment. These partnerships offer opportunities for shared ownership, increasing the number of people who are responsible for and invested in the success of the program initiative. Utilizing private funds this way may also stimulate an increase in public funding (Illinois, Maryland). Some states have established new appropriations for family resource efforts which are not tied to the program goals of other departments, thus making their use more flexible and better able to support program goals (Kentucky, Minnesota). In an approach that may be more readily achieved in the current climate of budget limitations, some states have consolidated categorical funds from existing federal, state, and local funding streams (Arkansas, Vermont). A somewhat similar strategy has been to redeploy funds from existing programs, utilizing them to fund pilot family resource programs which will then be examined as an alternate programming possibility (Connecticut, Nebraska) (Weiss, 1989a).

The funding questions that emerge relate to every legislative level: how can legislators be encouraged to make a commitment to ongoing, long-term funding for family resource and support? What new appropriations can be designated for prevention? How can legislators be convinced to commit major funding to such services now, based upon a belief in their cost-effectiveness? How can family resource program initiatives be funded without decreasing funds for other necessary services for children?

To secure its place in the human services, funding for family resource initiatives should be written into all childcare, welfare reform, and pre-school education legislation. Beyond that, legislation must be passed that would directly increase the capacity of states and local communities to initiate and maintain programs.

CONCLUSION

The challenges facing the family resource movement emerged from its significant effects on the social service and education systems and on the attitude and approaches of those seeking more effective ways to foster family health. While such challenges indicate the extent to which family resource programs and principles are reorienting thinking and planning for human services, they also point to the fact that this is a critical juncture in program development. As programs proliferate and systems are reorganized, their impact and success will depend upon the ability to maintain the program characteristics of flexibility, responsiveness, and partnerships with parents and communities, and to support training, rigorously evaluate effectiveness, and guarantee the funding base necessary to insure quality programs.

The enthusiastic embrace of family resource programs and principles speaks to the demand for services that can make a difference in an increasingly complex society, as it does to the demand for prevention services deemed to be cost-effective. It further speaks to values that strengthen the commitment of society to its families, and that recognize the link between independence and inter-dependence. It is perhaps not unrealistic to envision a time when community-based family resource programs will be available to all families regardless of economic status, race, ethnicity, ability or disability. Our next biggest challenge will be to move from a focus on *preventing* problems to one of *promoting* health through assuring a baseline of good beginnings which continues throughout the years of childhood.

REFERENCES

Benedek, T. (1970). Parenthood during the life cycle. In E.J. Anthony & T. Benedek (Eds.), *Parenthood its psychology and psychopathology* (pp. 185-206). Boston: Little Brown.

Bronfenbrenner, U. (1979). *The ecology of human development: Experiments by nature and design*. Cambridge, MA: Harvard University Press.

Bruner, C. (1989, April). *Legislating family support and education: Program development at the state level*. Paper prepared for the Public Policy and Family Support and Education Programs Colloquium, Annapolis, MD.

Children's Defense Fund. (1988). *A call for action to make our nation safe for children: A briefing book on the status of American children in 1988*. Washington, D.C., pp. iv, 6.

Committee for Economic Development. Research and Policy Committee. (1987). *Children in need*. New York.

Farrow, F. (1989, April). [Colloquium Presentation], The Public Policy and Family Support and Education Colloquium, Annapolis, MD.

Florin, P.R. & Dokecki, P. (1983). Changing families through parent and family education. In I. Sigel & L. Laosa (Eds.), *Changing families: Review and analysis* (pp. 23-63). New York: Plenum.

Garbarino, J. (1982). *Children and families in the social environment*. Hawthorne, NY: Aldine.

Gottlieb, B.H. (1983). *Social support strategies*. Beverly Hills, CA: Sage.

Gottlieb, B.H. (1988). Marshaling social support: The state of the art in research and practice. In B.H. Gottlieb (Ed.), *Marshaling social support* (pp. 11-51). Beverly Hills, CA: Sage.

Griffin, J.L. (1989, October 26). Crack, high baby death rate linked. Chicago *Tribune*, p. 20.

Kagan, S.L. (1987). Home-school linkages: History's legacy and the family support movement. In S.L. Kagan, D.R. Powell, B. Weissbourd, & E.F. Zigler (Eds.), *America's family support programs* (pp. 161-181). New Haven: Yale University Press.

Keniston, K. & The Carnegie Council on Children. (1977). *All our children*. New York: Harcourt Brace Jovanovich.

Levine, C. (Ed.). (1988). *Programs to strengthen families* (rev. ed.). Chicago: Family Resource Coalition.

Littell, J.H. (1985, November). *Research in family support programs*. Paper prepared for the National Association of Social Workers Conference, Chicago.

McCubbin, H.I. & Patterson, J.M. (1981). Broadening the scope of family strengths: An emphasis on family coping and social support. In N. Stinnett, J. DeFrain, K. Kind, P. Knaub, & G. Rowe (Eds.), *Family strengths 3 roots of well-being* (pp. 177-194). Lincoln, NE: University of Nebraska Press.

Mumma, E. (1989, Spring). Reform at the local level. *Public Welfare*, pp. 15-24.

Pizzo, P. (1987) Parent-to-parent support groups: Advocates for social change. In S.L. Kagan, D.R. Powell, B. Weissbourd, & E.F. Zigler (Eds.), *America's family support programs* (pp. 228-242). New Haven: Yale University Press.

Powell, D.R. (1988, June). *Seeking dimensions of quality in family support programs*. Paper prepared for the A.L. Mailman Family Foundation Symposium: "Dimensions of Quality in Programs for Children and Families," White Plains, NY.

Schorr, Lisbeth. (1988). *Within our reach: Breaking the cycle of disadvantage*. New York: Doubleday.

Spiegel, J. (1982). An ecological model of ethnic families. In M. McGoldrick, J.K. Pearce, & J. Giordano (Eds.), *Ethnicity and family therapy* (pp. 31-51). New York: Guilford.

Towle, C. (1965). *Common human needs* (rev. ed.). Silver Springs, MD: National Association of Social Workers.

Wandersman, L.P. (1987). New directions for parent education. In S.L. Kagan, D.R. Powell, B. Weissbourd, & E.F. Zigler (Eds.), *America's family support programs* (pp. 207-227). New Haven: Yale University Press.

Weiss, H.B. (1989a, April). *From grass roots programs to state policy: Strategic planning and choices for family support and education initiatives*. Paper prepared for the Public Policy and Family Support and Education Programs Colloquium, Annapolis, MD.

Weiss, H.B. (1989b). State family support and education programs: Lessons from the pioneers. *American Journal of Orthopsychiatry, 59*(I), 32-48.

Weissbourd, B. & Kagan, S.L. (1989). Family support programs: Catalysts for change. *American Journal of Orthopsychiatry, 59*(I), 20-31.

Services for Children
with Special Needs:
Partnerships from the Beginning
Between Parents and Practitioners

Eleanor Stokes Szanton

SUMMARY. This paper addresses what is meant by effective partnerships between parents of very young children with special needs and the professionals seeking to help them. It addresses the obstacles, both past and present, to effective partnerships as well as past successes. It examines the strategies for breaking down barriers in order to forge solid and lasting alliances for the benefit of all concerned.

A SHIFT IN PERSPECTIVE IN PROVIDING SERVICES TO CHILDREN WITH SPECIAL NEEDS

In the Past: A Child-Oriented Focus

It has been pointed out repeatedly that services designed to improve the lives of young children in the United States in this century have been hampered by a tradition both in theory and practice which focused too narrowly on the child, ignoring family and broader social setting. That is true of services for children with handicapping conditions as well. For example, when Title V of the Social Security Act was enacted, that part which created Crippled Children's Services called for "services and facilities to locate, diagnose, and treat children who are crippled or suffer from potentially crippling conditions" (Select Panel for the Promotion of Child Health, 1981, p. 18). It made no mention of the family as a system needing attention as a unit. Families existed to bring the child to services and to administer the prescribed activities with the child until time for the next visit to the professional. Certainly many gifted individual clinicians and service providers understood the importance of what has come to be called family centered care (Association for the Care of Children's Health, 1987). However, by and large, the focus was on the child.

A New Focus on the Family as the Unit of Intervention

Two important factors have contributed to the change from *child*-centered to *family*-centered intervention. First, a growing body of research has shown that the effects of intervention programs are relatively short term when focused on the child alone (Zigler & Freedman, 1987; Shonkoff, 1987; Jeppson 1988; NCCIP 1987).

Secondly, parents themselves have begun to insist on what to them is important about early intervention programs. Thus, when researchers were quibbling about whether children in a particular poverty program had slightly higher IQs than their counterparts who were not in the program, parents were pointing out with increasing vigor that for them the "effectiveness" was better measured by the degree to which family stress was diminished, or the degree to which the child developed stable social relationships with peers (Shonkoff & Hauser-Cram, 1987).

Effective Partnerships Between Parents and Professionals: What Does This Mean?

This paper then addresses what is meant by "effective partnerships" between parents of very young children with special needs and the professionals seeking to help them. It will address the obstacles, both past and present, to effective partnerships as well as the strategies for breaking down those barriers in order to forge solid and lasting alliances for the benefit of all concerned.

OBSTACLES TO AN EFFECTIVE PARTNERSHIP BETWEEN PARENTS AND PROFESSIONALS

Several distinctive features characterize most relationships between professionals and parents of infants or very young children with special needs or handicapping conditions.

Differing Levels of Expertise

Often there is an enormous and cumulative body of expertise held by professionals who work with special needs children—expertise which, at least initially, their families are entirely lacking. Whether the particular special need is extreme prematurity or need for pediatric surgery or venti-

lator dependence, it usually creates a large imbalance in sense of competence as between professional and parent. This is in contrast to many other
kinds of services for young children and their families, such as a parent
education program or a family support program, many of which are
staffed by individuals whose backgrounds are similar to those of the program participants.

Emotional Reactions of Parents and Distancing Practices of Professionals

Secondly, the professional is likely to be confronting a family in
shock—a family which is only beginning to adjust, both psychologically
and logistically—to the special needs of their child. Unless parents became aware of a genetic problem during pregnancy or purposely adopted a
baby with a handicapping condition, they generally are totally unprepared
for the kinds of adjustments which are demanded of them. These adjustments are far above the large demands on any new parents. Most parents
of a child with special needs have not expected to begin the parenting
process with a swarm of questions such as "How could this have happened?" "How could I have failed as a parent?" "How shall I deal with
the shock and questions of grandparents, friends, my other children?" As
one parent put it:

> When my son Nicholas was born prematurely, I felt more hostage
> than partner to a gang of powerful professionals who sustained his
> life and taught me the rules of a strange new variety of motherhood.
> I didn't question their competence in treating any of us: my husband
> and I needed to believe that someone had wisdom in this situation
> that had spun our lives out of control and made us wonder who we
> were and whether we were any good. The individuals stand out who
> helped me begin rebuilding a sense that I was worth something. . . .
> But so many of our contacts with professionals were frustrating or
> destructive to our self-esteem. (Oster, 1985, p. 27)

Professionals are likely to confront parents' painful shocks by insulating
themselves. Most professionals have been trained to believe that if they
become too emotionally involved with each set of grieving parents, they
may not be able to function "professionally." In the words of one parent:

Although the professionals I have met are always well-trained in how to greet parents, how to ask questions and conduct an interview, they rarely are comfortable relating to parents as real people with lives of their own. It both amuses and annoys me when I read reports or medical charts and see myself referred to as "the mother" or "mother." (Iris, 1988, p. 9)

Similarly, in the words of another:

I thought back to the time we 'learned' of Kevin's hearing loss. It actually had happened rather quickly, seemingly not really a big deal to the doctor who told us the test results over the telephone. He said our one-year-old son was deaf. Told us to get him some hearing aids, the kind that pick up vibrations, because he wouldn't really be able to hear anything anyway. Hearing this news could never be easy, but I knew that the way we were told was particularly insensitive. This man was cruel, I thought, and I hoped he didn't treat all parents in a similar manner. I later found out that many other parents do 'learn' of their children's special needs/disabilities in a similar way. (Bohlin, 1989, p. 13)

Professional Focus on Categorizing

A third attribute which is true for all families working with professionals but perhaps especially true for families of special needs children is that professionals are experts by virtue of having spent years learning to make generalizations about the phenomena they are confronting. An observation such as, "This looks like a severe intraventricular bleed. Let's quickly measure the size and calculate the degree to which functioning may be impaired" does not look at what is unique to this particular child who is bleeding. It *categorizes*. Wise clinicians and highly skilled service providers keep in mind what is unique to this child, her family, and the situation. However, it is tempting, particularly for the inexperienced practitioner, to look at what the child shares with other children with similar disorders rather than what she does not. Yet it is just exactly the individuality of the case to which families bring *their* expertise. The average family knows virtually nothing about spina bifida in general. However many parents know a great deal—even in the earliest days of life—about their particular baby. The unwillingness of many professionals to acknowledge this source of expertise is a wasted opportunity and a damaging experience for families.

Differing Views of the "Whole" Child

A fourth source of misunderstanding—or at least a different perspective between professionals and parents of infants and young children with special needs—is that professionals, of necessity "take the child apart" by examining past and present functioning of the pieces. (This, of course, is not unique to professionals working with special needs children.) Parents, on the other hand, powerfully see the whole child *and see his or her future*. One has only to compare a disabled child's medical record with a family photo of the child to understand what utterly different perspectives are operating. In the past, "good parent-professional relations" has meant helping the parent see the professional's perspective. Only now is it increasingly understood that professionals also need to see the child from the parent's perspective.

These observations are various ways of saying that the skilled services performed by a professional in working with a small child with a handicapping condition are only partially important. Aspirating a tube or measuring the degree of hearing loss are only enormously helpful if child and family perceive them as such, if they have developed a sense of being on the same team with the professional. Heretofore, there has been a tendency among professionals to say, "I did my thing. I can't help it if the family did not follow through." Now professionals are coming to see—and parents are helping them see—that "doing my thing" includes helping the entire family feel competent and motivated to follow through in a difficult situation.

STRATEGIES TO IMPROVE RELATIONS
BETWEEN PARENTS AND PROFESSIONALS

The Parent Movement

A combination of the consumer movement and a new look at education for all handicapped children brought on a major shift in relations between parents of special needs children and professionals (Jeppson, 1988; Szanton, 1988; Pizzo, 1983; Association for the Care of Children's Health, 1987). The parent movement among parents of children with special needs has been one of the remarkable developments of the past fifteen years in the area of human services. This movement had a double focus—on parent-to-parent counseling and on political activism. Increasingly, a third—training of professionals—has emerged.

1. Parent-to-parent counseling: This kind of peer counseling relied on

the typically American phenomenon of volunteerism. To quote a parent of a baby with special needs:

> Nick was nine months old before I met a mother whose baby had similar problems. I will never forget the incredibly intense feeling of recognition and kinship that I experienced during that hour-long talk in a hospital cafeteria. And later, as our parent group flourished, I saw so many other mothers and fathers experiencing the remarkable sense of connection that had kept a group of strangers talking in a hospital parking lot until midnight after our first meeting. (Oster, 1985, p. 32)

This kind of parent-to-parent activity was given greater legitimacy and a financial base under provisions of the Education for All Handicapped Children Act, described below. The new law actually required the establishment of a grant program to support organized parent-to-parent information and training activities for parents of children with special needs. The administrator of the program reported directly to the Assistant Secretary of the Department of Education for Special Education and Rehabilitative Services. Groups such as Parent Care, the Parent Network, SKIP, and the Parent Training and Information Projects, to name only a few, have organized national networks of caring parents, ready to help new parents of children with special needs as they have been helped. (Addresses of these organizations appear at the end of this chapter.)

2. Parent training of professionals: In recent years, the activities of parents of children with special needs have included not only counseling and support to other parents, but organized advice to professionals as well. There are a number of publications to this end. One such publication is *Equals in this partnership: parents of disabled and at-risk infants and toddlers speak to professionals* (NCCIP, 1985). This publication, used widely both for parent and professional groups, reports the words of five parents of children with various kinds of special needs. The presentations, themselves, were a "first" — being part of each plenary panel at a national conference for professionals held in 1984, cosponsored by the National Center for Clinical Infant Programs, the Office of Special Education and Related Services of the U.S. Department of Education, and the Division of Maternal and Child Health of the U.S. Public Health Service. The publication, *Four critical junctures: support for parents of children with special needs* (Edge and Pizzo [eds.], 1988), also sponsored by the National Center for Clinical Infant Programs as part of its work with families of children with special needs, outlines four points at which professionals should take particular care in their approach to parents.

The use of parents in the preservice training of professionals is also a very important new development. As Jill Bohlin, the Parent Advisor to Early Intervention training at Wheelock College described her decision to work in this area: "Maybe if I could just tell students about the insensitivity that many parents were experiencing, it would help eliminate it. Maybe I could make a difference" (Bohlin, 1989, p. 13). Thus, Bohlin visits a variety of courses in the program, discussing with the students her perspectives and experiences and those of other families. More educators are coming to use professionals in some capacity or another in training of those who work with very young children with special needs and their families. However, change occurs slowly.

3. A third focus of the parent movement has been political activism. The Education for All Handicapped Children Act (P.L. 94-142), enacted in the mid-1970s, was at once the culmination of one era and the beginning of another. Remarkably, parents were active in the process of drafting both the bill and the regulations which followed. To quote one parent who was involved in this process:

> After the bill passed, there was an extraordinary process for the regulations. You know, usually the administering agency curls up with some of its staff and they write regs and publish them in the *Federal Register*. People scream about them and then sometimes they change them and sometimes they don't. What happened on this one was that before they drafted them they got together about 150 people from all over the country. . . . They locked us up . . . for three days and said 'draft regs.' (Akerley in Pizzo, 1983, p. 139)

In 1981 a parent of a child with special needs was appointed to the position of Assistant Secretary of Education for Special Education and Rehabilitative Services. Since that time, the concepts of family centered services and family empowerment have been stronger than ever.

At the same time, the Office of Maternal and Child Health within the U.S. Public Health Service was promoting similar goals. Its support of the work of the Federation for Children with Special Needs and of the manual for professionals published by the Association for the Care of Children's Health on *Family-centered care for children with special health care needs* (ACCH, 1987) was an important parallel step to those going on in education. It spread the word to the health and public health communities, much as the Department of Education had to the state education agencies. Other MCH special projects of regional and national significance (including the National Center for Clinical Infant Programs' own Project Zero to Three) also supported active and vocal parent groups.

Parents have similarly been active at the state and local level on behalf
of programs for their young children with special needs and handicapping
conditions. In fact, their activism has given professionals an increased
recognition of their need for parent lobbyists. NCCIP's publication, *The
open door: parent participation in state policymaking about children with
special health needs* (Woll and Pizzo [eds.], 1988), is one good source of
information on this subject.

The Newest Legislation: Public Law 99-457

With the advent of P.L. 99-457, the amendments to the Education of
the Handicapped Act of 1987 which mandated services for children age
three and above and which provided states with strong incentives to plan
for services for children either with actual or potential special needs from
birth through age two, yet another historic chapter was written by parents
and for parents of special needs children. Instead of requiring an Individualized Education Plan to be written each year in consultation with the
parents and signed by the parents as per the requirements of PL 94-142,
the legislation required an Individualized *Family Service* Plan for families
of children from birth through age two. As a member of one of the two
Congressional committee staffs closest to the drafting process has since
said:

> Congress wanted the language of the bill to reflect our utmost re-
> spect for the family. The word 'family' must appear ten or fifteen
> times throughout the legislation; this was intentional. Congress was
> trying to say, 'Do not have professionals come into a family situa-
> tion and assume that the mom and dad don't know anything. Respect
> the family.' The language in the legislation which talks about
> strengths as well as needs is an attempt to recognize and provide
> respect for the family. . . . There is nothing more central to this
> legislation than respect for the family. (Silverstein, 1989, pp. A-3
> and A-4)

The existence of the IFSP (rather than the IEP) for families of children
birth through age two presents parents and professionals with a tremendous challenge. Will states assure, and service providers develop, procedures for administering IFSPs which truly address the needs of the family
as a nurturing system for children with special needs without being overly
intrusive? Will they build on the family's *strengths*, rather than simply
addressing the family's needs? These are not easy questions to answer.
Answers lie partially in the degree to which professionals have indeed
been trained to be sensitized to these issues, to what degree they can help

parents truly identify their own needs even when previously only half understood or articulated. They will also lie in the degree to which states come to view basic health and education as a resource which should be available to *all* very young children without the need for stigmatizing labels as a passport to funded services.

As those parents and professionals who drafted the (technical assistance) *Guidelines and recommended practices for the individualized family service plan* state in the introductory section:

> The purpose of the IFSP is to identify and organize formal and informal resources to facilitate families' goals for their children and themselves. The IFSP is a promise to children and families — a promise that their strengths will be recognized and built on, that their needs will be met in a way that is respectful of their beliefs and values, and that their hopes and aspirations will be encouraged and enabled. (NECTAS, 1989, p. 1)

The *Guidelines* then make a series of recommendations for operationalizing that goal. States have yet to fully implement the individualized family service plan, so it is too early to tell how well the recommendations are being utilized.

An Inspiration for ALL Parent-Professional Relationships?

A new and thrilling possibility emerges from the rhetoric of parents of special needs children and of professionals working together with them to redefine their mutual relationships: If they will respond to the opportunity, parents of children with special needs and handicapping conditions can help professionals and parents in a broader array of service relationships to better understand and support each other. How can this be? Because there are ways in which *all* parents whose young children are served by professionals share a perspective. Whether a mother is sincerely battling an addiction or is a young teenager or is severely depressed, she also must develop an alliance with the practitioner serving her and her child. She also must overcome her anxiety, her sense of failure in needing help, her reluctance to trust someone else with her child, and her sense that she can't "say it as well" as the professional. She also must find the strength to insist that the professional see the whole child and provide truly "family-centered care." And if women who have the time and self confidence to organize parents on behalf of children with special needs have expressed problems in doing those things, how much more difficult it must be for those with less self assurance and education! And how much easier for a professional to dismiss the parent as part of the problem instead of part of the solution! Obviously, there are ways in which parents from widely divergent backgrounds cannot really help each other. However, their perspectives converge significantly — probably more than they diverge. Perhaps those women and men who have helped professionals see their role afresh can broaden their mission to others whose family strengths must also be fostered but who are less skilled at articulating them.

CONCLUSION:
MUCH PROGRESS — MUCH MORE NEEDED

In summary, families of very young children with special needs and handicapping conditions have led the way in helping professionals beyond a child-centered, family-ignoring style of operation. Many professionals have responded and encouraged this process, learning to value parents' perspectives as consumers of services, as advocates for improved services, and as teachers for new practitioners. Some of this change has been reflected in new legislation; some has been because of the new legislation. However, this is merely a beginning, both for the families of children with special needs and, even more, for other kinds of families seeking outside help in meeting the needs of their children.

Organization Addresses

The Federation for Children with Special Needs
95 Berkeley Street, #104
Boston, MA 02116

National Network of Parent Centers
95 Berkeley Street, #104
Boston, MA 02116

Parent Care
101 1/2 So. Union Street
Alexandria, VA 22314-3323

Parent Training and Information Projects
c/o The Federation for Children with Special Needs
95 Berkeley Street, #104
Boston, MA 02116

SKIP
216 Newport Drive
Severna Park, MD 21146

REFERENCES

Association for the Care of Children's Health (ACCH) (1987). *Family-centered care for children with special health care needs.* Washington, D.C.

Bohlin, J. (1989). Teaching and learning: My first year as an advisor at Wheelock College. *Zero to Three.* X(1). Washington, D.C.: National Center for Clinical Infant Programs.

Edge, E., & Pizzo, P. (Eds.) 1988. *The four critical junctures: support for parents of children with special needs.* Washington, D.C.: National Center for Clinical Infant Programs.

Equals in this partnership: parents of disabled and at-risk infants and toddlers speak to professionals. (1985). Washington, D.C.: National Center for Clinical Infant Programs.

Iris, M.A. (1988). The parent/professional relationship: complex connections, intricate bonds. *Family Resource Coalition Report.* VII(2). Chicago, IL: Family Resource Coalition.

Jeppson, E. (1988). Parents take priority in family-centered care. *Family Resource Coalition Report.* VII(2). Chicago, IL: Family Resource Coalition.

National Center for Clinical Infant Programs (1987). *Charting change in infants, families and services: a guide to program evaluation for administrators and practitioners.* Washington, D.C.

National Early Childhood Technical Assistance System (1989). *Guidelines and recommended practices for the individualized family service plan.* Washington, D.C.: Association for the Care of Children's Health.

Oster, A. (1985). *Equals in this partnership: parents of disabled and at-risk infants and toddlers speak to professionals.* Washington, D.C.: National Center for Clinical Infant Programs.

Pizzo, P. (1983). *Parent to parent: working together for ourselves and our children.* Boston, MA: Beacon Press.

Select Panel for the Promotion of Child Health (1981). *Better health for our children: A national strategy.* II. Washington, D.C.: U.S. Department of Health and Human Services.

Shonkoff, J. P., & Hauser-Cram, P. (1987). Early intervention for disabled infants and their families—a quantitative analysis. *Pediatrics,* 80, 650-658.

Silverstein, R. (1989). *The intent and spirit of P.L. 99-457: A sourcebook.* Washington, D.C.: National Center for Clinical Infant Programs.

Szanton, E. (1988). States take leadership role in prevention/early intervention programs. *Family Resource Coalition Report.* VII(2). Chicago, IL: Family Resource Coalition.

Woll, J., & Pizzo, P. (Eds.) (1988). *The open door: Parent participation in state policymaking about children with special health needs.* Washington, D.C.: National Center for Clinical Infant Programs.

A Life-span Perspective on Care-giving

Richard C. Birkel

SUMMARY. In its simplest form, care-giving involves a personal commitment to the needs of another individual, and the entrainment, or close pacing, of two life trajectories. In order to study care-giving from a life-span perspective, five areas of research and thinking must be integrated: (1) life-span development, (2) care-giving across different life stages, (3) the origin and dynamics of care-giving, care-withholding and harm-inducing behaviors, (4) the psychological and the social/economic contexts of care, and (5) the personal versus the relationship dimensions of care-giving.

INTRODUCTION

Care-giving refers to a class of positive responses to the basic needs of others. Prods to care-giving are everywhere apparent: in our families, in our work relationships, and on the streets of our cities. Individual and organizational responses to the needs of others are highly variable; some give deeply and graciously in a wide array of situations, others ignore the basic needs of most everyone and inflict harm on those they interact with, while the majority of individuals and organizations choose to invest their time and energy in providing certain kinds of care for select groups or individuals. Individuals and organizations tend to make care-giving choices which reflect a personal logic and strategy of how to respond to the basic needs of others while at the same time pursuing one's own agenda.

It is not the objective of this paper to present a causal model or theory of care-giving across the lifespan. Such a task is well beyond the scope of this paper and perhaps not feasible given the current status of theoretical and empirical development in this area. Rather, I aim to present some conceptual tools and clarifications which may ultimately be useful in developing such a model. Specifically, I emphasize that a life-span model of care-giving must be able to integrate current research and thinking in five critical areas: (1) life-span development, (2) care-giving across different life stages, (3) the origin and dynamics of care-giving, care-withholding and harm-inducing behaviors, (4) the psychological and the social/economic contexts of care, and (5) the personal versus the relationship dimensions of care-giving. I deal with each of these issues briefly below.

A LIFE-SPAN DEVELOPMENT APPROACH

A developmental view of behaviors, including care-giving, implies the ability to link age to the behavior in question in a systematic way. The complexity of development, however, greatly reduces our ability to trace specific or exact pathways and interactions that both anticipate and produce the care-giving and care-withholding behavior of interest. The problem lies in tracing the maturational processes in the individual along with and in interaction with ongoing physiological, psychological, social and cultural events.

The life-span development approach presented by Baltes and his colleagues (Baltes, Reese and Lipsitt, 1980), sees behavioral development as shaped by three major systems of influence:

a. Normative, age-graded influences. Events that occur in similar ways for all individuals in a particular culture or subculture (e.g., biological maturation, entrances and exits from socially-defined roles in school, work, and family life, etc.).
b. Normative, history-graded influences (Cohort effects). Events that occur to most members of a given generation (a cohort) in a similar way (e.g., wars, economic depressions, etc.) although the actual experience of the event may differ both within and between generations.
c. Non-normative life events. Events that vary by individual and are not shared across a population (e.g., family illness, divorce, unemployment, etc.).

These three types of influence, age-graded, history-graded, and non-normative each impact on the development of individual and organizational predilections and behaviors in relation to care-giving.

In relation to age-graded influences, for example, opportunities to enter the "care-giver role" tend to cluster (in our society) in young adulthood at the time of parenthood, and in later adulthood at the time that one's own parents become dependent, and this normative pattern of entry into the role of care-giver exerts a powerful influence on the institutions and supports available to care-givers. For example, social supports for those who enter care-giving roles at non-normative times, such as during adolescence, are likely to be poorly developed or non-existent. Changes in the age of puberty, in the average age at first birth for women, and in the expected life-spans of men and women, will have direct bearing on these normative patterns, and subsequently on the nature of social supports available to care-givers.

In addition to normative patterns of entry into care-giving roles, an individual's unique history (non-normative life events) with care-giving powerfully shapes personal attitudes and predilections. For example, whether an individual's formative experiences with care-giving comes via responsibility for a younger sibling, through care of a parent or grandparent, as a result of traumatic injury or illness of a family member, through work as an aide, or babysitter, or through any of a large number of other formal and informal avenues, will have an important bearing on the skills and attitudes that individual brings to future care-giving responsibilities. More than just the quantity of care-giving experience, it is likely that who one cares for, at what age, and under what conditions, will be important from a life-span perspective.

Finally, in relation to history-graded influences, it is clear that increased longevity and the current and projected "tidal-wave" of aging individuals in our society have made parent-care a key concern for at least one cohort of adults in the latter part of the this century and into the next. Such concerns, however, are historically novel and may be unique. In summary, a life-span perspective on care-giving must chart individual development in relation to both history-graded and non-normative influences in order to accurately reflect the major systems of influence on behavior.

INTEGRATING CARE-GIVING ACROSS THE LIFE-SPAN

Current approaches to care-giving are disjointed in that there is a tendency to apply different frameworks to understand care-giving depending upon whether the care receiver is a child, an elderly person, or someone who is sick or disabled. In the aging literature and in instances in which the care receiver is ill or disabled, for example, the predominant model of care-giving is a stress and coping model which emphasizes both objective and subjective "burden" experienced by the care-giver, and views the attitudes and behaviors of the care receiver primarily as mediators of the care-giver's reaction to the demands of care-giving (Birkel, 1987).

On the other hand, when the care-receiver is a developing child, care-giving is generally couched within a framework which emphasizes the child's well-being and development, and largely ignores that of the care-giver. For example, the emphasis is likely to be on the psychological development of the child viewed as a product of his/her involvement in "progressively more complex, enduring patterns of reciprocal contingent interaction with persons with whom he has established a mutual and enduring emotional attachment," and the focus of activity is generally on "activity challenging to the child" (Bronfenbrenner, 1974). Because the parent has taken on a strong positive value for the child, he/she is able to teach him language, encourage him in task oriented behavior, and increase his/her attention and perseverence by engaging in reciprocal interaction.

These two examples serve to illustrate how disparate our attempts to understand care-giving are depending upon the life-stage of the care-receiver. Inherent in these different approaches are subtle evaluations of the social "value" of the elderly versus the new-born, of the satisfaction versus frustration of providing care to them, and of the legitimate needs of each. A truly life-span model of care-giving must address investment in care-giving from within the care-giver's own frame of reference, and harbor no inherent assumptions about the difficulty or ease of providing care to different populations.

CARE-GIVING, CARE-WITHHOLDING AND HARM-INFLICTING BEHAVIORS

A comprehensive approach to care-giving across the life span must be realistic in giving attention to care-withholding and harm-inducing behaviors, as well as to care-giving. Most current approaches to care-giving isolate and idealize "care-giving" as a behavioral standard, and look upon neglect, abuse, and failure in care-giving as anomalies. On the other hand, some family scholars have tended to identify violence as the standard and care-giving as an anomaly. Indeed, Gelles and Straus (1979), in reviewing the literature on family violence, state: "Some of our findings together with other indicators lead us to believe that violence is a pervasive and common feature of American family relations. It may be more common to the institution of family than is love" (p.550).

It is essential, from a life-span perspective, to study care-giving as part of a larger "class" of behaviors which includes indifference, neglect, exploitation, and abuse; in short, the whole range of responses which characterize interpersonal and family relations. In Table 1, I have presented some prototypic behaviors (as examples) within a grid resulting from the crossing of the nature of the behavior (care-giving, care-with-

Table 1.

CHARACTER OF INTERPERSONAL RELATIONSHIPS

	Care-Giving	Care-Withholding	Harm-Inflicting
Physical/ Biological	Nursing	Neglect	Abuse
Psychological	Mentoring	Inattention	Exploitation
Social/ Economic	Advocacy	Indifference	Discrimination

holding, and harm-inflicting) with the level of impact (biological, psychological, social).

Table 1 shows that care-giving can be viewed as one end of a continuum (the x-axis) of interpersonal relations. At the other end of the continuum are harm-inflecting behaviors, and toward the middle are care-withholding (or care-neutral) behaviors. The y-axis demonstrates that each class of behaviors can have primary impacts at the biological, psychological or social/economic levels. Such a scheme is offered only as a first pass. Development of such a model must address a number of important concerns including the fact that withholding care, under some conditions, is equivalent to inflicting harm.

THE PSYCHOLOGICAL AND SOCIAL/ECONOMIC CONTEXTS OF CARE

There is a tendency in the literature to emphasize direct, personal care as the central concern in the study of care-giving. Yet, this is a limited perspective. Table 1 presents the view that care-giving, care-withholding, and harm-inflicting behaviors are biopsychosocial phenomenon, and that while each class of behavior may occur primarily at one of these levels (biological, psychological, social), the overall impact of the behavior may be to potentiate related behaviors at different levels. For example, advocating for children infected with HIV virus is likely to lead to more psychological and physical care-giving for them, while discriminating against these children is likely to lead to their exploitation and abuse. Similarly, public indifference is likely to lead to inattention and neglect.

Thus, within this framework, it is important to recognize the central importance, for understanding care-giving, of a range attitudes and influences which provide the context for direct, personal care. Ultimately, the study of care-giving must expand to include consideration of the social customs and sanctions, as well as the laws, codes, ordinances and regulations which relate to defining who is dependent and how such individuals are to be treated in a particular society. This cultural and social policy framework has a direct bearing on more personal aspects of care-giving.

For example, Lozier and Althouse (1974), in studying a rural Appalachian community, found that repeated observations of a particular individual led to a public definition of his/her career, along with assessment of that career (e.g., "no-count," "down and out"). These assessments, either harmful or helpful, produced environmental conditions which constituted social sanctions and strongly influenced the quality of care they could rely on in their old age from their juniors.

In a similar manner, the esteem or disdain with which different groups of dependents in society are held has important implications for how their personal and psychological needs are addressed by individuals and by society. Systems of abuse, as well as systems of care, are biopsychosocial phenomenon.

A potentially useful framework for considering the relation between the various levels of care-giving is that of "strategy." I use the term strategy to refer to the unity of at least two key elements in such arrangements: the identification of where and by whom care should be provided, along with obfuscation of the true burden of personal and economic costs by a public rationale which supports the particular arrangement over other possible options. A focus on strategies is intended to emphasize the role of choice among a range of options, and to point to the critical role of public doctrine in supporting the choices made, while masking deeper and more unsettling issues related to the true burden of care.

The history of deinstitutionalization can serve as an example which allows us to examine the elements involved in a public care-giving strategy. Deinstitutionalization involved moving large numbers of mostly elderly patients in state-run mental hospitals into nursing homes and represented a massive shift of financial costs for care to the federal government using as a vehicle for the transfer the newly established Medicaid and Medicare programs. In addition, it re-defined the nature of dependency from primarily "psychiatric" in nature, to primarily "medical" in nature (Mechanic, 1980).

The public rationale for deinstitutionalization, however, emphasized removing the costs of institutionalization from the patients themselves. Individuals with mental illness were to benefit from the new arrangements by significant reductions in constrained freedom, increases in autonomy and civil liberties and reductions in the adverse consequences of long-term removal from the community.

What is critical to note is that the ultimate costs of this strategy in terms of community disruption, homelessness, family burden, increases in law violations and assaultive behavior by expatients, as well as the risk of patients being exploited in the community, were largely overshadowed by highly-touted prospects for community living (Mechanic, 1980).

In a similar vein, current strategists of care for young children often point to the dangers of daycare in terms of its impact on the quality of child attachment to his/her mother, and the possible consequences for psychological and cognitive development. While this rationale argues for us to move slowly in shifting the burden of care for young children away from mothers, it fails completely to acknowledge the paradox that the act of producing children by a male carries little assumption of responsibility for care-giving, while for women, it involves assumption of massive personal responsibility. The unstated foundation for mother-focused strategies is that while procreation in our society is viewed as a right, care-giving is largely viewed as elective responsibility, particularly for males.

It is worth noting in this regard that mother-focused strategies are consistent with the overall strategy of care-giving in our society which has been to take advantage of what Galbraith calls "convenient social virtues" which ascribe merit to " . . . any pattern of behavior however uncomfortable for the individual involved that serves the comfort or well being of, or is otherwise advantageous for the more powerful members of a community" (Galbraith, 1958). This strategy has reinforced and provided rationale for a highly inequitable distribution of the costs of care-giving in our society, with women and families bearing the major burden of costs for all dependent groups. These costs include psychological strain, career disadvantage, economic injury, and the sacrifice of personal autonomy. The "winners" in this strategy have largely been men who have maintained significant career advantages and economic gains as well as advantages in personal autonomy.

In summary, a life-span perspective on care-giving must strive to understand care-giving within the broader context of social policy and cultural pressures. A focus on social "strategies" for dealing with dependency may be useful for this purpose.

CARE-GIVING (AND RECEIVING) AS BOTH A RELATIONSHIP AND A PERSONAL ODYSSEY

Much care-giving literature emphasizes the interaction of care-giver and receiver, but fails to illuminate the personal experience of either giving or receiving care. A life-span view of care-giving must allow examination of both the relationship dimension and the personal dimension (and how they are related) of giving and receiving care.

Care-givers Are Individuals with Agendas

In this regard, it is critical to view care-givers primarily as individuals with their own agendas. Individuals are not born into care-giving relationships nor do they give up control of their lives easily. Thus, the care-giver's history and direction, his/her goals and ambitions must undergird any understanding of the meaning and the experience of care-giving in their lives.

Yet, in carrying out their life's agenda, individuals often operate in a somewhat automatic fashion. In fact, according to Berscheid (1985), a large proportion of a person's daily activities are organized response sequences and /or portions of higher order plans that are in the process of being completed: "An organized action sequence is a series of actions that are emitted as a whole, or as a single unit; where the first action in the sequence occurs, the others in the series tend to follow" (p. 150). She refers to this as the "automatic" characteristic of organized behavior.

It is in this regard that the impact of care-giving is best understood. That is, using Berscheid's model, the care-giving relationship can be viewed as intrachain connections which serve to facilitate, interrupt, or have no affect on the care-giver's ability to carry out his/her higher order plans. Similarly for the care-receiver. Hence, care-giver and receiver may operate in parallel fashion (*"un-meshed"*) . . . "where there are no causal connections between the two intrachain sequences simultaneously occurring (disengaged), or their behavior may be *meshed* when they are simultaneously executing highly organized intrachian sequences, and events in each person's chain facilitate the performance of the other's sequence. Finally, they may be *non-meshed*, wherein the causal connections between the two intrachain sequences interfere with the enactment of one or both" (Berscheid, 1985, p. 152). Negative emotions are most likely when the behavioral sequences of care-giver and care-receiver are non-meshed, whereas harmony may prevail when these sequences are meshed.

In summary, care-givers are individuals who enter into demanding relationships with those who benefit from their care. In order to understand care-giving behavior we must develop models which allow us to view care-givers (and receivers) as individuals with personal agendas and to understand the impact of the care-giving/receiving relationship on the fulfillment of those agendas.

CONCLUSION

There are a number of forces which are making it increasingly important for us to develop a life-span perspective on care-giving. First, there is growing awareness that decisions involving care-giving responsibilities are among the most important decisions individuals and families make. They are seminal and potentiate or forestall a wide range of subsequent choices and options. Despite their importance, however, they are often made at such an early age, or in the face of such compelling conditions that the realistic weighing of the potential impact of care-giving is precluded. Indeed, care-giving responsibilities often descend upon individuals and families with great speed, as when a parent or spouse becomes disabled, and sweep one up in a backwash of consequences which continue unabated long after care-giving responsibilities end.

Second, from the study of care-giving situations such as teenage childbearing, caring for an aging parent during middle age, and caring for a spouse during one's own old age, we are beginning to understand the fundamental economic ramifications of care-giving for both individuals and society. Corporations are coming to understand that they share in the cost of providing care for the dependent or sick family members of employees through employee absenteeism, the cost of health benefits to the corporation, and through the various care-giver morbidities including injuries from lifting, family conflict, stress and fatigue. Similarly, issues of child care and early childhood education are directly tied to the ability of corporations to maintain an active labor force now, and the viability of the labor force in the future.

As a result, the business community has begun to look for opportunities to invest in the communities in which they are located. These investments are a good example of the kind of care-giving I refer to (in Table 1) as "sponsorship." Increasingly, business sees supporting care-giving as an investment in the future labor force, and looks to the provision of child-care and eldercare as investments in their current labor force. In addition, providing support for care-givers and dependents is, in itself, a big business with important and far-reaching economic implications (e.g., see Estes, 1979).

Finally, we have begun to understand the critical importance of care-giving issues to understanding the development of men, as well as women. For example, in recent years we have found that men are a significant portion of care-givers for the elderly in our society (Stone, Cafferata & Sangl, 1986) and, for them, care-giving is of a different quality and may have a different life course impact than for women. Further, there has been increasing recognition that fathers play unique roles in the development of their children, and that divorce and remarriage make important care-giving demands on each parent. Ultimately, by disentangling issues of gender and care-giving, we may come to see that care-giving decisions and responsibilities are of fundamental importance to human development, regardless of gender.

REFERENCES

Baltes, P.B., Reese, H.W. & Lipsitt, L.P. (1980). Life-span developmental psychology. *Annual Review of Psychology, 31,* 65-110.

Berscheid, E. (1985). Compatibility, Interdependence, and Emotion. In W. Ickes (Ed) *Compatible and incompatible relationships.* New York: Springer-Verlag, pp.143-161.

Birkel, R.C. (1987). Toward a social ecology of the home-care household. *Psychology and Aging, 2*(3), 294-301.

Bronfenbrenner, U. (1974). Is early intervention effective? *Teachers College Record,* 76, 279-33.

Estes, C.L. (1979). *The Aging Enterprise.* San Francisco: Jossey-Bass.

Galbraith, J.K. (1958). *The affluent society.* Boston: Houghton Mifflin.

Gelles, R.J. & Straus, M.A. (1979). Determinants of violence in the family: Toward a theoretical integration. In W.R. Burr, R. Hill, F.I. Nye & I.L. Reiss (Eds) *Contemporary Theories about the family: Research-based theories, Vol. 1.* New York: The Free Press, 549-581.

Lozier, J. & Althouse, R. (1974). Social enforcement of behavior toward elders in an appalachian mountain settlement. *The Gerontologist, 14,* 69-80.

Mechanic, D. (1980). *Mental health and social policy.* Englewood Cliffs, N.J.: Prentice Hall.

Stone, R. Cafferata, G.L. & Sangl, J. (1986). Caregivers of the frail elderly: A national profile. Paper presented at the 32 Annual Meeting of the American Society on Aging, San Francisco, March.

Families, Policy,
and Family Support Policies

Brian L. Wilcox
Janet E. O'Keeffe

SUMMARY. An historical perspective on family policy is presented along with issues shaping future directions. Two prevention-oriented policies in particular are discussed: respite care services to assist persons caring for elderly infirm family members and family (parental) leave for new parents. The goals of previous family policies are challenged and recommendations are made for more realistic approaches to formulating successful family policies.

Family policy seems to have come of age over the past decade. While politicians have invoked the family in policy pronouncements throughout the history of politics, attention to family policy as a genre of social policy is relatively recent (Steiner, 1981). Serious discussions concerning the nature of family policy—what it might be and what it might accomplish—are typically dated to the writings of Daniel Patrick Moynihan (1967; U.S. Dept. of Labor, 1965). At that time, Moynihan wrote that "American social policy until now has been directed toward the individual. Thus, our employment statistics count as equally unemployed a father of nine children, a housewife coming back into the labor market in her forties, and a teenager looking for a part-time job after school" (1967, p. 387). This individual focus, Moynihan argued, made it virtually impossible for the nation to respond to the myriad problems facing Americans living in diverse family situations and, more importantly, failed to recognize the need for a policy response designed to ensure the viability of American families. What was needed, Moynihan stated, was a family policy:

A national family policy need only declare that it is the policy of the American government to promote the stability and well-being of the American family; and the social programs of the Federal government will be formulated and administered with this object in mind. . . . (1967, p. 390)

Unfortunately, the controversy surrounding Moynihan's focus on the status of the Black family cut short consideration of an explicit "family policy" during the remaining years of the Johnson administration.

The call for a family policy arose again in the mid-1970's. Senator Walter Mondale, chairman of the Senate Subcommittee on Children and Youth, seriously entertained a proposal to extend the concept of environmental impact statements to policies as they might affect families. The family impact statement would analyze the likely intended and unintended consequences of proposed government policies on family structure and function. Although several noted developmentalists supported Mondale's efforts (Bronfenbrenner, 1974; Zigler, 1974), enthusiasm for the proposal never developed within the Congress. While the Foundation for Child Development provided funds for a feasibility study of the family impact statement process, no action was subsequently taken by either the Congress or the Administration.

Family policy discussions did not cease, however. Jimmy Carter, mounting a campaign for the presidency, picked up the theme of family policy. Early in the campaign, Carter stated: "It is clear that the national government should have a strong pro-family policy, but the fact is that our government has no family policy, and that is the same as having an anti-family policy . . . (O)ur government's policies have often actually weakened our families, or even destroyed them" (Carter, 1978, p. 463). Carter proposed that, if elected, he would require a family impact statement for each new policy proposal.

Campaign rhetoric and political reality often diverge, and such was the case with the Carter pledge to establish family impact analysis as a routine in the policymaking process. Indeed, the major "family" activity initiated by the Carter Administration was the White House Conference on Families. The pathetic history of this event is detailed by Steiner (1981). The failure of the conference to produce anything other than exceptionally vague policy statements and fighting between liberal and conservative constituencies surprised few and illustrates many of the dilemmas facing those advocating a national family policy.

Interestingly, Carter's successor, Ronald Reagan, also sounded the pro-family policy theme in words nearly identical to Carter's, stating that government policies were often the culprits responsible for "family breakups, welfare dependency, and a large increase in births out of wedlock" (cited in Levitan, Belous, & Gallo, 1988, p. 131). Unlike Carter, Reagan's inclinations were noninterventionist and, sometimes, anti-interventionist. Reagan's goals for family policy, every bit as inexplicit as Carter's, included the "return of money from the federal budget to the family budget" (p. 131).

President Reagan did pursue two family policy related activities late in his presidency. First, he asked Gary Bauer, then Under Secretary of the Department of Education, to chair an Administration working group "that would study how government at all levels could be more supportive of American families" (Gary Bauer letter to President Reagan, personal communication). The Working Group, dominated by young neo-conservatives in the White House and the Federal agencies, produced a report more polemical than analytical, filled with factual inaccuracies, clear misrepresentations of data, and rhetorical fusillades against the "liberal establishment" (Bauer, 1986). Undermined by the controversy surrounding it (Senator Moynihan referred to the report as a "temper tantrum"), the report and its recommendations never generated serious discussions. Second, President Reagan issued an Executive Order requiring all federal agencies issuing regulatory or statutory proposals to append a family impact statement addressing the likely effect of the proposal on families. There is no evidence, however, that this order had an effect on the policy process.

As a general theme, family policy has proven attractive to scholars and politicians alike. Presidents as ideologically dissimilar as Carter and Reagan were able to rally around the concept. Moving beyond the concept to specific policy directions has proven problematic, for as Steiner has noted, "Family policy is unifying only so long as the details are avoided. When the details are confronted, family policy splits into innumerable components. It is many causes with many votaries" (1981, p. 215).

BARRIERS TO FAMILY POLICY

The barriers to a family policy are numerous. The White House Conference on Families was nearly undone by the problem of defining the term "families." Also, if family policy is seen as encompassing all or most policy actions having a potential effect on families, the concept broadens to the point of incomprehensibility, including as it would nearly all areas of social and economic policy. Additionally, there is a strong national noninterventionist bias when it comes to "family matters." The tension between the contrasting ideologies of public versus private responsibility for family well-being has been a constant throughout the history of American social policy (Grubb & Lazerson, 1982). Both the American tradition of respecting the sanctity of the family and the limitations which the Constitution places on federal legislative intervention in family matters limits the probability of a comprehensive national family policy. Finally, there is little agreement on what actions will actually strengthen or support the American family. Opponents of abortion and proponents of reproductive choice both argue that their own position is pro-family and their opponent's position is anti-family. Proponents of comprehensive child care legislation argue that such legislation is clearly pro-family; some conservatives argue, however, that child care legislation encourages women to work outside the home, abandoning their caretaking roles to persons less capable of providing a nurturing environment for the child, and are thus inherently anti-family.

FAMILY POLICIES: REALISTIC AND UNREALISTIC GOALS

If comprehensive family policy is unlikely for the reasons above, there is more hope for specific family-oriented policies. Such policies would typically have relatively modest, concrete goals. Respite care and parental leave are discussed later as two examples of specific family-oriented policies.

Scholars and politicians alike often assume either explicitly or implicitly that government policy actions can and do have effects on family structural variables such as marriage, divorce and fertility rates. We will briefly examine the validity of these claims and then discuss what we see as the appropriate and realistic goals of family-oriented policies.

Federal welfare programs were described as anti-family policies by Presidents Carter and Reagan. Joseph Califano, Carter's Secretary for Health, Education, and Welfare, told the Senate Subcommittee on Public Assistance in 1978 that the Aid to Families with Dependent Children (AFDC) welfare program breaks up families. When pressed for specifics and data supporting this claim, Califano was able to provide none (Moynihan, 1986). By this time, the presumed anti-family effects of welfare policy had entered political lore.

The strongest argument supporting the contention that welfare policies have destructive consequences for families was made several years later by Charles Murray (1984). According to Murray, welfare benefits: allow women to have and support children without marrying; allow men to father children without fear of financial responsibility; encourage women receiving welfare to have additional children in order to increase the size of the benefit; and encourage couples to divorce in order to qualify for benefits. Murray argued that increases in divorce and out-of-wedlock birth rates and decreases in marriage rates occurring throughout the 1970s and early 1980s were closely and causally related to increases in social welfare spending, especially with respect to the AFDC program.

Numerous scholars (e.g., Ellwood & Bane, 1984; Ellwood & Summers, 1986; Gottschalk, 1985; Greenstein, 1985) have criticized Murray's claims, principally on empirical grounds. For example, Ellwood and Summers (1986) carefully compared time trends for welfare policies (and benefits) and changes in family structural variables. Numerous findings contradicted Murray's claims. They found that between 1972 and 1982, while AFDC participation rates were virtually constant, the proportion of children living in female-headed families rose 6 percent. During roughly the same period, the out-of-wedlock birth rate for Black women fell by 13 percent while the rate for white women rose by 27 percent. Murray's claim that AFDC is a major influence on the birth rate for unmarried women is contradicted by empirical reality. Ellwood and Summers also examined the relationship between state AFDC benefit levels and various family structure variables: divorce rates, proportion of single-parent families, and out-of-wedlock births. Since state AFDC benefits vary considerably, Murray's position would hypothesize a strong relationship among benefit levels and family structural variables. In fact, Ellwood and Summers found no significant relationships among the measures. Ellwood and Bane (1985) found only very small effects of AFDC on similar family variables, certainly nothing of the magnitude posited by Murray.

Bane and Jargowsky (1988) examined a variety of policy contexts, including family law, adolescent pregnancy prevention, family supports, welfare, and economic policy, in order to assess the relationship between changes in government policy and family structure. In each case they found policy changes to be very poor predictors of changes in family structure. They conclude that "direct government policy is neither the problem nor the solution, at least in terms of 'causing' or 'preventing' marital breakup and unmarried parenthood" (p. 245). Bane and Jargowsky, along with Ellwood and Summers (1986), conclude that the demographic shifts which have generated legitimate concern amongst policymakers are due to a host of very broad social forces which have created dramatic changes in societal attitudes concerning marriage, divorce, parenting and work.

The conclusion that policy tools are relatively ineffectual means for triggering changes in family structural variables should not be taken as suggesting that policies designed to assist families are not worth pursuing. There are, of course, a variety of potential policy goals other than changing family structures. We agree with Bane and Jargowsky (1988) that more modest but nonetheless important goals of family oriented policies should include (a) the alleviation of the economic stresses facing disadvantaged families and (b) the reinforcement of societal concern for the support of families. The former category might include more stringent child support enforcement policies and expansion of the earned income tax credit. The latter category would include a variety of family support policies, including child care, family leave, and respite care. We will now examine the latter two policy issues, respite care and family leave, more closely.

RESPITE CARE

Background

The growing need for long-term care for the elderly and the potentially high cost of a long-term care program are major issues with which policy makers at both the state and federal level are grappling. Currently, Medicare covers only acute and post-acute services, and Medicaid, which provides coverage only for the very poor, is biased towards institutional care. For those not eligible for Medicaid, nursing home care (which averages about $25,000 per year) and in-home and community-based services are often unaffordable.

In the absence of a comprehensive state or national policy to address the needs of the chronically ill and impaired elderly, families provide the majority of long-term care (LTC) for this population. Only twenty percent of the impaired elderly are living in nursing homes. The remainder are cared for in the community, and it is this informal care provided by family members and friends that is a major factor in preventing or delaying nursing home utilization (U.S. House of Representatives, 1987). The majority of caregivers are female — generally wives and adult daughters — and they provide care an average of four hours a day, seven days a week (U.S. Department of Labor, 1986). Many of these women have competing family obligations and work conflicts. Thirty percent of caregivers (excluding spouses) have simultaneous responsibility for children under 18, and many women must combine caregiving with the demands of a full-time job (Commonwealth Fund Commission, 1989).

Several demographic trends suggest that, in the future, conflicts between work and family obligations — and between elder care and child care — will be more prevalent. Longer life expectancies, delayed childbearing, an increase in the median age of the labor force, and increasing female labor participation rates will together result in increasing numbers of women working and caring for dependent family members — both children and the elderly (U.S. Department of Labor, 1986).

Numerous studies, surveys and anecdotal reports have documented the tremendous burdens that family members must bear when faced with the care of a disabled elderly spouse or parent. The stress of caregiving, particularly when a family member is severely disabled, may itself constitute a serious health problem for many caregivers. A major review of the literature (U.S. House of Representatives, 1987) found that caregivers frequently reported symptoms of depression and anxiety, and that many used psychotropic drugs and alcohol to cope with the emotional strains of caregiving. The stresses associated with caregiving have also been cited as a factor in elder abuse (State of Wisconsin, 1987).

Concerns about escalating nursing home expenditures under Medicaid and a recognition that families need support if they are to continue providing care in the community have generated various public and private strategies to support family caregivers. These include support groups, counseling services, training, and respite care (Gorsche, Mastalish & Shepard, 1987). Respite care involves the provision of care for infirm elderly persons who are regularly cared for by family members, thereby providing that regular caretaker with a respite from the burdens associated with providing care. At the federal level, Section 2176 of the 1981 Omnibus Reconciliation Act allows state Medicaid programs to offer in-home and community-based services, including respite care, under a special waiver. Under the 2176 Waiver Program, states obtain waivers from Medicaid regulations — such as the requirement for state-wide services to experiment with the provision of non-institutional long-term care services. However, these home and community-based services must be targeted toward those at risk for institutionalization, and the cost cannot exceed comparable care in a nursing home. By 1986, 46 states had waivers to cover such services and many included respite care (U.S House of Representatives, 1987).

Other federal programs providing a limited amount of funds for home and community-based services include the Social Services Block Grant, Title II of the Older Americans Act, ACTION's Senior Companion Program, and the Veterans Administration Respite Care Program. At the state level, there has been considerable legislative activity in the area of respite care with funding appropriated for both demonstration projects and ongoing programs (Stone, 1985). Because of the great demand for services, restrictive eligibility criteria and the limited funding available, both state and federal respite care programs serve only a small proportion of those in need (Cohen & Warren, 1985).

Policy Issues in Respite Care

While respite care is recognized as a necessary long-term care benefit in both state and federal legislation, there are policy issues related to the creation of a respite benefit that remain to be addressed. Most important is the determination of appropriate goals of a respite benefit and the definition and operationalization of the benefit to meet these goals. A narrow definition of respite care may restrict the usefulness of the benefit for many families and undermine its goal. On the other hand, overly optimistic goals may cause respite care programs to be viewed as failures.

The goal of many respite care programs and demonstration projects has been to provide support to family members in order to prevent or delay institutionalization. To achieve this goal, many programs have targeted individuals considered "at risk for institutionalization," e.g., those who have requested nursing home replacement. This strategy, however, is often ineffective because the caregiving burden generally reaches crisis proportions before families seek nursing home placement (Meltzer, cited in Cohen & Warren, 1985, p. 144). If respite care is offered only to those individuals at risk of nursing home placement, the services may be too little, too late to achieve the intended outcome.

Another factor to consider when determining the appropriate goals of a respite benefit is whether the maintenance of a severely impaired family member in their own home is in the best interest of the care recipient and the caregiver. There will be situations where nursing home placement is appropriate, and a program whose only goal is to delay institutionalization may well achieve its goals at the cost of extending an unreasonable family caregiving burden (Hawes, Kane, Powers & Reinardy, 1988).

Determining what types and levels of services will be most useful to families is another important respite care policy issue. Respite care is often categorized as one of many LTC services required by the disabled elderly. In fact, the term "respite" more accurately defines the intent rather than the type of service. Although all respite care programs don't offer all services, respite care services encompass the full range of LTC services, including volunteer in-home companions, home health aides, skilled nursing services, adult day care and nursing home care. A caregiver with a disabled spouse in the early stages of Alzheimers disease may require only companion services. However, as the illness progresses leading to physical impairment, she may require specialized nursing services. If respite services are limited to just one type or one level of care, there will be many family caregivers whose needs will not be met.

The delivery of respite services must also be flexible enough to meet the diverse and changing needs of family caregivers. Respite care is often defined as the provision of "temporary" or "intermittent" services for short periods of time. Service hours are generally capped and the number of hours allowed per year is very low relative to need. Such limited benefits restrict the usefulness of respite care because they do little to provide regular relief to overburdened caregivers. Respite care which is limited to an annual 14 day institutional care benefit can create an incentive to "save" the benefit for a crisis. Respite care in crisis situations is certainly needed, such as when a caregiver becomes ill. However, families need respite care on a regular basis as well. To be useful to families, and to prevent breakdown in family caregiving, a respite benefit should include the widest array of services available and should allow families to schedule the services to meet their needs.

Apart from fiscal constraints, the major reason underlying the creation of a respite benefit distinct from other LTC services and the limited nature of such benefits, is the concern that the provision of formal in-home and community based services will lead families to abandon their caregiving responsibilities—often termed the "substitution effect." However, in a major review of the literature, Hawes et al. (1988) found no evidence of this effect among primary family caregivers. In fact, caregivers substantially underutilize respite services relative to need, in part because of a reluctance to leave their family members with respite workers.

Family members are also reluctant to use formal services because of cost concerns—both current and future anticipated costs for institutional care (Gwyther, 1987). In a 1982 national survey, approximately a third of caregivers were poor or near-poor and 57 percent reported incomes in the low to middle range (Stone, Cafferata & Sangle 1986). Thus, affordability is a major factor in determining family utilization of respite services. In the absence of subsidized care, i.e., free services or payment according to a sliding scale, many families will not receive the services they need.

Families provide support to frail and disabled spouses, siblings, and parents for as long as they are able. The literature is replete with accounts of caregivers who have provided care to severely impaired relatives, day and night for many years, with little or no respite. The fact that the overwhelming majority of disabled elderly live in the community attests to the continuing involvement of families in providing long-term care. The fear that the provision of formal services will undercut or replace family care seems unfounded. The majority of research in this area has concluded that such services do not replace family care, rather they *complement and support* the family's caregiving. However, unless a respite benefit includes a full range of affordable long-term care services that are available when caregivers need them and for as long as they need them, respite services will not meet the needs of millions of families and will not achieve the goals of preventing or delaying institutionalization.

FAMILY LEAVE

Background

The profound changes affecting labor force participation of women, particularly mothers, have created substantial new burdens with which families must cope. As of March 1988, 48 percent of all infants and one-year-olds had mothers in the labor force, representing an increase of over 100% since 1970 (U.S. Department of Labor, 1988). Financial concerns are paramount among the reasons why many women return to work soon after giving birth (Kamerman, Kahn, & Kingston, 1983). Projections suggest that trends such as these will continue into the 21st century. By the year 2000, nearly two-thirds of women will be employed and will thus comprise nearly half of the total workforce (Hudson Institute, 1988).

Developmentalists have grown increasingly concerned about the conflicts between work and family roles and the implications of those conflicts for both child development and family functioning (Bronfenbrenner & Crouter, 1982; Brazelton, 1985; Hopper & Zigler, 1988). Particularly troubling to many researchers is the trend toward early return to work following the birth of a child. Relying on findings from many research areas but particularly from the attachment literature, scholars have suggested that this pattern of returning to work within the first few weeks of giving birth can have significant negative effects on the mother-infant attachment process and subsequent social development of the infant (Harwood, 1988; Hopper & Zigler, 1988). Brazelton (1988) further argues that the early months are critical for family development as well: "All the evidence that we have concerning pregnancy, labor and delivery, and the development of attachment between parents and their young infants demonstrates that this is an important time to aid and support families in creating a sense of mutual understanding, trust, and love" (p. 47). Brazelton, Zigler, Bronfenbrenner and their colleagues have argued that mothers should be given approximately six months of leave following the birth of the child, and that fathers should spend a significant amount of time at home with the new family as well (Yale Bush Center in Child Development and Social Policy, 1985).

Policy responses to these family needs have been limited. The federal

Pregnancy Discrimination Act requires employers to treat pregnancy-related disabilities, including normal post-childbirth recovery, as they would any other temporary disability. While this provides new mothers with some limited protection against job and income loss, disability leave is limited to the time medically needed to recover from childbirth, often no more than a few weeks. A leave this limited cannot be responsive to the psychosocial needs of infants and parents. Further, not all employers provide disability coverage to employees, and those that do often provide only partial wage replacement and may exclude part-time employees.

In the absence of federal family leave policy, states and the private sector have been left to develop some response. That response has varied considerably. Six states have passed laws which guarantee men and women time to care for a new child, ranging from 8 to 24 weeks of family leave. A number of other states require that all employers provide temporary disability insurance for employees, including coverage for pregnancy and childbirth related disabilities. The lengths of these leaves are often unspecified; those laws that specify leave length tend to offer between six and eight weeks. Clearly, even the best of these state laws falls well short of the leave parameters recommended by child and family development experts.

Family leave policies in the private sector are exceedingly variable. Factors affecting leave policies include the size of the company and whether the employees are union members (Butler & Wasserman, 1988; Sheinberg, 1988). Several studies have examined corporate leave policies, the most thorough being the Columbia University (Kamerman et al., 1983) and Catalyst (1986) studies. The Catalyst study of Fortune 1500 companies found that a slight majority of companies offered some unpaid maternity leave for women with a job guarantee. Thirty-seven percent offered unpaid, job-protected leave for new fathers, but a majority of these companies indicated that they disapproved of men taking such leaves. The Columbia University study of a random sample of small to medium firms found that 88 percent of those companies provided some maternity leave, though in most cases the leave was limited to two or three months or less, and that the typical leave was wholly unpaid or partially paid only for the "medical disability" period. Paternity leave was offered by one quarter on the companies, but typically for only a few days. Many of the companies did not, however, continue to provide health care benefits during the leave period.

In sum, the likelihood that new parents will have a reasonable period of leave available to them following the birth of their child, a leave that would allow them to develop as a family, is dependent on the state they reside in and the particular policies of their employer. State employees in Connecticut may take six months of family leave. IBM employees may take 3 years of unpaid, job-protected leave with company-paid benefits. Employees in many small businesses have no guarantees with regard to job-security should they take even so few as three weeks of leave following the birth of a child. The modal state and corporate policy provides just enough unpaid or partially paid leave to allow the new mother to physically recover from childbirth. Most women feel fortunate if their employer allows them to take as much as four months of unpaid leave.

This situation appears all the more appalling when one examines the standards of other nations. The U.S. is virtually alone among industrialized nations in not offering some form of parental leave as a universal benefit to new parents (Kamerman, 1988; Kamerman & Kahn, 1981). Over 130 countries, including some Third World nations, provide maternity benefits to new mothers. Most of these countries provide partial or full salary replacement for some portion of the leave. France, for example, guarantees a 16 week job-protected leave for new mothers, along with a substantial cash benefit. Parents may also take an unpaid, job-protected supplementary leave of up to two years to care for a child.

Policy Issues in Family Leave

Before examing specific policy options relating to family leave, we must return to the issue of policy goals. It should be noted that many nations adopted parental leave benefits for pronatalist reasons. Faced with declining or stable populations, policymakers believed that these policies would facilitate child rearing. While parental leave policies likely do ease child rearing, the empirical evidence suggests that they are not effective in raising national birthrates (Demeny, 1986).

Possibly the most important goal served by a family leave policy would be to signal to the American public that families are indeed valued and critical to the well-being of society. Family support policies such as parental leave have important symbolic value that may well "enhanc[e] the status and dignity of families having and raising children" (Bane & Jargowsky, 1988, p. 252). Federal leadership in this arena might trigger changes in corporate policy further recognizing the needs of families. The cumulative symbolic, indirect and direct effects of such action should contribute to enhanced child development and family functioning, and in the long run, possibly to family structural variables. In the short run, though, providing direct support to families to facilitate family adjustment is enough of a goal to justify policy action.

In designing a parental leave policy, numerous policy choices must be made. One important decision concerns the length of the leave. The expert panel convened by the Yale Bush Center (1985) recommended a minimum leave of six months. This length was considered the minimum time needed to allow new parents to recover from childbirth and to care for the newborn and establish equilibrium in the family. Legislation being considered by Congress would provide only 10 weeks of leave.

A second policy decision concerns coverage, namely, whether coverage should include adoptive parents and foster parents. Most countries have extended parental leave to adoptive but not foster parents on the grounds that adoptive parents make the same lifelong commitment to their new children as do natural parents and will need time to make the transition to parenthood.

A critical decision involves the types of supports provided employees on leave. We believe that to make such leave a practical option for many parents, it must include some level of wage replacement. Low income families are unlikely to be able to afford anything more than a very brief leave if they must forego all income. An unpaid leave policy might be regressive in the sense that higher income families would be more likely to use the benefit. To make such a benefit manageable, policymakers might limit income replacement to 90 percent of income for three or four months, followed by two or three months where the benefit level drops to some lower amount (e.g., 50 percent). Another support of concern to families is health benefits. Most existing policies require continuation of health benefits, although since most policies in the U.S. are for unpaid leave, beneficiaries must pay their contribution for health care even though they receive little or no income. The legislation being considered by Congress would provide unpaid leave but would protect both job and benefits.

Once the issues of eligibility, coverage, and benefit levels are decided upon, one must establish a means for financing and administering the benefit. Most European nations, for example, finance the benefit through a social insurance mechanism where costs might be shared by the government, employers and employees. The proposal for unpaid leave pending before Congress would require employers to cover costs associated with the benefit.

We concur with the Yale Bush Center (1985) that the issue of family leave requires immediate national attention. State and private sector responses have been uneven and too limited. The federal government should establish a minimum policy upon which the states and the private sector can expand. Family leave is a policy supported broadly by the public and represents an action which can send an unequivocably clear message from policymakers to families concerning the centrality of family well-being to societal well-being.

FUTURE TRENDS IN FAMILY POLICY

We began this article with a discussion of some of the dilemmas facing family policy advocates. We noted, for example, the general lack of consensus concerning the types of policies that might strengthen families. Some opponents of respite care policies have argued that federally supported respite care usurps family authority and undermines family responsibility. We also noted the traditional tension between ideologies of public versus private responsibility for family matters. Opponents of parental leave policy proposals argue that parental leave is a concern of employees and employers, not the federal or state governments. We are unable to provide an example of a problem where there is unanimity of opinion regarding both the nature of the problem and the appropriate policy response. Still, the opposition to these policies, particularly in the case of family leave, centers on the Federal government's role in addressing the problem and not on the correctness of the policy itself. Also, both policies further the goals of reducing family economic stress and reinforcing societal concern for family wellbeing.

There is a growing consensus among policymakers that stable, well-functioning families are fundamentally important to the health of the nation and that families are increasingly strained by broad changes in social and economic circumstances. In such an environment, traditional opponents of state intervention may well soften their stance and accept state responsibility in circumstances where the failure to act might well have short and long term negative consequences for both the state and individual families. For example, there is unprecedented agreement emerging regarding the worthiness of comprehensive child care legislation. While disagreement continues to exist concerning the exact form such legislation should take, it is noteworthy that key sponsors of this legislation in the Senate include Senators Kennedy and Hatch. There is also growing agreement that the federal government must respond more vigorously to the problems facing poor families, particularly the working poor (Ellwood, 1988). Specific policies attracting considerable support include expansion of the earned income tax credit and innovations in the area of child support enforcement.

For the foreseeable future, all policy actions will be constrained by the nation's budget deficit. The consequences of this situation for family policies are two-fold. First, policymakers will naturally be attracted to policies which are self-financing (e.g., will not require new government expenditures) or are demonstrably cost-effective. Second, policies which target the most needy are more likely to attract support than those reaching a broader population.

In this type of political environment there is a tendency among advocates to overpromise particular policy actions. Some advocates of early childhood education have made fairly wild claims about the likely benefits of a national early childhood education policy on the basis of a few very expensive experimental programs. Exaggerated claims are almost always counterproductive in the end. Advocates of family support policies must avoid the overadvocacy trap and, instead of arguing that such policies will reverse trends in family formation, dissolution and birthrate, convince policymakers that actions facilitating children's development and family dignity are inherently in the nation's interest. Of course, evidence of likely cost-benefits is always welcomed by policymakers.

REFERENCES

Bane, M.J., & Jargowsky, P.A. (1988). The links between government policy and family structure: What matters and what doesn't. In A.J. Cherlin (Ed.), *The changing American family and public policy* (pp. 219-261). Washington, DC: Urban Institute Press.

Bauer, G.L. (1986, November). *The family: Preserving America's future* (Report of the Working Group on the Family). Washington, DC: U.S. Department of Education, Office of the Undersecretary.

Brazelton, T.B. (1985). *Working and caring*. Boston: Addison-Wesley.

Brazelton, T.B. (1988). Issues for working parents. In E.F. Zigler & M. Frank (Eds.), *The parental leave crisis: Toward a national policy*. New Haven: Yale University Press.

Bronfenbrenner, U. (1974). Testimony before the Subcommittee on Children and Youth of the Senate Labor and Public Welfare Committee, 93rd Congress. Washington, DC: Government Printing Office.

Bronfenbrenner, U., & Crouter, A.C. (1982). Work and family through space and time. In S.B. Kamerman & C.D. Hayes (Eds.), *Families that work: Children in a changing world* (pp. 39-83). Washington, DC: National Academy Press.

Butler, B., & Wasserman, J. (1988). Parental leave: Attitudes and practices in small businesses. In E.F. Zigler & M. Frank (Eds.), *The parental leave crisis: Toward a national policy* (pp. 223-232). New Haven: Yale University Press.

Carter, J. (1978). A statement in New Hampshire, August 3, 1976. In *The presidential campaign, 1976, vol. 1: Jimmy Carter* (pp. 460-464). Washington, DC: Government Printing Office.

Catalyst. (1986). *Report on a national study of parental leaves*. New York: Catalyst.

Cohen, S. & Warren R.D. (1985). *Respite care: Principles, programs and policies*. Texas: PRO-ED, Inc.

Commonwealth Fund Commission on Elderly People Living Alone. (1989). *Help at home–long-term care assistance for impaired elderly people*. Baltimore, MD: Author.

Demeny, P. (1986). Pronatalist policies in low fertility countries: Patterns, performance and prospects. *Population and Development Review, 12*(supplement), 350-366.

Ellwood, D.T. (1988). *Poor support: Poverty and the American family*. New York: Basic Books.

Ellwood, D.T., & Bane, M.J. (1984). *The impact of AFDC on family structure and living arrangements* (Contract No. 92A-82). Washington, DC: U.S. Department of Health and Human Services.

Ellwood, D.T., & Summers, L.H. (1986). Poverty in America: Is welfare the answer or the problem. In S.H. Danziger & D.H. Weinberg (Eds.), *Fighting poverty: What works and what doesn't* (pp. 78-105). Cambridge, MA: Harvard University Press.

Gorsche, N., Mastalish, R.C. & Shepherd, P. (1987). *Caregivers of the elderly*. Washington, DC: National Association of Area Agencies on Aging.

Gottschalk, P. (1985). Testimony before the Subcommittee on Fiscal and Monetary Policy of the Joint Economic Committee of the U.S. Congress, 99th Congress. Washington, DC: Government Printing Office.

Greenstein, R. (1985). Testimony before the Subcommittee on Fiscal and Monetary Policy of the Joint Economic Committee of the U.S. Congress, 99th Congress. Washington, DC: Government Printing Office.

Grubb, W.N., & Lazerson, M. (1982). *Broken promises: How Americans fail their children*. New York: Basic Books.

Gwyther, L.P. (1987). *Catastrophic health care: the role of respite care*. Testimony before the Subcommittee on Health and the Environment of the House Committee on Energy and Commerce. Washington, DC: Government Printing Office.

Harwood, R. (1988). Parental stress and the young infant's needs. In E.F. Zigler & M. Frank (Eds.), *The parental leave crisis: Toward a national policy* (pp. 55-76). New Haven: Yale University Press.

Hawes, C., Kane, R.A., Powers, L.L. & Reinardy, J.R. (1988). *The case for a continuum of long-term care services: lessons from the community-based care demonstrations*. Washington, DC: American Association of Retired Persons, Public Policy Institute.

Hopper, P., & Zigler, E. (1988). The medical and social science basis for a national infant care leave policy. *American Journal of Orthopsychiatry, 58*, 324-338.

Hudson Institute. (1988). *Workforce 2000*. Washington, DC: U.S. Department of Labor.

Kamerman, S.B. (1988). Maternity and parenting benefits: An international comparison. In E.H. Zigler & M. Frank (Eds.), *The parental leave crisis: Toward a national policy* (pp. 235-244). New Haven: Yale University Press.

Kamerman, S.B., & Kahn, A.J. (1981). *Child care, family benefits and working parents*. New York: Columbia University Press.

Kamerman, S.B., Kahn, A.J., & Kingston, P. (1983). *Maternity policies and working women*. New York: Columbia University Press.

Levitan, S.A., Belous, R.S., & Gallo, F. (1988). *What's happening to the American Family: Tensions, hopes, realities*. Baltimore: Johns Hopkins University Press.

Moynihan, D.P. (1967). A family policy for the nation. In L. Rainwater & W.L. Yancey (Eds.), *The Moynihan report and the politics of controversy* (pp. 387-393). Cambridge, MA: MIT Press.

Moynihan, D.P. (1986). *Family and nation*. New York: Harcourt, Brace Jovanovich.

Murray, C. (1984). *Losing ground*. New York: Basic Books.

Sheinberg, R. (1988). Parental leave policies in large firms. In E.H. Zigler & M. Frank (Eds.), *The parental leave crisis: Toward a national policy* (pp. 211-222). New Haven: Yale University Press.

State of Wisconsin Department of Health and Human Services. (1987). *Wisconsin Elder Abuse Reporting System, Annual Report*. Madison, WI: Author.

Steiner, G.Y. (1981). *The futility of family policy*. Washington, DC: Brookings Institution.

Stone, R. (1985). *Recent developments in respite care services for caregivers of the impaired elderly* (Grant No. 90-AP0003). Washington, DC: Administration on Aging.

Stone, R. (1987). *Informal caregivers of the frail elderly and the need for respite care*. Testimony before the Subcommittee on Health and the Environment of the House Energy and Commerce Committee. Washington, DC: Government Printing Office

Stone, R., Cafferata, G.L. & Sangle, J. (1986). Caregivers of the frail elderly: A national profile. *The Gerontologist, 27*, 616-626.

U.S. Department of Labor, Office of Policy Planning and Research. (1965). *The negro family: A case for action*. Washington, DC: Government Printing Office.

U.S. Department of Labor, Bureau of Labor Statistics. (1988). *Marital and family characteristics of the labor force from the March 1988 Current Population Survey*. Washington, DC: Government Printing Office.

U.S. Department of Labor, Women's Bureau. (1986). *Facts on U.S. Working Women* (Fact Sheet No. 86-4). Washington, DC: Author.

U.S. House of Representatives, Select Committee on Aging, Subcommittee on

Human Services. (1987). *Exploding the myths: caregiving in America*. (Comm. Pub. No. 99-611). Washington, DC: Government Printing Office.

Yale Bush Center on Child Development and Social Policy. (1985). *Statement and recommendations of the advisory committee on infant care leave*. New Haven: Yale University.

Zigler, E.H. (1974). Testimony before the Subcommittee on Children and Youth of the Senate Labor and Public Welfare Committee, 93rd Congress. Washington, DC: Government Printing Office.

FAMILY SUPPORT
ACROSS THE LIFE SPAN
AND WITHIN DIFFERENT SETTINGS

Early Family Intervention:
Focussing on the Mother's
Adaptation-Competence
and Quality of Partnership

Christoph M. Heinicke

SUMMARY. Two general hypotheses relating to studies of early family intervention are discussed: (1) Pervasive and sustained gains in family development are correlaries of changes in the multi-risk mother's adaptation-competence and partnership quality, and (2) Efforts to change this functioning are most likely to be successful if the mother can develop a sustained and working relationship with the intervenor. The paper reviews sources which support these hypotheses: (1) Eight controlled follow-up intervention studies assessing and attempting to intervene in different family domains; and (2) Current ongoing studies focussing on the nature of the mother's relationship to the intervenor.

The author wishes to acknowledge the generous financial support of the Lawrence Welk Foundation.

The efforts of the UCLA Family Development Service to enhance the multi-risk family as a nurturing system has been guided by the assumption that lasting change is not likely to occur unless the adaptation-competence and/or quality of the primary caretaker's partnership is also changed in a progressive direction. In this paper we will (1) Define adaptation-competence and partnership in the context of other dimensions of family functioning; (2) describe the approach and give the outcome results of early family intervention studies that have also been guided by the above assumption; and (3) describe the home-visiting approach being used by the UCLA Family Development Service.

Adaptation-competence is defined as the person's effective and flexible coping with the balance of internal and external demands. It has been specified empirically by a factor including ratings of the ability to meet one's own needs, flexibility in adaptation, low anxiety, and effective use of support systems (Heinicke, Diskin, Ramsey-Klee & Oates, 1986). The mother's capacity for partnership is defined as the ability to maintain a mutually satisfying personal relationship. One example of such a partnership, the husband-wife relationship, has been specified empirically by a factor including ratings of the husband's fostering the confidence of his wife, the mother's sense of success as a wife, the husband's empathy towards his wife, and ratings of her perception of the positivity and communication in the marriage (Heinicke et al., 1986).

It is recognized that the concepts of adaptation-competence and capacity for partnership can be measured in different ways. Equally important, if they are used in family intervention studies they must be placed in a family systems context. Previous publications have provided such a theoretical framework (Belsky, 1984; Heinicke, 1984; Cowan & Cowan, 1987). It is also recognized that any one aspect of the interacting family system can influence and be influenced by another aspect. Thus, it has been shown that the pre-birth characteristics of maternal warmth and adaptation-competence as well as husband-wife adaptation interacting with early stable infant characteristics such as soothability and visual attention are significant predictors of the positive parent-child mutuality in the first two years of life (Heinicke et al., 1986). Moreover, maternal warmth and adaptation-competence, measured before birth predict assessments of the same qualities in the pre-school years and are at that time part of a cluster of variables including positive parent-infant mutuality (Heinicke & Lampl, 1988). It follows that changes in these parental qualities as a function of intervention are likely also to have an impact on the positive parent-child mutuality. More generally, one can argue that the more pervasive and sustained positive outcome of intervention is not likely to occur unless parental characteristics as well as the quality of the family interaction and the child's development are addressed.

OUTCOME OF INTERVENTION AND CHANGE IN PARENT ADAPTATION-COMPETENCE AND QUALITY OF PARTNERSHIP

What evidence is there that those early family intervention studies showing a *pervasive* as well as *sustained* effect included both an explicit effort to alter and in fact reported success in changing the adaptation-competence and/or the quality of the partnership of the parents?

In a recent review of controlled studies of early family intervention (Heinicke, Beckwith, & Thompson, 1988), ten studies were reported that showed *pervasive* effects as defined by three or more positive findings in different subcategories of family functioning. Two further studies meeting the criteria of pervasiveness have come to our attention since publication of this review (Wieder, Poisson, Lourie & Greenspan, 1988; Lally, Mangione & Honig, 1988). Of these twelve (12) studies, eight (8) also demonstrated through follow-up that the results were sustained for at least a year after the intervention had ceased. In all eight studies there was both an explicit effort to change and reported success in actually changing the adaptation-competence and/or quality of the partnership of the parents.

Before turning to the specific documentation of this characteristic of the studies, other common descriptors should be noted. All eight of these intervention programs involved a minimum of 11 contacts over a 3 month period, but the variation in the number of contacts was considerable with the median being 75. Six of the eight targeted low-income multi-risk families and were at the same time "comprehensive" in providing more than one kind of service. Most important, in all eight instances the delivery of the services was made possible through the ongoing relationship to the intervenor. In seven of the eight instances that relationship was to a home visitor. In the paragraphs below we will briefly summarize for each of the eight studies the functions targeted and which indices of parent adaptation-competence and/or quality of partnership changed.

The first of these projects intervened with mentally retarded, poverty level mothers with full term babies (Heber & Garber, 1975; Garber & Heber, 1981). The project offered comprehensive family intervention that included occupational training, job placement, home-making, and childrearing training for the mothers and center-based education for the child in order to prevent cultural-familial retardation in infants. An ongoing relationship with a home visitor provided much of this information. Intervention focused on changing family ecology, maternal adaptation-competence, and child cognitive development. Various assessments determined that the intervention not only enhanced many aspects of the mother-child interaction and the child's development but led to the mother's increased literacy, a more stable work history, and increased earnings. The adaptation-competence of the mothers clearly was improved.

Nurcombe, Howell, Rauh, Teti, Ruoff, Brennan, and Murphy (1984) intervened with married couples raising a premature infant. A programmed series of contacts with a pediatric intensive care nurse included enhancing sensitivity of parents to cues of the premature infant and promoting enjoyment of play. Both hospital contact and home visits were involved. Functions targeted were maternal adaptation, parent-infant interactional synchrony, affective closeness, and infant temperament. The authors report that in addition to positive effects in the family interaction and child development domains, the mothers who experienced the intervention showed greater role satisfaction and confidence than the mothers in the control group.

Similarly, Minde, Shosenberg, and Thompson (1983) found that their intervention with low socio-economic status families of premature infants affected not only the mother-child interaction and the child's development, but led to the mother's improvement in her relationship with others generally, a greater knowledge of community resources, and a greater sense of autonomy. In this project a self-help group provided ongoing support, specific assistance, and a forum for discussion in order to improve parents' sense of mastery and autonomy and their interaction with a stressful premature infant. The group was led by a veteran mother and nurse group coordinator who was also available for individual support between group meetings.

Olds, Henderson, Tatelbaum and Chamberlin (1986a; 1986b) intervened with teenage, mostly single, poverty mothers. A nurse home visitation program including parent education, enhancing the informal support system, and linking families to community resources was designed to improve maternal health behaviors, the quality of parenting including prevention of abuse, the effective use of support, and the health of the infant. In addition to an ongoing relationship with a nurse visitor, free transportation to clinics and developmental screening were provided. Changes in the mother child interaction and the child's development were found and mothers experiencing the intervention showed a more positive adaptation: They made better use of community resources and informal support, had fewer kidney infections, better diets, and reduced their smoking.

Seitz, Rosenbaum, and Apfel (1985) has reported the evaluation of comprehensive family services for single, inner city, poverty-level mothers designed to enhance the mother's adaptation, the quality of her relationship to her child, and the child's development. An ongoing relationship with a home visitor, pediatric care, high quality day care, and developmental examinations were provided. Changes in the family interaction and the child behavior as well as changes in the adaptation-competence and relationship capacity of the mothers were found. At the seven and a half year post-intervention follow-up the program mothers were characterized as follows: They completed more years of education, waited longer to have a second child, were more frequently a part of a nuclear family, were more frequently self-supporting, more frequently initiated contacts with teachers, and made greater use of remedial and supportive services.

Cowan and Cowan (1987) have evaluated the impact of couples groups for first-time parents. The groups were led by married couples and provided ongoing support, normalization of experiences, and discussion of all family issues to enhance positive marital quality and parent adaptation. At follow-up, couples attending the group when compared with a control group showed greater improvement in the following different dimensions: Marital satisfaction, self-esteem, and mutual role arrangements.

Wieder, Poisson, Lourie and Greenspan (1988) have reported the five-year follow-up of 32 multi-risk families who received intensive, comprehensive services through the Clinical Infant Development Program (CIDP). Three components made up this intervention:

1. Organizing basic services for adequate food, housing, medical care and educational opportunities, to deal with day-to-day survival and future family stability;
2. Providing a constant emotional relationship with the family through which trust could be established with the parents and the infant; and
3. Providing specialized services to the infant and parents geared to meet the challenges at each stage of development, given each infant's and parent's individual vulnerabilities and strengths.

The follow-up assessments were relevant to these three goals. In so far as the first goal was to deal with basic survival and sustenance, when compared with both the beginning and the end of intervention point, both the adult and especially the adolescent mothers had made striking gains in their work status and in being independent of public assistance. The increased freedom to work outside the home was very likely due to avoiding the repeat pregnancies which in the past further drained the limited resources.

The provision of an ongoing relationship opportunity by the CIDP staff was reflected in the mother's *increasing capacity to form mutually satisfying partner relationships*. Five years after the intervention ended, 42% of adult mothers were married or had sustained relationships. There was a striking decline in the abusive aspects of these relationships as well as those with their children. Thus, spousal abuse for the older mothers decreased from 60% to 5.3% and from 50% to 18% for the adolescents.

Wieder et al. (1988) also cite findings on the children which indicate average IQ performance (103), placement in regular as opposed to special education classes, and active involvement in team sports and local youth organizations.

Although it would seem clear that the persistent, clinically skilled and comprehensive program outlined above did indeed produce sustained gains in parent and child functioning, some reservation is introduced by the fact that a comparison group was not available to highlight which positive changes were a function of the intervention and which might have occurred without intervention.

Another major project, the Syracuse University Family Development Program has also recently published dramatic follow-up results (Lally, Mangione, Honig & Wittner, 1988; Lally, Mangione & Honig, 1988). The intervention was designed to influence the permanent environment of the child, the family and the home. A poverty, largely black, young, mostly single population was recruited in late pregnancy. The contact with the parent was viewed as primary and child care as supplementary.

A cadre of paraprofessional home visitors called Child Development Trainers (CDTs) was recruited and trained intensively to encourage strong, nurturing mother-child relationships that involved giving affectionate bodily contact, respecting children's needs, and responding positively to young children's efforts to learn. CDTs offered positive support and encouragement to mothers as they interacted with their children and also responded positively and actively to the parent's need to fulfill her aspirations for herself. Many mothers came to rely on the CDT as an advisor and confidant on personal relations, finances, career changes, and education. The CDT served as a liaison between the family and community support services, including the child care component of FDRP; in addition, she helped families to learn to find and use neighborhood resources on their own; for example, giving families specific practice in learning how to make and maintain contact with school personnel as children reached school age.

In addition, parent associations were encouraged and the Children's Center provided child and pre-school education to three age groups: 6 to 15 months, 15 to 18 months, and 18 to 60 months.

The follow-up conducted ten years after the end of the program revealed that the program children showed both a significantly lower rate of delinquency (6% vs. 22%) and the offenses they did commit were less severe than those reported for the control group.

Girls in the program group, but not boys, were performing significantly better in school than their counterparts in the control group. Interestingly, these positive findings only began to appear during early adolescence; information on the elementary school years indicated no differences between the program and control group. Teachers rated girls from the program group as having more positive attitudes toward themselves and other people.

Compared to control-group parents, parents who had been in the program reported feeling proud about the positive social attitudes and behaviors of their children and the degree of unity in their family. They were also more likely to advise young people to learn something about themselves and accomplish all they could, while control parents were more inclined to counsel young people to concentrate just on "getting by."

Compared to control-group children, those in the program group felt more positively about themselves in early adolescence and were more likely to expect education to be a continuing part of their lives. Fifty three percent of the program group but only 28% of the controls anticipated that they would be in school at age 17 or 18.

Summarizing the above, pervasive and sustained changes in family functioning were found in each of the eight studies. Included in these developments were changes in parental adaptation-competence and/or partnership quality. It is also true that all of these successful interventions involved a sustained and working relationship to the intervenor. Furthermore, there is additional evidence that the ongoing relationship to the intervenor is likely to be crucial to effective outcome.

THE ONGOING RELATIONSHIP TO THE INTERVENOR

Three current projects provide further indication that the effectiveness of intervention in enhancing the family as a nurturing system depends on the formation of a sustaining and working relationship between the mother and the intervenor.

Osofsky, Culp, and Ware (1988) evaluated an intervention program for adolescents that included a home visiting program. Comparison with a health department project group revealed very few significant differences including no differences in the child's attachment. However, when those mothers who established a working relationship and followed through on activities and goals ("takers") were compared with those who were "non-takers," several significant differences emerged. The "takers" scored significantly higher on the emotional and verbal responsivity scale of the HOME at 1 month and by 20 months differed from the "non-taker" mothers on five of the six HOME scales. The "takers" had significantly higher maternal play scores at 6 and 13 months, and higher Bayley Mental Scale and feeding interaction scores at 13 months. The authors suggest that it is likely that at least some of these outcome differences were related to "taking" the intervention.

Barnard, Magyary, Sumner, Booth, Mitchell, and Spieker (1988) have reported the results of comparing two forms of nurse home visiting interventions: The Mental Health Model and the Information/Resource Model. The primary focus of the first model was to develop a relationship with the mother and to use this relationship as a way of dealing with interpersonal situations and solving problems. The objective of the Information/Resource model was to provide information — facts, procedures, and practices — to the mother.

Contrasting the outcome of the two forms of intervention, there were no differences in the child's attachment classification at 13 months nor in Bayley Mental or Motor Scales at 2 years. Striking differences were found that speak to the interaction of the mother's initial status and type of intervention experienced. On various self-report inventories the mothers in the Mental Health model had a more positive view of their world and were rated higher on parental competency scales and the HOME Inventory. These changes were very likely related to the fact that the Mental Health Group had more nurse contacts, that more of the treatment goals were attained and that the attrition rate was 20% as opposed to 47% for the Information/Resource group. In summary, mothers in the Mental Health group experienced a more sustaining and working relationship to the intervenor.

Beckwith (1988) has reported the results of evaluating a 13 month home visiting program for pre-term infants. The program was individualized and parent directed and based on the belief that multiproblem parents can not focus on the infant until they have themselves been nurtured. Beckwith and her colleagues set out to develop a trusting, supportive relationship; to do so by mediating between the family and community resources such as child care, family planning, medical care; to do so also by providing concrete help to the family such as clothes, equipment, toys, photos, and transportation; to help parents develop observational skills in relation to their infants; and to place the infants' behavior in the context of normal development. Beckwith (1988) reasoned that the supportive relationship of the intervenor to the parent would promote parental self-confidence and competence and would modify the parent's perceptions of the infant's behavior, so as to make it more understandable in terms of normal development.

Similar to the previously reported study, the attrition rate differed considerably; 36% for the control group and 5% for the intervention group. It was further determined that those mothers who dropped out of the control group as opposed to those who stayed received no pre-natal care in the first half of pregnancy and came from less stable, more abusive homes. The failure to obtain adequate pre-natal care could be seen as an index of poor adaptation-competence while a less stable family background could well influence the young mother's capacity to form and sustain a relationship.

When intervention and control groups equivalent on the background variables were compared, those mothers receiving home visitor services were more satisfied with themselves, were involved and responsive with their infants, and thought about their infants with more realistic developmental expectations.

The above three projects illustrate the importance of the interaction of certain characteristics in the mother and the development of a sustained relationship to the intervenor. Fraiberg (1980) was among the first to delineate what needed to be known about the nature of the relationship to the intervenor to make it effective.

MODELS OF INTERVENTION INSPIRED BY THE PIONEERING STUDIES OF SELMA FRAIBERG

As is true for the UCLA Family Development Service to be described in the next section of this paper, two current projects to be described below acknowledge their debt to the pioneering studies of Selma Fraiberg (1980).

Lyons-Ruth, Coll, Connell and Odom (1987) have outlined the central goal of their intervention service targeted at low-income socially at risk mothers:

1. Provision of an accepting and trustworthy relationship.
2. Increasing the family's competence in accessing neighborhood resources, including social, legal, health and educational services.
3. Modeling and reinforcing more interactive, positive and developmentally appropriate exchanges between mother and infant, with emphasis on the mother's dual role as both teacher and source of emotional security for her infant.
4. Increasing social contacts with other mothers in the neighborhood through encouraging weekly participation in parenting groups (professional service) or monthly participation in a drop-in social hour (paraprofessional service).

The paraprofessional service relied more on a detailed curriculum and a toy demonstration model while the professional service emphasized the psychodynamically-based model pioneered by Selma Fraiberg (1980). Various comparisons of High Risk Treated and Untreated infants at infant age 18 months revealed a significantly higher proportion of secure attachments in the treated group.

Selma Fraiberg (1980) was originally one of the collaborators of an early family intervention project recently reported by Lieberman, Weston, and Paul (1989). These investigators have described their intervention approach as follows: "Our goal was to free and enhance the mother's emotional availability and empathy for her child, and in order to accomplish this we engaged in a parallel process of being emotionally available and empathetically responsive to the mother. The intervenor met with each mother-infant dyad once a week for about 1 1/2 hours, either in their home or in our office playroom, as preferred by the mother. The sessions were unstructured, with the mother and child setting the tone of the visit, but the intervenor had at least two major simultaneous agendas in mind. The first agenda was to become the advocate for the mother's affective experience, speaking for her and on her behalf about the mother's rights to and longing for protection and safety, both when she was a child and currently as an adult. The second agenda was to seek linkages between the mother's reported experiences and the mother-child interaction as it unfolded in the course of the session. In this context, the intervenor tried to expand the mother's empathy for her child by focusing on contingency to signals, the provision of developmental opportunities for exploration, and the negotiation of conflicts between mother and child in a way that was mutually face-saving and could promote a goal-corrected partnership. Whenever feasible, the intervenor also brought a concrete element of protection to the family's life by helping the mother to secure needed goods and services, including medical care, food stamps, and housing. In this sense, the intervention approach involved an integration of several modalities, particularly elements from psychotherapy, developmental guidance and social work."

Systematic evaluation of this intervention model led to the finding that by two years of age (the intervention having started at 12 months) the children in the intervention group showed less proximity avoidance during an experience of reunion with their mother than the matched control group. However, the children experiencing intervention did not differ from the control in the Waters (1986) Q-sort security measure. Equally important, the contrast of intervention and control group revealed no significant impact as a function of intervention on the following maternal dimensions: Awareness of complexity in child rearing, encouragement of reciprocity, and control of aggression. However, ratings of whether the mother developed a good relationship with the intervenor correlated significantly with the emergence of more adaptive maternal attitudes towards the control of aggression, with higher child scores on the Waters Q-sort for security of attachment, and with less child avoidance of mother on reunion. Once more the "takers" evidenced a different result than the "non-takers." "Takers" is again defined as developing a sustaining and working relationship with the intervenor. In that sense the intervention nurtured and enhanced the nurturing potential of the family system.

THE INTERVENTION MODEL
OF THE UCLA FAMILY DEVELOPMENT SERVICE

Given the above emphasis on the importance of intervening at various levels of family functioning, we developed an early family intervention approach that recognized the importance of the relationship to the intervenor as the vehicle of change and used it to address the adaptation-competence and partnership quality of the mother to sustain progress in her relationship to her infant.

The UCLA Family Development Service, a home visiting intervention, is available to families receiving care in the UCLA Obstetrical-Gynecological and Pediatric Continuity Care Clinics. Referral to the service is facilitated by a pediatric clinical social worker, thus insuring continuing liaison between the pediatric house staff and the home visiting intervenor. Families are recruited if they are asking for help in the non-medical care of their physically normal infant, and whose inadequate financial and support resources put them at risk for maladaptive parenting.

Following the referral, a preventive intervention plan consisting of the following elements is formulated: (1) Initial relationship-building with the family and problem identification; (2) Objective assessments of the family's functioning; and (3) The actual intervention. These steps are spelled out in three operational manuals (UCLA Family Development Service, 1989).

The first manual describes the initial response to the family's interest in the service. In various ways we convey that promoting early infant development involves enhancement of the parent's parenting, their more general family functioning, and their environmental supports. A first task of the home visitor is to listen and help the parents clarify what they feel good about and what they experience as difficult. Listening and shared observation help to clarify areas of distress and their antecedents. Priority is given to building an ongoing relationship by the home visitor offering to be available on a regular (usually weekly) and convenient basis and by encouraging telephone contacts. Expertise is kept in the background except where advice or reassurance is appropriate to enhance the family's experience of receiving support. Before leaving the house great care is taken by the home visitor to schedule the next contact.

The initial contacts permit subjective definition of the experienced difficulty and offer a committed enhancing relationship. The primary mode of gaining access to the family system is the relationship between the intervenor and the parents. It has been our experience that these areas can be addressed if there is also an awareness and discussion of those aspects of the relationship when the parents need to repeat with the intervenor parts of their unresolved past and present relationships. This aspect of our work follows the pioneering research of Fraiberg and her colleagues (Fraiberg, 1980).

The initial contacts also permit observation of the salient features of the infant's caretaking environment. Although the primary observational stance is to note whatever emerges, the following five domains that are important in family development are observed:

1. The social and economic support available to the family
2. The quality of the marital or partner relationship
3. The individual personality of each parent, including their adaptation competence
4. The quality of the transaction between parent and infant, including their positive mutuality, and
5. The early emerging and relatively stable characteristics of the infant such as his/her soothability.

Further guidelines for observation are defined within these five foci. The initial approach to gathering valid knowledge is to have the family members define through words and actions what is important rather than their responding to a set of prestructured questions. We assume that effective and lasting change is most likely to occur if intervention is directed at what the caretaker feels is important and wants to change. A further step in intervention is to continue our evaluation using objective assessment techniques. A second manual defines ratings covering the five data domains discussed above, guides the administration of four inventories filled out by the parents, and outlines the semi-structured interview conducted with the mother (Loranger, 1988). Once a trusting positive relationship is initiated then other key needs and functions as defined by both parents and intervenor can be addressed. A third manual defines the various intervention roles that have been articulated on the basis of our experience:

A. Enhancing Communication and Adaptation to Areas of Greatest Concern.

1. *Listening* to the parent and
2. *Clarifying* the area of concern including how the mother has attempted to cope with the issue and how she felt about her efforts.
3. *Providing Understanding* of areas of concern including the antecedents of the observed difficulties.
4. *Articulating alternatives* in relation to issues of experienced support, partnership, relationships in general, anxiety, depression, confidence as parent, in order to increase the parent's adaptation in any or all of these areas. Articulation of these personal adaptation and relationship issues are guided by the real relationship and transference to the intervenor. The concerns specifically relating to the parent-infant interaction are given in the next section.

B. Enhancing Alternate Approaches to Parent-child Interaction. In addition to *listening to*, *clarifying*, and *providing understanding* involved in concerns emerging from the parent-child interaction, certain specific intervention roles are used in this specific focus.

5. *Observing and teaching observation of parent-child interaction.* The intervenor may address a concern by observing the parent-infant at the same time as the parent or guiding the parent in that observation.
6. *Providing developmental information.* As one response to the area of concern, the issue may be resolved by providing information on family development.
7. *Articulating alternate approaches.* Another method of resolving parental concerns about the parent-infant interaction is to articulate alternate approaches. This is based on all the previous steps of

listening, clarifying, and providing understanding and parallels in form the articulation of alternatives in relation to personal adaptation issues defined above.

8. *Modeling alternate approaches.* Part of the process of enhancing alternate approaches to parent-child interaction is to involve the parent by modeling alternate ways of approaching a particular concern or dealing with the child.

C. Enhancing Experienced Support. Three specific roles have been identified as enhancing the parent's experienced support.

9. *Specific affirmation of the parent as a person or a parent.* Although the very arrangement and continued commitment of the home visitor serves as an affirmation, there are times when the intervenor specifically affirms, praises, or recognizes in a positive way the parent as a person or a parent.

10. *Enhancing the parent's instrumental competence in dealing with external problems.* Once certain alternatives and goals have been defined, the home visitor may assist the parent in rehearsing steps to achieve a particular goal. For example, discussing how one might go about obtaining day care or extending one's education.

11. *Direct assistance to the parent.* At times the intervenor provides direct assistance as opposed to or in addition to facilitating alternate approaches to a problem. For example, the intervenor accompanies the parent and helps her sign up for a class.

The particular profile of intervention roles is developed and changed to meet the needs of the parents and their infant. In order to sustain a working relationship the intervenor keeps as a high priority that the mother needs to experience being given to (the real relationship to the intervenor) and that the distortions of that relationship will be understood (transference).

CONCLUSION

Theoretical considerations, a review of eight controlled follow-up studies of early family intervention, and descriptions of current projects support the general hypotheses that: (1) Pervasive and sustained gains in family development are correlaries of changes in the multi-risk mother's adaptation-competence and/or partnership quality, and (2) Efforts to change this functioning are most likely to be successful if the mother can develop a sustained and working relationship to the intervenor.

REFERENCES

Barnard, K.E., Magyary, D., Sumner, G., Booth, C.L., Mitchell, S.K., & Spieker, S. (1988). Prevention of parenting alterations for women with low social support. *Psychiatry*, 248-253.

Beckwith, L. (1988). Intervention with disadvantaged parents of sick, pre-term infants. *Psychiatry*, *51*, 242-247.

Belsky, J. (1984). The determinants of parenting: A process model. *Child Development*, *55*, 83-96.

Bronfenbrenner, V. (1977). Toward an experimental ecology of human development. *American Psychologist*, *32*, 513-631.

Cowan, C.P., & Cowan, P.A. (1987). A preventive intervention for couples becoming parents. In C.F.Z. Boukydis (Ed.), *Research on support for parents and infants in the post-natal period*. Norwood, NJ: Ablex.

Garber, H., & Heber, R. (1981). The efficacy of early intervention with family rehabilitation. In M.J. Regab, H.C. Haywood, & H.L. Garber (Eds.), *Psychosocial influences in retarded performance: Vol. 2. Strategies for improving competence* (pp. 71-88). Baltimore: University Park Press.

Fraiberg, S. (1980). *Clinical studies in infant mental health: The first year of life*. Basic Books: New York.

Heber, R., & Garber, H. (1975). The Milwaukee Project: A study of the use of family intervention to prevent cultural-familial mental retardation. In B.Z. Friedlander, G.M. Sterritt, & G.E. Kirk (Eds.), *Exceptional infant* (pp. 399-433). New York: Brunner/Mazel.

Heinicke, C.M. (1984). Impact of pre-birth parent personality and marital functioning on family development: A framework and suggestions for further study. *Developmental Psychology*, *20*, 1044-1053.

Heinicke, C.M., Beckwith, L., & Thompson, A. (1988). Early intervention in the family system: A framework and review. *Infant Mental Health Journal*, *9*, 111-141.

Heinicke, C.M., Diskin, S.D., Ramsey-Klee, D.M., & Oates, D.S. (1986). Pre and postbirth antecedents of 2-year-old attention, capacity for relationships, and verbal expressiveness. *Developmental Psychology*, *22*, 777-787.

Heinicke, C. M. & Lambi, E. (1988). Pre and post birth antecedents of three and four year old attention, IQ, verbal expressiveness, task orientation, and capacity for relationships. *Infant Behavior and Development*, *11*, 381-410.

Lally, J.R., Mangione, P.L., & Honig, A.S. (1988). The Syracuse University Family Development Research Program: Long-range impact of an early intervention with low-income children and their families. In D.R. Powell (Ed.), *Parent education as early childhood intervention*, (pp. 79-104). Norwood, NJ: Ablex.

Lally, R.J., Mangione, P.L., Honig, A.S., & Wittner, D.S. (1988). More pride, less delinquency: Findings from the 10-year follow-up study of the Syracuse University Family Development Research program, *Zero to Three*, *8*, 13-18.

Lieberman, A.F., Weston, D., & Paul, J.H. (1989). Preventive intervention with anxiously attached dyads. Abstracts, biennial meeting, Kansas City, Society for Research in Child Development, Vol. VII.

Loranger, H.W. (1988). Personality disorder examination (PDE) Manual. Yonkers, NY, DV Communications.

Lyons-Ruth, K., Botein, S., & Grunebaum, H.U. (1981). Reaching the hard-to-reach: Serving isolated and depressed mothers with infants in the community. In B. Cohler & J. Musick (Eds.), *Intervention with psychiatrically disabled parents and their young children*, 95-122. San Francisco: Jossey-Bass.

Lyons-Ruth, K., Coll, D., Connell, D.B., & Odom, R. (1987). Maternal depression as mediator of the effects of home-based intervention services. Abstracts, biennial meeting, Baltimore, Society for Research in Child Development, Vol. VI.

Minde, K., Shosenberg, N., & Thompson, J. (1983). Self-help groups in a premature nursery, infant behavior and parental competence one year later. In E. Galenson & J. Call (Eds.), *Frontiers of infant psychiatry*, 266-271. New York: Basic Books.

Nurcombe, B., Howell, D.C., Rauh, V.A., Teti, D.M., Ruoff, P., Brennan, J., & Murphy, B. (1984). An intervention program for mothers of low birth-weight babies: Outcome at six and twelve months. In J. Call, E. Galenson, & R. Tyson (Eds.), *Frontiers of infant psychiatry*, Vol. 2, 201-210. New York: Basic Books.

Olds, D., Henderson, C., Tatelbaum, R., & Chamberlin, R. (1986a). Improving the delivery of prenatal care and outcomes of pregnancy: A randomized trial of nurse home visitation. *Pediatrics*, *78*, 16-28.

Olds, D., Henderson, C., Tatelbaum, R., & Chamberlin, R. (1986b). Preventing child abuse and neglect: A randomized trial of nurse home visitation. *Pediatrics*, *78*, 65-78.

Osofsky, J.D., Culp, A.M., & Ware, L.N. (1988). Intervention challenges with adolescent mothers and their infants, *Psychiatry*, *51*, 236-241.

Seitz, V., Rosenbaum, L.K., & Apfel, N.H. (1985). Effects of family support intervention: A ten-year follow-up. *Child Development*, *56*, 376-391.

UCLA Family Development Service: Operational Manuals for Preventive Intervention Plan. Los Angeles, CA, University of California, Department of Psychiatry and Biobehavioral Sciences, 1989. [The three operation manuals are available from the author (CMH), Department of Psychiatry and Biobehavioral Sciences, University of California, Los Angeles, 760 Westwood Plaza, Los Angeles, California 90024-1759.

Waters, E. (1986). Attachment Behavior Q-Set: Revision 2.0. Unpublished manuscript: SUNY Stony Brook.

Wieder, S., Poisson, S., Lourie, R.S., & Greenspan, S.I. (1988). Enduring gains: A five-year follow-up report on a clinical infant development program, *Zero to Three*, *8*, 6-11.

The Challenges of Multiple Roles:
The Interface Between Work and Family
When Children Are Young

Angela Barron McBride

SUMMARY. This paper reviews the problems and benefits associated with combining work and family when children are young, then proceeds to discuss both implications for research and some strategies (individual and structural) for easing tensions between the two domains.

At a time when some combination of work and family is the lifestyle preference of most Americans, but the two domains remain largely described as espousing conflicting values, it is important that the issues affecting any interface be explored for possible directions for future research and practice. This paper begins with a review of the problems and benefits associated with combining work and family, then proceeds to urge that thinking in this area move beyond simplistic linear models to a full appreciation of the many variables which influence an individual's short-term reactions and resulting long-term consequences when balancing multiple roles. At the end, some suggestions are made for easing tensions between work and family based on the current state of knowledge.

CONFLICTING OBLIGATIONS
VS. ENHANCING OPPORTUNITIES

Combining work and family when children are young has long been regarded as difficult, if not impossible, for women, though men traditionally have been expected to carry both roles. The reason for this situation becomes obvious if one reads traditional prescriptions for functional role division in the family: "Father's primary goal may be to support his family; mother's may be not only to keep everybody fed, clothed, and looked after but hopefully, to keep everybody happy" (Ames, 1970, p. 273).

That division of labor makes being a good father and a successful worker one and the same, but keeping everybody happy is a never-ending (probably impossible) job which leaves no time for employment outside the home.

Both the lay and the social science literatures point to the difficulties women have juggling multiple roles. A large part of the feminist debate has centered on how women can meet both the needs of others and their own (McBride, 1976). This dilemma is expressed in the very title of Radl's (1979) book, *How to Be a Mother and a Person, Too*. Tuthill (1980) described combining marriage and career as not an easy choice, and likely to lead to divorce. Grieff and Munter (1980) expressed doubts about whether a dual-career family can live happily ever after with all the pressures. Television commercials which celebrate the woman's making the bacon, then serving it up in a pan, while having time to look attractive for her loved ones leave many women wondering if they are not just being sold a bill of goods, which is not *good* for them.

When the Associate Director for Special Populations of the National Institute of Mental Health convened a panel of experts to propose a research agenda for women's mental health in October 1986, the concern receiving the most attention in the initial position papers was the effects on mental health of women's multiple roles (Eichler & Parron, 1987). This area was subsequently selected by that group as one of its final five priorities (McBride, 1988). In making this selection, the panel built on the report of the Public Health Service Task Force on Women's Health Issues (1985) which assumed that one of the most important social changes affecting women's health today is the unprecedented entry of women, especially women with infants and young children, into the labor force. Indeed, the model woman at the end of the twentieth century is parent, spouse, and worker (Hayghe, 1984: Reading & Amatea, 1986).

Women experience appreciably more change than do men in becoming parents (Belsky, Lang, & Huston, 1986; Cowan et al., 1985; Gore & Mangione, 1983: Harriman, 1983; Hobbs & Cole, 1976). The subsequent stress particularly affects single women, working class women and working women with sick or difficult infants (Cleary & Mechanic, 1986; McKim, 1987; Reilly, Entwisle, & Doering, 1987). New parents have to balance multiple role responsibilities (Myers-Walls, 1984; Steffenmeier, 1982; Ventura, 1987; Weinberg & Richardson, 1981), and this is made difficult by the drastic difference in time now available for various activities (LaRossa, 1983).

Combining the roles of parent, spouse, and worker means very different things for women and men because the job descriptions are likely to be very different. The employed wife-mother plays her roles out in a different world from the working husband-father. More of the stress in a typical dual-earner family is felt by the woman because childcare and housework continue to be considered her responsibilities, even when she is employed full time (Alpert & Culbertson, 1987; Blumstein & Schwartz, 1983; Hare-Mustin, 1988; Ross & Mirowsky, 1988). Mothers feel responsible for the continuing success and happiness of their children, and are often blamed when anything goes wrong in their children's lives (Caplan & Hall-Mc-Corquodale, 1985). Those who are employed outside the home must also deal with the stresses associated with their occupational role (Riesch, 1984; Sund & Ostwald, 1985; Woods, 1985), often without any reassignment of domestic expectations (Gilbert, Holahan, & Manning, 1981). Working wives' dissatisfactions with the level of their husbands' contributions to family matters is much greater than whatever distress they feel about the amounts of time they spend on work and family roles (Pleck, 1985).

Role strain is likely to be additive for women (Galambos & Silbereisen, 1989); it is not just the number of events in their own lives that affect women but what happens to those about whom they care (Kessler & McLeod, 1984). Women are often in a situation where they have not only to deal with their own work pressures but also to serve as a sounding board for the problems experienced by their husbands (Bolger, DeLongis, Kessler, & Wethington, 1989; Hunt & Hunt, 1982; Ladewig & McGee, 1986). Their husbands, on the other hand, may remain relatively unaffected by their wives' juggling, and may even ignore their accomplishments (Hiller & Philliber, 1986). It is also important to realize that women and men who hold the same occupational title may still be expected to do different things. For example, women flight attendants are expected to serve as shock absorbers with difficult passengers more than are their male counterparts (West & Zimmerman, 1987).

A so-called scarcity hypothesis, originally put forward by Goode (1960), expects family roles to leave women too drained to meet the demands of the workplace: "The more roles one accumulates, the greater the probability of exhausting one's supply of time and energy and of confronting conflicting obligations, leading to role strain and psychological distress" (Barnett & Baruch, 1987, p. 124). A revisionist position, however, began to take hold in the 1970's emphasizing the advantages which accrue to those juggling a number of roles (Crosby, 1987). If multiple role involvement has traditionally enhanced men's lives (Gove & Tudor,

1973), then "the more roles, the better" might also hold true of women's experience. After all, home has not been for women the stress-free sanctuary it was sometimes portrayed as being by men (Baruch, Biener, & Barnett, 1987). Getting out of the house and having their own economic tie to the larger society might actually be beneficial for women, even when they remain saddled with the roles of housekeeper and of primary parent, because the independence and resources of the former can have a buffering effect on the latter.

According to this line of reasoning, problems can accumulate across roles, but so can opportunities and benefits. Some women with multiple role identities have reported better health than their stay-at-home contemporaries (LaRosa, 1988; Mostow & Newberry, 1975; Thoits, 1983); some employed women have a more autonomous sense of self as a result of working (Meisenhelder, 1986; Warren & McEachren, 1985); and a number of dual-earner families rate their lifestyles positively (Skinner, 1980). Participation in several roles may cancel some of the negative effects generated by a particular role; e.g., the woman who does not want to have to nurse her ailing mother-in-law all the time may be pleased that her job affords an excuse for setting limits.

It is not just work versus family roles that is the issue, but the costs and benefits of various patterns of employment and intimate relationships (Shehan, 1984). Roles which require drastically different value systems or capabilities, and are unsupported by significant others, would lead presumably to very different reactions and consequences than roles which are perceived to complement each other and to provide gratifications, security, and a sense of purpose. Holding a responsible position in a company can enhance the authority the woman has at home, making her husband and children take her perspective on issues more seriously than they might otherwise do. On the other hand, being told one can work outside the home as long as the normal routine is not altered can place tremendous pressure on the person trying to balance career and hearth values who simply does not have enough hours in the day to meet everyone's expectations. Depending upon the circumstances and personality of the individual husband, the woman's paycheck can either be threatening to his ego or mean freedom from having to work overtime. Even the same role may elicit a very different response at different times in the life cycle. For example, the mother-scientist with a toddler may feel torn because the roles in which she is engaged have nothing in common, but may feel pleased with herself as a mother when her teenage daughter needs help with her science homework. Difficulties are particularly likely when women and men remain influenced by the norms that define traditional gender relations at the same time that they are acting out alternatives to the old-role ideology (Ulbrich, 1988).

BEYOND SIMPLISTIC THINKING

The link between multiple roles and negative consequences is definitely not linear, nor is it easily explained merely by demographic variables (Thoits, 1987). The roles an individual plays can vary in terms of number, type, quality of transition, requirements, overlapping values/activities, social status, and whether they are freely chosen. Roles assumed are themselves affected by *background factors*, e.g., genetic endowment, kind of childrearing personally experienced, gender-role socialization, societal values, federal policies, and expectations of significant others; as well as by a host of *personal moderating variables*, e.g., personality, self-esteem expectations for success, attributional style, level of physiological arousability, vigor, social support (emotional, material, informational), age, education, race, marital status, and socioeconomic status. *Short-term reactions* to roles can be affective, perceptual/cognitive, behavioral, physiological, social, and economic. These reactions, in turn, have *long-term consequences* for quality of life, health, adaptation, and social status (McBride, 1989). It is only in conducting research aware of these complexities that investigators can hope to understand fully the experience of parents when their children are young.

Weaving into some integrative whole what is known about the interface between work and family when children are young is difficult because so many variables are thought to bear on the general area. A coherent statement of the relationships between and among institutional policies, family support, and individual/family well-being remains to be drafted, largely because extant models are not sensitive to the *individual-to-family* fit and the *family-to-community* fit, which are so important because women particularly live out their lives embedded in a context full of feedback loops. Looking at the professional literature, one is confronted by many seemingly unconnected pieces of information: Mothers with young children may be more depressed and less satisfied (Amaro, Russo, & Johnson, 1987; Gross, 1989); women may be more demoralized by work than men (Lennon, 1987); childcare availability strongly influences employment, especially for those doing shift work (Floge, 1989; Greenstein, 1986; Presser, 1986); homemakers may have different health problems than their employed counterparts (Berns, 1988; Freedman & Bisrsi, 1988); women's greater household responsibilities account in part for their lower pay (Shelton & Firestone, 1989); employment opportunities for some women are predicated on the assumption of traditional mothering work by poor women who have little or no help in their own juggling of work and family roles (Rothman, 1989). The task ahead is for research efforts to be conceptualized in terms of a theoretical framework which allows for examining individual psychology in terms of impinging social structures—a true systems approach to the phenomena under study.

The emphasis to date has been on individuals changing, not society (Orthner & Pittman, 1986; Voydanoff, 1984), yet the individual's experience is powerfully shaped by social factors. If one focuses on the link between the work-family interface and depression, for instance, the extent to which the personal is influenced by societal forces in women's lives becomes obvious. Depression is associated with having both low income and low job status—the demographic profile of more women (particularly divorced women) than men—which, in turn, means fewer resources for handling the requirements of other roles (Golding, 1988). Depression is associated with having less control over important events in one's life, and women trying to combine work and family roles often complain of the little control they have over where they will live (husband's job traditionally takes precedence and may cause frequent relocations), and of the "on call" quality of their various work and family roles which require them either to "cover the desk" or to "fill in the spaces" (Brown & Siegel, 1988). Certain self-evaluation and attributional styles have been significantly associated with depression—an absence of self-serving biases (Alloy & Ahrens, 1987; Crocker, Alloy, & Kayne, 1988; Golin, Sweeney, & Shaeffer, 1981; Tennen & Herzberger, 1987), constant social comparison (Weary, Elbin, & Hill, 1987), and a ruminating response set (Greenberg & Pyszczynski, 1986; Nolen Hoeksema, 1987; Pietromonaco & Rook, 1987; Pyszczynski & Greenberg, 1987; Segal, 1988)—which are features of women's lives in a society where humility is extolled as a feminine virtue, "fitting in" is expected, appearances are more important than actions, and it is necessary to be twice as good to be considered any good.

The anecdotal evidence for the distress of women juggling multiple roles is extensive. Systematic research is needed that replaces a count-the-burdens approach to understanding experience with one that analyzes the relationships between reactions to roles and eventual consequences in full awareness of the importance of a host of background factors and moderating variables. For example, a *couple's* ambivalence about combining work and family cannot be equated with the woman's *personal* feelings about how she is managing the interface, and both perspectives are played out in a society with normative expectations; thus, any study of conflict would not be complete without understanding these inter-relationships (Neal, Groat, & Wicks, 1989). In getting away from simplistic either/or thinking, the investigator must appreciate that high commitments to both work and parenting are theoretically as likely to lead to positive consequences as to any negative effect (Greenberger & Goldberg, 1989), and that the childless might be likely to have more traditional views of the work-family interface than those with children (Callan, 1986). It is not just work and family, but the meaning of each domain to individuals, their families, and communities which must be investigated if the phenomena in question are to be understood.

INDIVIDUAL CHANGE STRATEGIES

Individual strategies for easing tensions between work and family typically aim to change the affected person's beliefs and behaviors. Making use of Hollister's typology of primary prevention (1977), one can ease tensions between work and family on the personal level by: (a) stressor management, (b) stressor avoidance, (c) stress resistance building, and (d) stress reaction management.

With *stress management*, the focus is on dealing with stressors before they have an impact on the person or family. This tactic involves the affected individual in identifying those stressors—external, interpersonal and/or self-imposed—, which can be changed in the short or long term, and eliminating or modifying them. One of the most obvious ways of proceeding is to come to terms with unrealistic goals and role expectations, especially "straitjacket scripts" which were absorbed during the formative years, and rethinking them in terms of the exigencies of modern life. *Stressor avoidance* means that those who are most vulnerable should either withdraw from disabling situations or avoid as many day-to-day hassles as possible. This strategy involves identifying problems and arranging alternative ways of dealing with them which remove the affected person from some onerous responsibilities, leaving the individual to focus on what she or he does best. Illustrating this approach are such commonplace measures as getting relatives and friends to help with what one finds anxiety-producing and buying help for what one does not want to do.

With *stress resistance building*, the major effort is to mobilize strength-building experiences. This strategy includes all individuals can do to prepare generally to cope better with stress, e.g., regular exercise, sound nutrition, learning relaxation techniques, and anticipating problems by reading about the experience ahead of time or taking classes. With *stress reaction management*, the focus is on preventing the person's response to stressors from compounding the problem further. This strategy includes avoiding those cognitive distortions which blow a situation out of proportion and lead to bouts of rumination, e.g., overgeneralizing what happened on a particular afternoon into "I'm no good; I was never cut out to be a mother" or magnifying one mistake into "I loused up my child's whole life."

STRUCTURAL CHANGE STRATEGIES

Beyond these representative, individual strategies for successfully combining work and family, modifications have to be made in the very structure of family and work, so that disjunctures between the two domains can cease to be treated only as personal problems (as they often are now). This could involve a number of structural changes at local, regional and national levels — home economics courses required of all boys and girls in middle school and high school, quality child care which is easily available and affordable, flextime, job sharing, parental leave, lenient sick leave, revamping house and apartment structures to include service centers to deal with emergencies and repairs, and tax credits for support services (Cook, 1988). Instead of always expecting family subordination to work rules and structures, which is the current practice, employers and policy makers have to begin to accommodate to family needs (Gerstel & Gross, 1987). The Scandinavian countries have led the way in developing parental leaves and shorter hours of work for parents of preschool children (Moen, 1989), but the United States has left intact male-defined standards of achievement which expect workers to be free of home responsibilities or at least to act as if that were the case. Women and men with young children are likely to have the most precarious work situations — least seniority, lowest salary, least desirable job — just when they are assuming intense family responsibilities, so some structural changes are needed to help them through this period.

Friedman (in press) notes how the subject matter of employee assistance programs is expanding to include a range of family supportive information. However, relatively few employers currently weigh the benefits of providing child care and flexibility more heavily than the costs associated with responding to family needs. For fundamental change to take place in this arena, a new set of values has to take hold which accepts collective responsibility for the development of the next generation (as opposed to glorifying rugged individualism), recognizes that family needs cannot be dismissed as merely a "woman's problem," and, in calculating cost-benefit ratios, includes more variables—e.g., the importance of a stable, satisfied work force or of a public reputation for being a corporation that cares about people—than just dollars spent in the next quarter.

CONCLUSION

Functional role division—he's the head and she's the heart—overlooked the fact that every family needs at least two heads and two hearts, if not more. Children can best learn to combine head and heart—being assertive *and* nurturing—if they see adults struggle with balancing such values. To the extent that separation of work and family is urged, children will be thwarted in becoming whole persons and their parents will tend to be one-sided, too. The interface between work and family when children are young may sometimes seem only pressure-laden, but the tensions between the two areas can literally be energizing. Balance is not a steady state, even though it is frequently associated with reaching plateaus, but is achieved only through a constant juggling of competing values. The balancing act of day-to-day life, with its competing pressures and expectations, should not be regarded as merely a distraction, but as the main event of adult development, for it is in this give and take that the individual, as well as a society, eventually forges something approaching a balanced perspective—maturity.

REFERENCES

Alloy, L. B., & Ahrens, A. H. (1987). Depression and pessimism for the future: Biased use of statistically relevant information in predictions for self versus others. *Journal of Personality and Social Psychology, 52*, 366-378.

Alpert, D., & Culbertson, A. (1987). Daily hassles and coping strategies of dual-earner and non-dual earner women. *Psychology of Women Quarterly, 111*, 359-366.

Amaro, H., Russo, N., & Johnson, J. (1987). Family and work predictors of psychological well-being among Hispanic women professionals. *Psychology of Women Quarterly, 11*, 523-532.

Ames, L. B. (1970). *Child care and development*. Philadelphia: J.B. Lippencott Co.

Barnett, R. C., & Baruch, G. K. (1987). Social roles, gender, and psychological distress. In R. C. Barnett, L. Biener, & G. K. Baruch (Eds.), *Gender and stress* (pp. 122-143). New York: The Free Press.

Baruch, G. K., Biener, L., & Barnett, R. C. (1987). Women and gender in research on work and family stress. *American Psychologist, 42*, 130-136.

Belsky, J., Lang, M., & Huston, T. L. (1986). Sex typing and division of labor as determinants of marital change across the transition to parenthood. *Journal of Personality and Social Psychology*, *50*, 517-522.

Berns, J. S. (1988). The health status of mothers employed inside and outside the home. *Health Values*, *12*(6), 9-19.

Blumstein, P., & Schwartz, P. (1983). *American couples: Money, work, sex*. New York: Morrow.

Bolger, N., Delongis, A., Kessler, R. C., & Wethington, E. (1989). The contagion of stress across multiple roles. *Journal of Marriage and the Family*, *51*, 175-183.

Brown, J. D., & Siegel, J. M. (1988). Attributions for negative life events and depression: The role of perceived control. *Journal of Personality and Social Psychology*, *54*, 316-322.

Callan, V. J. (1986). The impact of the first birth: Married and single women preferring childlessness, one child, or two children. *Journal of Marriage and the Family*, *48*, 261-269.

Caplan, P. J., & Hall-McCorquodale, I. (1985). The scapegoating of mothers: A call for change. *American Journal of Orthopsychiatry*, *55*, 610-613.

Cleary, P. D., & Mechanic, D. (1983). Sex differences in psychological distress among married people. *Journal of Health and Social Behavior*, *24*, 111-121.

Cook, A. (1988). Working the double day. *The Women's Review of Books*, *6*(1), 20-21.

Cowan, C. P., Cowan, P. A., Heming, G., Garrett, E., Coysh, W. S., Curtis-Boles, H., & Boles, A. J., III. (1985). Transitions to parenthood: His hers, and theirs. *Journal of Family Issues*, *6*, 451-481.

Crocker, J., Alloy, L. B., & Kayne, N. T. (1988). Attributional style, depression, and perceptions of consensus for events. *Journal of Personality and Social Psychology*, *54*, 840-846.

Crosby, F. J. (Ed.). (1987). *Spouse, parent, worker. On gender and multiple roles*. New Haven: Yale University Press.

Eichler, A., & Parron, D. L. (Eds.). (1987). *Women's mental health: Agenda for research*. Rockville, MD: National Institute of Mental Health.

Floge, L. (1989). Changing household structure, child-care availability, and employment among mothers of preschool children. *Journal of Marriage and the Family*, *51*, 51-63.

Freedman, S. M., & Bisrsi, M. (1988). Women and workplace stress. *Health Values*, *12*(2), 30-35.

Friedman, D. E. (in press). Corporate responses to family needs. In D. G. Unger & M. B. Sussman (Eds.), *Families in community settings: Interdisciplinary perspectives*. New York: Haworth Press.

Galambos, N. L., & Sibereisen, R. K. (1989). Role strain in West German dual earner households. *Journal of Marriage and the Family*, *51*, 385-389.

Gerstel, N., & Gross, H. E. (Eds.). (1987). *Families and work*. Philadelphia: Temple University Press.

Gilbert, L. A., Holahan, C. K., & Manning, L. (1981). Coping with conflict between professional and maternal roles. *Family Relations*, *30*, 419-426.

Golding, J. M. (1988). Gender differences in depressive symptoms. Statistical considerations. *Psychology of Women Quarterly, 12*, 61-74.

Golin, S., Sweeney, P. D., & Shaeffer, D. E. (1981). The causality of causal attributions in depression: A cross-lagged panel correlational analysis. *Journal of Abnormal Psychology, 49*, 14-22.

Goode, W. (1960). A theory of strain. *American Sociological Review, 25*, 483-496.

Gore, S., & Mangione, T. W. (1983). Social roles, sex roles and psychological distress: Additive and interactive models of sex differences. *Journal of Health and Social Behavior, 24*, 300-312.

Gove, W. R., & Tudor, J. (1973). Adult sex roles and mental illness. *American Journal of Sociology, 78*, 812-835.

Greenberg, J., & Pyszczynski, T. (1986). Persistent high self-focus after failure and low self-focusing style. *Journal of Personality and Social Psychology, 50*, 1039-1044.

Greenberger, E., & Goldberg, W. A. (1989). Work, parenting, and the socialization of children. *Developmental Psychology, 25*, 22-35.

Greenstein, T. N. (1986). Social-psychologica factors in perinatal labor-force participation. *Journal of Marriage and the Family, 48*, 565-571.

Greiff, B. S., & Munter, P. K. (1980). Can a two-career family live happily ever after? *Across the Board, 17*(19), 40-47.

Gross, D. (1989). Implications of maternal depression for the development of young children. *Image: Journal of Nursing Scholarship, 21*, 103-107.

Hare-Mustin, R. T. (1988). Family change and gender differences: Implications for theory and practice. *Family Relations, 37*, 36-41.

Harriman, L. C. (1983). Personal and marital changes accompanying parenthood. *Family Relations, 32*, 387-394.

Hayghe, H. (1984). Working mothers reach record number in 1984. *Monthly Labor Review*, December, 21-34.

Hiller, D. V., & Philliber, W. W. (1986). Determinants of social class identification in dual-earner couples. *Journal of Marriage and the Family, 48*, 583-587.

Hobbs, D. F., Jr., & Cole, S. P. (1976). Transition to parenthood: A decade replication. *Journal of Marriage and the Family, 38*, 723-738.

Hollister, W. G. (1977). Basic strategies in designing primary prevention programs. In D. C. Klein & S. E. Goldston (Eds.), *Primary prevention: An idea whose time has come* (pp. 41-48). Rockville, MD: National Institute of Mental Health.

Hunt, J. G., & Hunt, L. L. (1982). The dualities of careers and families: New integrations or new polarizations? *Social Problems, 29*, 499-510.

Kessler, R. C., & McLeod, J. D. (1984). Sex differences in vulnerability to undesirable life events. *American Sociological Review, 46*, 443-452.

Ladewig, B. H., & McGee, G. W. (1986). Occupational commitment, a supportive family environment, and marital adjustment: Development and estimation of a model. *Journal of Marriage and the Family, 48*, 821-829.

LaRosa, J. H. (1988). Women, work and health: Employment as a risk factor for coronary heart disease. *American Journal of Obstetrics and Gynecology*, *158*, 1597-1602.

LaRossa, R. (1983). The transition to parenthood and the social reality of time. *Journal of Marriage and the Family*, *45*, 579-589.

Lennon, M. (1987). Sex differences in distress: The impact of gender and work roles. *Journal of Health and Social Behavior*, *28*, 290-305.

McBride, A. B. (1976). *Living with contradictions: A married feminist*. New York: Harper Colophon Books.

McBride, A. B. (1988). Mental health effects of women's multiple roles. *Image: Journal of Nursing Scholarship*, *20*, 41-47.

McBride, A. B. (1989). Multiple roles and depression. *Health Values*, *13*(2), 45-49.

McKim, M. K. (1987). Transition to what? New parents' problems in the first year. *Family Relations*, *36*, 22-25.

Meisenhelder, J. B. (1986). Self-esteem in women: The influence of employment and perception of husband's appraisals. *Image: Journal of Nursing Scholarship*, *18*, 8-14.

Moen, P. (1989). *Working parents. Transformation in gender roles and public policies in Sweden*. Madison: University of Wisconsin Press.

Mostow, E., & Newberry, P. (1975). Work role and depression in women: A comparison of workers and housewives in treatment. *American Journal of Orthopsychiatry*, *45*, 538-548.

Myers-Walls, J. A. (1984). Balancing multiple role responsibilities during the transition to parenthood. *Family Relations*, *23*, 267-271.

Neal, A. G., Groat, H. T., & Wicks, J. W. (1989). Attitudes about having children: A study of 600 couples in the early years of marriage. *Journal of Marriage and the Family*, *51*, 313-328.

Nolen-Hoeksema, S. (1987). Sex differences in unipolar depression: Evidence and theory. *Psychological Bulletin*, *101*, 259-284.

Orthner, D. K., & Pittman, J. F. (1986). Family contributions to work commitment. *Journal of Marriage and the Family*, *48*, 573-581.

Pietromonaco, P. R., and Rook, K. S. (1987). Decision style in depression: The contribution of perceived risks versus benefits. *Journal of Personality and Social Psychology*, *52*, 399-408.

Pleck, J. H. (Ed.). (1985). *Working wives/working husbands*. Beverly Hills, CA: Sage.

Presser, H. B. (1986). Shift work among American women and child care. *Journal of Marriage and the Family*, *48*, 551-563.

Public Health Service Task Force on Women's Health Issues. (1985). *Women's health: Report of the public health service task force on women's health issues*, Vols. I & II. Washington, DC: U.S. Department of Health and Human Services.

Pyszczynski, T., & Greenberg, J. (1987). Self-regulatory preservation and the depression self-focusing style: A self-awareness theory of reactive depression. *Psychological Bulletin*, *102*, 122-138.

Radl, S. L. (1979). *How to be a mother—and a person, too.* New York: Rawson, Wade Publishers.

Reading, J., & Amatea, E. S. (1986). Role deviance or role diversification: Reassessing the psychosocial factors affecting the parenthood choice of career-oriented women. *Journal of Marriage and the Family, 48,* 255-260.

Reilly, T. W., Entwisle, D. R., & Doering, S. G. (1987). Socialization into parenthood: A longitudinal study of the development of self-evaluation. *Journal of Marriage and the Family, 49,* 295-308.

Riesch, S. K. (1984). Occupational commitment and the quality of maternal infant interaction. *Research in Nursing and Health, 7,* 295-303.

Ross, C., & Mirowsky, J. (1988). Child care and emotional adjustment to wives' employment. *Journal of Health and Social Behavior, 29,* 127-138.

Rothman, B. K. (1989). Women as fathers: Motherhood and child care under a modified patriarchy. *Gender and Society, 3,* 89-104.

Segal, Z. V. (1988). Appraisal of the self-schema construct in cognitive models of depression. *Psychological Bulletin, 103,* 147-162.

Shehan, C. L. (1984). Wives' work and psychological well-being: An extension of Gove's social role theory of depression. *Sex Roles, 11,* 881-899.

Shelton, B. A., & Firestone, J. (1989). Household labor time and the gender gap in earnings. *Gender and Society, 3,* 105-112.

Skinner, D. A. (1980). Dual-career family stress and coping: A literature review. *Family Relations, 29,* 473-480.

Steffenmeier, R. H. (1982). A role model of the transition to parenthood. *Journal of Marriage and the Family, 44,* 319-334.

Sund, K., & Ostwald, S. K. (1985). Dual earner families' stress levels and personal and life-style-related variables. *Nursing Research, 34,* 357-361.

Tennen, H., & Herzberzer, S. (1987). Depression, self-esteem, and the absence of self-protective attributional biases. *Journal of Personality and Social Psychology, 52,* 72-80.

Thoits, P. A. (1983). Multiple identities and psychological well-being. *American Sociological Review, 48,* 174-187.

Thoits, P. A. (1987). Gender and marital status differences in control and distress: Common stress versus stress explanations. *Journal of Health and Social Behavior, 28,* 7-22.

Tuthill, M. (1980). Marriage and a career. No easy choices and a good chance of divorce. *Nation's Business, 68*(5), 75-78.

Ulbrich, P. M. (1988). The determinants of depression in two-income marriages. *Journal of Marriage and the Family, 50,* 121-131.

Ventura, J. N. (1987). The stresses of parenthood re-examined. *Family Relations, 36,* 26-29.

Voydanoff, P. (1984). *Work and family: Changing roles of men and women.* Palo Alto, CA: Mayfield.

Warren, L. W., & McEachren, L. (1985). Derived identity and depressive symptomatology in women differing in marital and employment status. *Psychology of Women Quarterly, 9,* 133-144.

Weary, G., Elbin, S., & Hill, M. G. (1987). Attributional and social comparison processes in depression. *Journal of Personality and Social Psychology, 52,* 605-610.

Weinberg, S. L., & Richardson, M. S. (1981). Dimensions of stress in early parenting. *Journal of Consulting and Clinical Psychology, 49,* 686-693.

West, C., & Zimmerman, D. H. (1987). Doing gender. *Gender and Society, 1,* 125-151.

Woods, N. F. (1985). Employment, family roles, and mental ill health in young married women. *Nursing Research, 34,* 4-10.

The Schools
and Family-Oriented Prevention

Sharon L. Kagan
Deborah M. Lonow

SUMMARY. School-based family resource programs are examined as an illustration of a promising programmatic direction in family-school relations. A brief historical review of family-school interactions is provided and a continuum of family-school interactions is set forth. The article describes examples of diverse family resource programs, identifies problems in implementing and evaluating family resource programs, and suggests needed directions in strengthening the potential of school-based, prevention-oriented services to families.

Since the inception of public education in the United States, schools have had the often contradictory responsibility of socializing youngsters to society's standards and working as catalysts to reform those standards. Although this dialectic permeates all aspects of education, it is nowhere more clearly manifest than in the historic controversy over the nature of the relationship between schools and families. Long unresolved, family-school relations have vacillated dramatically between guarding the status quo and reforming it.

The purpose of this article is to explore this dialectic, delineating how changing positions mirror the zeitgeist of the times. The article suggests that today's emerging relationships, as evidenced in family resource programs, are both reflective of the current times and represent a new step in the evolution of family-school relations, a step that underscores the role of schools as catalysts for social reform. While presenting challenges associated with implementing and evaluating family resource programs, the article contends that they can be an effective strategy for preventing social problems as well as a potent vehicle for school change.

FAMILY-SCHOOL RELATIONS IN PERSPECTIVE

The Evolution of Family-School Relations

What was to become a legacy of family-school separation took root in colonial times when schools and families had distinct missions; schools taught academic basics, while family and church were responsible for imparting ethical character. Gradually, recognition that this separation was dysfunctional mounted, so that by Horace Mann's era in the early 19th century some educators and parents began to form parent-school organizations. With parents involved, albeit minimally, schools slowly expanded their role to address critical civic needs necessitated by industrialization and the influx of large waves of immigrants. Responding to the crises of the era, some schools provided or accessed direct services for families: they fed the poor, taught English, and accultured immigrants to American values. Recognizing the viability of such school reforms, parents, primarily mothers, advocated school change that benefited not only the "new" Americans but their own children as well. At their behest, domestic science, play gardens, and kindergartens became part of American public schooling, further legitimizing an advocacy role for parents. Indeed, schools were opening up to accommodate societal need.

Efforts to encourage interaction among families, schools, and communities continued, peaking during the 1930s and again in the 1960s at times of particular social need. Although the 1930's community school movement never gained full acceptance, it was important because it visioned schools not simply as conduits of academic instruction. Schools were seen as hubs for an array of diverse community services that would enrich the total family and community. Later, in the 1960s, propelled by overwhelming social sentiment, the nature of family-school relations took another turn. Empowerment became the by-word as community control and parent participation encouraged citizens to become actively involved in school decision making. Authority for schools was decentralized in some communities and formerly underrepresented parents participated on school boards and committees. Mandated as a condition of federal funding for Title I of the Elementary and Secondary Education Act and Head Start programs, parents became more active in shaping their children's education.

Though accurate, this brief review masks the fact that for all the attention accorded and effort expended on family-school relations, progress was highly episodic and limited in scope. Although many advocated an interactive orientation, full cooperation between families and schools was difficult to achieve for many reasons. Not all parents appreciated efforts to link schools and homes—quite the contrary, irrespective of socioeconomic class, many parents felt that such efforts violated cherished family privacy. Similarly, as professionalism grew, school personnel questioned the "intrusion" of parents into their domain. After all, teaching was a science and teachers were the scientists. Parents could be observers or helpers, but, without specialized training and experience, their input was of modest value at best and meddlesome at worst. Further, beyond personal sentiments that inhibited family-school interactions, there were few systemic rewards that motivated school personnel to involve families. In fact, there were numerous disincentives: family involvement took time; derailed efficiency; and sometimes engendered acrimony. Short on incentives and long on disincentives that fostered family-school relations, school officials, besieged by overloaded agendas, sought to invest time, energy, and dollars elsewhere.

A Continuum of Family-School Relations

Because the nature of family-school relations has been highly-episodic and dramatically influenced by the zeitgeist of the time, approaches to family-school relations vary tremendously. And because such approaches undergird today's efforts, it is important to more clearly distinguish different forms of family-school interactions that have emerged over time. Perhaps these differences can best be envisioned as a continuum that varies by source of support, information, or knowledge and by amount of respect or power accorded each party. At one end of the continuum is the relationship in which parents provide support while schools retain power—the historically conventional and predominant form of "parent involvement." In this most benign form, parent roles include fund raising, volunteering in classrooms, and assisting on field trips. Parents are the "extra pair of hands," the willing volunteers, the passive recipients of information. Accepting the status quo, their involvement perpetuates it.

"Parent participation" as compared to "parent involvement" represents another step in the continuum. Although parent participation may resemble parent involvement because it incorporates some of the activities of the former type, its rationale is entirely different. Parents still provide the support and they are accorded greater power. Characteristic of the 1930s and the 1960s approaches to school reform, parents participate in hopes of altering the system: the status quo is insufficient. Parent participation is pro-active and acknowledges the rightful role parents have in making decisions that affect their children's educational experience—even such critical decisions as curriculum, staffing, and budgeting. The fundamental role of parents in this mode of involvement centers not solely on supporting the school, but on enhancing the broader environment so that the school experience will be more effective for children.

Though operative for a long time, these approaches are being replaced by an entirely new form of family-school interaction, called family resource programs. Building upon parenting education, self-help, and the settlement house movement (Pizzo, 1987; Wandersman, 1987; Weissbourd, 1987), family resource programs foster equal relationships among parents and school personnel, and on the importance of advancing total family competence. Non-hierarchical relationships and non-deficit perspectives prevail. All parents are respected for having special knowledge about their children that is essential for effective teaching and learning. The focus is on supporting not just children or schools or parents but all three. As such, family resource programs represent the most egalitarian and broad-based approach to family-school interactions to date.

If the premise that approaches to family-school interaction reflect their times is true, then to fully understand this new form of family-school interaction, we need to examine the zeitgeist from which it emerged.

TODAY'S ZEITGEIST: THE BEDROCK OF FAMILY RESOURCE PROGRAMS

Changing Families: Changing Schools

There can be no doubt that the quality of American family life is undergoing a massive transformation. With more mothers in the work force, fewer children per family, and more variegated family patterns, the very structure and function of families are being tested and modified. Now well documented, poverty has taken on dimensions and proportions never before evidenced (Ellwood, 1988; Wilson, 1987). Exacerbated by economic recessions and underemployment, structural changes are evidenced in increased rates of divorce, single parent families, and women and children in poverty. Even in traditional nuclear families, despite women's efforts to compensate for the reduced earnings of their spouses, real family income has remained below the 1973 level for over a decade (Rosewater, 1989). Increased family stress is ubiquitous and blatantly evidenced in growing annual percentages of child and spousal abuse (National Committee for the Prevention of Child Abuse, 1988; U.S. Bureau of Justice Statistics, 1986) and in increasing alcohol and drug abuse (National Institute on Drug Abuse, 1987). The need for support and the press to strengthen families has never been more necessary, yet more elusive.

Simultaneously, while families are experiencing such change, public schools are bombarded by charges of ineffectiveness and mediocrity. The schools reverberate with cries of too few resources, more challenging children, and unwieldy layers of regulation. Besieged by dissatisfaction, schools are called upon to challenge the old verities, to address the metaphor of "giving" an education, and to recognize that "nothing is beyond questioning" (Sizer, 1987). Reflecting deep public concern about the ability of individual schools or districts to achieve needed reform, a majority of recently-polled Americans reversed a historic commitment to local control and called for national goals and curriculum (Elam & Gallup, 1989).

Clearly, schools are being asked to do more and to do it better, to emphasize effectiveness and equity. In response, "restructuring" has gained currency in educational parlance. As a comprehensive reform strategy, restructuring involves nothing less than a fundamental realignment of schools' authority structure. Autonomy for teachers, choice for parents, and more of both for children hallmark the effort. No longer entities ruled by bureaucratic dictum, schools are being asked to reform conventional approaches to decision-making and include teachers, community, and families in meaningful ways. Underscoring the difficulty of the challenge, Mary Hatwood Futrell, departing a successful six-year presidency of the National Educational Association, dubbed education reform efforts to date a "mission not accomplished" (Futrell, 1989).

Is it mere coincidence that families and schools — the two institutions that most directly affect the developing child — are in such flux simultaneously? And is it coincidence that both need additional support to execute their functions effectively? We think not. Such a realignment recognizes a changing ethos for families and schools as they function independently and as they synergistically interact.

Changing Theory, Changing Research, and Changing Mandate

Once seen as disparate domains, families and schools have been motivated toward greater interaction by important theoretical advances and research findings. A body of theoretical work, spearheaded by Urie Bronfenbrenner's seminal work on the ecology of human development (1979), has underscored the significance of the interrelatedness of the various parts of a child's life. How children deal with school events and challenges affects, and is affected by, their families, legitimating the need for close family-school ties. In the aggregate, families and schools are linked because, as nurturing institutions, they are engaged in complementary tasks. Together, they not only contour an individual child's development but form the social infrastructure of communities. No longer can schools ignore families, and most are aware that doing so is a social, political, and strategic error.

Research from the past few decades has attested to the practical benefits of stronger family-school interactions. Studies looking at the impact of parental or family involvement in schools vary in their focus, with some examining child effects; others, parental or familial effects; and still others, schools and community outcomes. Great variability also exists in the interpretation of results reported in reviews of the research, with most suggesting at least some positive effects (Powell, 1989; Wallet & Goldman, 1979). Considerably more optimistic, other chroniclers (Davies, 1976; Epstein, 1989; Henderson, Marburger & Ooms, 1986; Seeley, 1981) suggest that research conducted over two decades has convincingly shown that parental involvement favorably affects children's learning, their attitudes toward school, and their aspirations. Epstein (1989) even suggests that new research in inner-city schools shows that school practices are more important than family characteristics in determining parents' long-term commitment to their children's education.

A separate body of research comparing early intervention programs also helped advance a growing recognition of the importance of family-school interaction. Studies on high-quality early intervention programs verified their positive effects, particularly for low-income children (Berrueta-Clement, Schweinhart, Barnett, Epstein & Weikart, 1984; Lazar & Darlington, 1982). Since many of the early intervention programs had strong parent components, some believe that parental support and involvement were critical components of children's success.

Buoyed by these data and the cost-effectiveness of intervening early, educators and policy makers began to shift their emphasis from remediation of academic and behavioral problems to prevention. As agencies serving all children, schools were viewed as one logical vehicle for institutionalizing this prevention concept. Yet, because schools typically begin to serve children in kindergarten, there was some concern that intervention, even at that age, might commence too late to effectively deter problems. Consequently, many school-based early intervention efforts began before formal kindergarten and included an important role for parents. Many states crafted home-based programs that directly involved parents and their young children, altering the question from "if" or "to what degree" families should be involved to "how" best to accomplish it.

Beyond theoretical and empirical rationales, practical forces converged to alter the zeitgeist for improved family-school interactions. Mandates, emerging since 1954, have encouraged greater responsiveness of schools to citizens and families. There can be little doubt that collectively *Brown v. Board of Education*, Head Start, the Elementary and Secondary Education Act, and the Education for All Handicapped Children Act dramatically influenced parent-school relations. Gradually, legitimated by law, parents made their way not simply to but into the schools.

Not surprisingly, these forces converged to create a new receptivity for family-school interactions. The challenge for schools was to meld a renewed desire to render support for families and communities with escalating pressure for student performance and institutional accountability. While there was little question that efforts to involve families and to improve student performance were synergistic, there were only limited effective models within the schools. Turning outside, educators discovered the family resource movement that had already gained considerable momentum.

TODAY'S FAMILY RESOURCE PROGRAMS AND THE SCHOOLS

Family Resource Programs

As uneasiness about the quality of American family life mounted, parents, regardless of income, yearned not for massive intervention programs, but for comparatively modest support. Many turned to kith and kin, others to family resource programs that: (a) enhance the capacity of parents in their child-rearing roles; (b) create settings in which parents are empowered to act on their own behalf and become advocates for change; and (c) provide a community resource for parents.

Essentially, family resource programs are unique from their predecessors in that they focus on preventing problems before they begin, acknowledge that parenting is a developmental process, and accept the universal value of support. Transforming these principles into activities means that programs typically include at least one or more of the following: (a) parent education and support groups; (b) parent-child activities that focus on child development and promote healthy family relationships; (c) drop-in centers that enable families to interact with one another and with program staff; (d) child care while parents participate in other program activities; (e) information and referral to other community services, including child care, health care, nutrition programs, and counseling; (f) home visits; and (g) developmental checks or health screening for children.

It is not surprising that many pioneering programs that espoused the principles above and enacted the specified activities took root in informal settings, outside conventional bureaucracies. Unencumbered by the structures, regulations, and cultures that accompany complex bureaucracies, free-standing family resource programs have been able to contour their efforts with slightly more freedom. This is not to imply that the early family resource programs were isolated from community needs or free from financial concerns; certainly not. Their free-standing nature imposed special challenges, particularly because they lacked the institutional stability that fostered continuity of service.

Consequently, on the one hand, fragile family resource programs began to look to more stable institutions as comfortable homes. On the other hand, institutions, recognizing the value of family resource programs, turned to them as vehicles for improving direct service delivery and as catalysts for reform (Weissbourd & Kagan, 1989). A synergistic melding of free-standing and institutionally-based programs took hold. And given the programs' focus on prevention and on beginning early, schools were one logical institution for planting the seed of family resource programs. As a result, schools today are providing a significant context for family resource programs.

School-based Family Resource Programs

Kentucky's Parent and Child Education Program (PACE) provides one example of a school-based family resource program. It is designed to end the intergenerational cycle of under-education and to promote parents as educational role models for their children. A unique feature of the PACE program is that parents attend school along with their three-or four-year-old children. For part of the day, parents are involved in adult education and life skills classes while their youngsters attend pre-school programs. At other times, parents and children engage in joint activities. A recipient of the 1988 Innovation in State and Local Government Award given by the Ford Foundation and Harvard's John F. Kennedy School of Government, PACE has made significant strides in helping children and their families.

Project Enlightenment in the Wake County public school system in Raleigh, North Carolina is another successful school-based family resource program with a slightly different orientation. It aims to keep children in the mainstream of the educational process by accentuating their strengths and by training parents, teachers, and child care workers to identify problems and develop techniques and skills to deal with them. Multiple services include parent workshops and classes, family counseling, a demonstration preschool, and a parent-teacher resource center. Supported by school district, mental health, Junior League, and Children's Trust Fund dollars, Project Enlightenment has been awarded an Outstanding Achievement Award by the North Carolina Department of Mental Health and a Significant Achievement Award by the American Psychiatric Association.

Another school-based program, the Early Childhood and Family Education Program of Minneapolis, Minnesota is a local example of a statewide program. It works to build the confidence and competence of parents so they can provide optimal parenting. The program, open to all parents of children from birth to kindergarten and expectant parents, builds partnerships among the home, school district, and city and community agencies. Families spend several hours a week involved in developmentally appropriate activities that foster exploration and family learning. Classes also involve parent-child interaction and parent discussion groups. Working in collaboration with numerous community agencies, this family resource program is an effective link for parents and community institutions.

Practical Parent Education in the Plano Independent School District, Plano, Texas, was established to assist parents, through training and support, in rearing responsible, self-confident, mentally healthy children who function at maximal capacity in their educational experiences, their personal lives, and in a complex society. Four- to six-week classes, workshops, and inservice training are customized to participants' specific needs and include issues of building self-esteem, setting limits, teaching responsibility, communicating, and establishing values. A family resource library and brief personal consultations and referrals are also provided. The program trains volunteers to be associate parent educators.

The Parent Resource Center (PRC) of the Corning-Painted Post School District in Corning, New York is an effort to give parents needed information and support to foster parenting skills and to combat the dearth of quality child care in the county by providing child care resources and referral services. Of particular concern are the large number of families whose income falls below the federal poverty guidelines and escalating rates of teen pregnancy and child abuse. This drop-in center encourages parents to interact with children and peers and to seek assistance from staff. Books, toys, and other resources may be borrowed from the Resource Center. Workshops, classes, and activities for parents address specific parenting issues. With another local agency, PRC offers training for family day care providers to increase the number and quality of local child care options. The Center combines public and private funds from the New York State Education Department, the Corning-Painted Post Area School

District, the Corning Glass Works Foundation, and the Steuben Child Care Project.

These programs provide a sampling of school-based family resource programs. While other volumes chronicle the growth and diversity of such programs more fully (Family Resource Coalition, 1989; Levine, 1988), even this cursory overview suggests two propositions that undergird any analysis of school-based family resource efforts. First, given the nature of American schools and society, there is no single response or program. States, municipalities and individual schools will contour their responses to meet local needs. Second, whatever form family resource programs take, they build upon what has gone before. They are an incremental, though important, alteration of past practice, rather than a massive paradigm shift.

The Challenges of Implementing School-based Family Resource Programs

While schools are a fertile setting for family resource programs (and an interesting lens through which to view the general institutionalization process), they represent a significant departure from past practice. As such, they are harbingers of school innovation and pose particular challenges.

The philosophical base and resultant characteristics that distinguish family resource programs from other services are often in direct conflict with conventional school practices. Operationalizing the recognition that all parents, like all children, vary in their developmental stages is a particular challenge. Although personalizing programs for parents is often only a secondary commitment of schools, it is a primary requirement for family resource programs. In fact such personalizing of adult services often flies in the face of rigid bureaucratic practices that favor established schedules, routines, and predictable programming.

Nor is the commitment to self-help and to egalitarian relationships among families and staff that characterizes family resource programs typical of school staffing patterns. While family resource programs shy away from formal staff hierarchies and seek to make parents less dependent on professionals, this may not be possible in schools that require certification for program providers. For family resource to be maximally effective, new attitudes toward professionalism must take root in systems that historically endorse strict hierarchical relationships. Moreover, because family resource programs give personnel new responsibilities with different staff functions, they rarely mesh with existing job descriptions. Consequently, school-based family resource programs usually require the development of new staff lines and additional training.

Though consistent with current efforts to restructure schools, empowering staff is only matched in difficulty by empowering parents. While family resource programs encourage parents to be actively involved with their children and to advocate for them, school bureaucrats may prefer that parents limit their involvement to more conventional activities. Further, there is a troublesome contradiction in having family resource programs empower parents only to have the rest of the school system reject them once the child enters school.

In addition to limiting the role of individual parents, schools may psychologically and strategically isolate the programs from the mainstream of school life. Often viewed in the schools, but not of them, such programs are kept at arm's length or regarded as special. Although being "special" may seem to accord unique privileges, the programs are often the least entitled, battling for space, materials, and dollars. As new and discrete programs, they are most vulnerable and may be forced to move when space is tight or fend for dollars when funds are limited. They must "continually repackage" themselves to accord with new district priorities (Weiss, 1989).

Such battles are waged at high costs. Uncertain of sustained funding, high-quality personnel often prefer other programs, accelerating turnover and generating discontinuity of services. Program leaders are forced to devote their energies to survival tactics rather than program refinements or improvements. Such program instability is a universal nemesis of family resource programs.

Are Family Resource Programs Worth the Effort?

Given the above challenges, one must question whether or not the programs are worth the incredible efforts they demand. Weiss and Halpern (1989), in analyzing 20 evaluations of family resource programs, have found encouraging effects. The findings, not limited to programs in schools, speak to the success of family resource programs regardless of location. For parents, they found short-term effects on one or more dimensions of maternal behavior, including involvement and reciprocal interaction with the child, praise for accomplishments, restrictiveness and appropriate control, and verbal and material stimulation. Parents were also more aware of their roles as teachers and of appropriate expectations for their children. In addition, general parent coping, adaptation, and efforts at personal development increased. They report, however, that long-term effects were "less clearly positive" with only a few studies finding some residual effects. Although intervention was for parents, children were indirectly affected as shown by their developmental test performance. Weiss and Halpern (1988) suggest that effects on children stem from parents improving their families' life circumstances as a result of enhanced self-esteem, and coping and problem-solving behaviors. Improved life circumstances may also stem from programs that improve chances for economic self-sufficiency through job, school, or vocational training placement.

In addition, anecdotal reports indicate that family resource programs reap benefits for schools and communities that adopt them. The sponsorship of such programs signals a strong commitment to families and suggests that schools are innovative and responsive to family needs. Schools that have incorporated family resource programs report greater parent involvement throughout the grades, which reinforces parents' commitment to and knowledge of the learning process. Parents become advocates for their children, for the school system, and for education in general. Nevertheless, while such findings are indeed promising, as are the apparent impacts on children and families, much more research is needed to verify these accounts and to ascertain more precisely which kinds of programs (and more specifically which program variables) affect individual outcomes.

The Challenges of Evaluating School-based Family Resource Programs

The need for more research and evaluation, while clear, poses very real challenges for those concerned about school-based family resource programs. Paradoxically, the precise characteristics that make family resource programs unique are those that make them difficult to evaluate — prevention, ecological orientation, flexibility, and individuality of program services. Evaluating preventive programs poses a particular challenge because it is difficult to measure what one is attempting to prevent. The non-occurrence of events cannot be tallied. Further, the ecological perspective hampers easy evaluation because we are faced with multiple points of intervention (children, families, schools) and their interaction. Because programs vary on every measurable characteristic, it is difficult to obtain a sufficient sample of similar programs for comparison. And because individual programs vary over time in response to changing needs of participants (Powell, 1989), researchers are often faced with "sequential" interventions within a single program. Though bearing the same name, locale, and staff, the program may vary dramatically from September to June. The difficulty of evaluating family resource programs is further complicated by their commitment to direct service. Program participants often find the demands of quantitative evaluation design (e.g., random assignment, controls for contamination) an obstacle to the efficient and equitable delivery of services. Finally, evaluation is complicated by disagreement about appropriate outcomes of family resource programs (Powell, 1989) and a lack of reliable and valid measures of child and family functioning. Evaluating family well-being or children's social competence is much more difficult than chronicling the occurrence of specific events or measuring children's intellectual capacities.

Though challenging, the evaluation dilemma is being hurdled. Rather than relying on quantitative measures, providers and evaluators are launching qualitative and ethnographic studies. Aware of the need to document program efficacy and accomplishment, they are chronicling outcomes, as well. Volumes about evaluating family resource programs have appeared, and technical assistance regarding evaluation is being provided.

Despite their success, such efforts are limited in number and scope, so that more sustained and systematic evaluation over time is needed to ensure the rightful place of family resource programs in the long history of family-school interactions.

THE FUTURE OF SCHOOL-BASED FAMILY RESOURCE PROGRAMS

When all is said and done, school-based family resource programs remain vulnerable. Three related strategies are necessary in order to increase their long-term viability within American schools.

The Need for Evaluation

Long-term evaluations, emphasizing the utility of qualitative evaluation, need to be supported. Over-reliance on quantitative data will delay the aggregation of data supporting the viability of family resource programs. To legitimate a role for ethnographic evaluation, professionals must be trained in its use and in how to garner data on different kinds of programs. Such evaluation data should include two often-neglected components that are critically important to program planners and policy makers. First, the lack of robust data to demonstrate the cost-effectiveness of family resource programs hampers advocating for their expansion. Second, evaluations should seek to assess process (Powell, 1989) in order to determine if and how the implementation of family resource programs has altered the climate or ethos of schools. For example, are schools with rich family resource programs more receptive to "restructuring" strategies? Are they more conducive to maintaining staff and families? If, in fact,

family resource programs are catalysts for institutional change, then
chronicling the process and nature of that change will help those concerned about school reform.

The Need for School Support

The second strategy in stabilizing school-based family resource programs is to establish an ethos for them and for the principles they espouse
within schools. If school personnel internalized the idea of working with
families as a critical component of their work and an essential ingredient
of their success, greater receptivity to family resource programs would
prevail. Teacher training institutions need to consider making their entire
curriculum family-sensitive. An elective course on family-school relations, sometimes considered a herculean step forward, is insufficient.
Schools must be seen as community institutions serving children *and* families, and school personnel must feel accountable to both as united entities.

Conventionally within the purview of other institutions, families in
need are served by an array of non-school agencies. Coming to grips with
how a community can integrate its services most appropriately and determining what roles schools can play within the array of community services are essential. Thus, establishing an ethos for family resource programs means that schools must be effective collaborators not just with
parents but with community institutions, as well.

The Need for Sustained Funding and Public Policy

Finally, stabilizing school-based family resource programs will occur
only when funding is secured. The pilot or demonstration strategy used so
often in public education has its merits. It is an excellent vehicle for deep-
ening our understanding of issues related to implementing programs in
particular settings. But the degree to which demonstration efforts can be
generalized has long been debated and is particularly questionable in the
case of family resource programs, given their idiosyncratic nature.
Launching pilots is a safe strategy, but alternates must be considered as
well.

Family resource programs need a policy commitment that accords
schools a role in the delivery of these services. Accompanying such legiti-
mation, funds are needed to ensure that the programs become a natural
and integrated part of school service delivery. An excellent example of
such commitment exists in Project Giant Step, New York City's effort for
four-year-old children. In every classroom, in addition to a teacher and an

assistant teacher (the conventional staffing pattern), a family worker was added to bridge the gap between home and school. Not a separate program, but a new strategy, the Giant Step experience suggests that supporting families can emerge from and become part of existing programs. Subjecting existing curriculum, staffing patterns, and mechanisms for decision-making to a "family impact and support" test would be productive in identifying areas where change could be made. We need to remember that adding on new programs is not the only answer; altering the extant system in subtle and important ways certainly can solidify family-school links.

Publicizing what works is another effective vehicle for securing a commitment to families. Through the print and broadcast media, informing the public and policy makers about advances in supporting families can engender additional support for these efforts.

CONCLUSION

Stabilizing a meaningful commitment to families by schools can be a surprisingly difficult task, but the kind of commitment necessary *is* happening in isolated schools, with others conceptually embracing such commitments.

As Kierkegaard said, however, "We live our lives forward and understand them backwards." No adage better describes the evolving relationship of schools and their commitment to families. Family-school relations seem to have been alive and well for decades in our country. Yet we seem able to understand them only in retrospect. The thesis of this article suggests that, by building on years of experience and on many practicable efforts, we can incorporate decades of understanding these efforts "backwards" and move them "forward," post-haste.

REFERENCES

Berrueta-Clement, J.R., Schweinhart, L.J., Barnett, W.S., Epstein, A.S., & Weikart, D. P. (1984). *Changed lives: The effects of the Perry preschool program on youths through age 19.* Ypsilanti, MI: The High/Scope Press.
Bronfenbrenner, U. (1979). *The ecology of human development: Experiments by nature and design.* Cambridge, MA: Harvard University Press.
Davies, D. (Ed.). (1976). *Schools where parents make a difference.* Boston, MA: Institute for Responsive Education.
Elam, S.M. & Gallup, A.M. (1989). The 21st annual Gallup poll of the public's attitudes toward the public schools. *Phi Delta Kappan, 71*(1), 41-54.

Ellwood, D.T. (1988). *Poor support: Poverty in the American family*. New York: Basic Books.

Epstein, J.L. (1989). Building parent-teacher partnerships in inner-city schools. *Family Resource Coalition Report*, *8*(2), 7.

Family Resource Coalition. (1989). Family support and the schools. *Family Resource Coalition Report*, *8*(2).

Futrell, M.H. (1989). Mission not accomplished: Education reform in retrospect. *Phi Delta Kappan*, *71*(1), 9-14.

Henderson A.T., Marburger, C., & Ooms, T. (1986). *Beyond the bake sale: An educator's guide to working with parents*. Columbia, MD: National Committee for Citizens in Education.

Lazar, I. & Darlington, R. (1982). Lasting effects of early education: A report from the Consortium for Longitudinal Studies. *Monographs of the Society for Research in Child Development*, *47*(2-3, Serial No. 195).

Levine, C. (Ed.). (1988). *Programs to strengthen families, revised edition*. Chicago, IL: Family Resource Coalition.

National Committee for the Prevention of Child Abuse. (1988, April). Newsletter.

National Institute on Drug Abuse. (1987). *National trends in drug use and related factors among American high school students and young adults*. Washington, DC: U.S. Department of Health and Human Services.

Pizzo, P. (1987). Parent-to-parent support groups: Advocates for social change. In S.L. Kagan, D.R. Powell, B. Weissbourd, & E. Zigler (Eds.), *America's family support programs*. New Haven, CT: Yale University Press.

Powell, D.R. (1989). *Families and early childhood programs*. Washington, DC: National Association for the Education of Young Children.

Rosewater, A. (1989). Child and family trends: Beyond the numbers. In F. J. Macchiarola & A. Gartner (Eds.), *Caring for America's children*. New York: The Academy of Political Science.

Seeley, D.S. (1981). *Education through partnership*. Cambridge, MA: Ballinger Publishing Company.

Sizer, T.R. (1987, October). Address at School-Based Reform Symposium, NEA, Minneapolis, MN.

U.S. Bureau of Justice Statistics. (1986, August). *Preventing domestic violence against women*. Washington, DC: Author.

Wallet, C. & Goldman, R. (1979). *Home/school/community interaction: What we know and why we don't know more*. Columbus, OH: Charles E. Merrill Publishing Company.

Wandersman, L.P. (1987). New directions for parent education. In S.L. Kagan, D.R. Powell, B. Weissbourd, & E. Zigler (Eds.), *America's family support programs*. New Haven, CT: Yale University Press.

Weiss, H.B. (1989, April 26-28). *From grass roots programs to state policy: Strategic planning and choices for family support and education initiatives*. Paper prepared for the Public Policy and Family Support and Education Programs Colloquium. Annapolis, MD.

Weiss, H.B. & Halpern, R. (1988, April 7). *Community-based family support and education programs: Something old or something new?* Paper for the National Resource Center for Children in Poverty. New York.

Weiss, H.B. & Halpern, R. (1989, April 26-28). *The challenges of evaluating state family support and education initiatives; An evaluation framework.* Paper for the Public Policy and Family Support and Education Programs Colloquium. Annapolis, MD.

Weissbourd, B. (1987). A brief history of family support programs. In S.L. Kagan, D.R. Powell, B. Weissbourd, & E. Zigler (Eds.) *America's family support programs.* New Haven, CT: Yale University Press.

Weissbourd, B. & Kagan, S.L. (1989). Family support programs: Catalysts for change. *American Journal of Orthopsychiatry, 59* (1), 20-31.

Wilson, W.J. (1987). *The truly disadvantaged: The inner city, the underclass and public policy.* Chicago: University of Chicago Press.

Social Network Intervention in Intensive Family-Based Preventive Services

James K. Whittaker
Elizabeth M. Tracy

SUMMARY. This paper describes two agency-based research and development projects designed to enhance the social support resources available to families at risk of disruption through the placement of one or more children in out-of-home care. Included are (a) descriptions of the development of an instrument (Social Network Map, Tracy & Whittaker, in press) for rapidly assessing client network resources and strains; and (b) description of needs assessment, development of staff training in network assessment, development of collaborative case consultation model for pilot testing and empirical evaluating social support interventions. Issues for future research and clinical applications are explored.

This paper describes two agency-based research and development projects designed to identify, enhance, and augment the social network resources of families at risk of disruption through the unnecessary placement of a child. "Family preservation services," as they have come to be called, are a major focus of concern for public and voluntary child welfare services. As a result of Public Law 96-272 passed by Congress in 1980, states must satisfy a judicial authority that "reasonable efforts" have been extended to keep the family together before placement can be justified. The brief, crisis-focused, intensive, in-home services described later in

The Family Support Project was supported by a grant from the Edna McConnell Clark Foundation and was a joint research effort of the University of Washington, School of Social Work and Behavioral Sciences Institute ("Homebuilders") of Federal Way, Washington. The Social Networks Project is an applied research effort at Boysville of Michigan funded, in part, by the Skillman Foundation of Detroit. The authors wish to thank both foundations and the clinical and administrative staffs of Homebuilders and Boysville for making both research projects possible.

this paper represent an attempt to define and operationalize these "reasonable efforts" (Whittaker, Kinney, Tracy, & Booth, 1990).

The first pilot effort, *The Family Support Project* (Whittaker, Tracy, & Marckworth, 1989), was carried out with Homebuilders of Washington State, perhaps the best known and widely cited model of intensive, in-home crisis services for families at imminent risk of placement (Kinney, Haapala, Booth, & Leavitt, 1988). A primary aim of this effort was the development and pilot testing of a measure for rapidly assessing the social support resources and related network characteristics of high-risk families (Tracy & Whittaker, in press).

A successor project, *The Social Networks Project*, is currently in progress with several similar "Family Preservation Programs" in a large, multiservice midwestern youth and family agency, Boysville, of Michigan (Tracy & Whittaker, in press). Clients are, for the most part, multiproblem, inner-city families with a child at imminent risk of placement. Our primary focus in this present effort is twofold: first, to assess the clinical utility and predictive validity of our social network measure (the *Social Network Map*) in routine agency data collection and, second, to develop and pilot test a variety of network-based interventions designed to improve the fit between professionally delivered clinical services and the client's social network. Both projects were based on the simple assumption that better understanding of the personal social networks of primary caregivers in high-risk families was a necessary, though not sufficient component of accurate assessment and effective intervention. We believe clinical research evidence is accumulating which supports this assumption. For example, in youth and family services there is growing recognition that certain characteristics of neighborhood and extended family networks are frequently correlated with successful service outcomes (Dumas & Wahler, 1983; Whittaker & Pecora, 1984). Treatment efforts can be made more permanent and enduring through the supportive assistance of kin, friends, neighbors, and other "informal helpers" who can help families sustain and consolidate the gains made in professional helping. Techniques for assessing and strengthening these network resources are not numerous, though some pilot efforts indicate much promise with certain high-risk families (Gaudin, Wodarski, Arkinson, & Avery, 1988; Tracy & Whittaker, 1987). *Network interventions offer no panacea.* Despite some early "overenthusiasm" in the human services field, such interventions should be seen as a necessary but not sufficient component of a comprehensive service plan which likely will include family treatment, parent education, case management, and related services. Nor is it wise to assume that network members will always be supportive: kin and friends can be the source of excessive demands as well as support and sometimes can reinforce self-injurious behaviors as in drug abuse. Indeed, we believe the potential *negative* effect of network members on the clients' treatment goals constitutes, in and of itself, a powerful reason for better understanding of network strengths and liabilities for high risk families.

Our conviction is bolstered by recent empirical research with low-income, inner-city, single-parent-headed black families at risk of abuse/neglect and a host of other adverse outcomes. This research points clearly to the criticality of systematically assessing, as part of ongoing treatment, network strengths/deficits (including the client's perception of various types of support) as well as culturally relevant patterns of helping (Linblad-Goldberg & Dukes, 1985; Lindblad-Goldberg, Dukes, & Hasley, 1988). While these last two studies do not support a stress buffering hypothesis for social support or particular network characteristics per se, they do suggest the wisdom of assessing more precisely the various types of support as a guide to planning interventions.

The remainder of this paper will briefly (a) describe the service context for our two projects: intensive, in-home family and preventive services; (b) provide a brief summary of *The Family Support Project* and *The Social Networks Project*; and (c) enumerate several issues for future intervention research and development.

UNDERSTANDING THE SERVICE CONTEXT
FOR INTENSIVE, IN-HOME FAMILY-BASED
PREVENTIVE SERVICES

Intensive, in-home family-based preventive services, or, as they are increasingly identified in the child welfare field, intensive family preservation services (IFPS), are characterized by highly intensive services, delivered generally in the client's home for a relatively brief period of time. Family preservation services are closely related to "family-centered social services" (Hutchinson, 1983; Bryce & Lloyd, 1981; Lloyd & Bryce, 1984) in philosophy and rationale, but generally provide more intensive services to families over a shorter time period. The primary goals of IFPS are (a) to protect children (0-17) at imminent risk of placement, (b) to maintain and strengthen bonds within the family, (c) to stabilize the crisis situation, (d) to increase the family's skills and competencies, and (e) to facilitate the family's use of a variety of formal and informal helping resources. Typically, IFPS focus on the current situation; the intent is not to "cure" the family. The time-limited nature of these services sets upper limits on what outcomes can reasonably be expected; however, the intensity of service, coupled with referral at the point of imminent risk of placement, produces a situation capable of dramatic change.

While there is no clear consensus on the exact nature of family preservation services, and wide variation in how such services are delivered—or even by what name they should be called—such services are increasingly popular in child welfare. The National Resource Center on Family-Based Services (Iowa) currently lists over 200 such programs; by comparison, the first directory in 1982 listed only 20 programs. Over 60 separate programs are administered by state and county agencies, and a number of states have passed home-based legislation and are developing statewide programs. Still, many communities have limited preventive services.

Family preservation services differ along a number of dimensions: *staffing patterns, auspice (public/private), target population, client eligibility, intensity of service,* and *components of service.* Pecora, Fraser, Haapala, and Bartlome (1987) have identified key dimensions in the areas of treatment technique and services, program structure, and program outcomes that can be used to compare and contrast different IFPS programs. These dimensions are helpful in making comparisons among different programs and in identifying key components of IFPS. The primary setting for our initial effort, *The Family Support Project,* was the Homebuilders model, which is described more fully by Kinney et al. (1988), and which represents one end of the continuum of intensity and brevity of services.

Notwithstanding differences among programs, there are a number of shared characteristics and features. Some reflect the nature of services delivered, while others reflect staff attitudes and values which are distinctive to this type of service. Elements common to both Homebuilders and other family preservation services programs include:

- Only families at risk of imminent placement are accepted.
- Services are crisis-oriented. Families are seen as soon as possible after referral is made.
- Staff are accessible, maintaining flexible hours seven days a week. For example, Homebuilders give out their home phone numbers to families.
- Intake and assessment procedures insure that no child is left in danger.
- Although problems of individuals may be addressed, the focus is on the family as a unit, rather than on parents or children as problematic individuals.
- Workers see families in their own homes, making frequent visits

convenient to each family's schedule. Many services are also provided in school and neighborhood settings.
- The service approach combines teaching skills to family members, helping the family obtain the necessary resources and services, and counseling based on an understanding of how each family functions as a unit.
- Services are generally based on identified family needs rather than strict eligibility categories.
- Each worker carries a small caseload at any given time. A limited number of programs make use of teams. Homebuilders work individually with team backup but have caseloads of only two families at a time.
- Programs limit the length of involvement with the family to a short period, typically between one and five months. Homebuilders typically work with a family over a four to six week period.

In short, the service delivery features of intensive preservation programs are designed to engage families in service (even those families who have "failed" in other counseling attempts), to keep families in service intensively for a time-limited period, and to increase the likelihood that they will benefit from service. IFPS provide a combination of services designed to deal with crisis situations, to enhance family functioning, to meet both concrete and clinical service needs, and to decrease the family's isolation. Most IFPS programs work from family strengths and include use of extended family, community, and neighborhood resources (Lloyd & Bryce, 1984). These services make maximum use of a variety of worker tasks and roles — counselor, parent trainer, advocate, consultant, and resource broker.

THE FAMILY SUPPORT PROJECT

The Family Support Project (Whittaker, Tracy, & Marckworth, 1989) sought to identify practical strategies for assessing and enhancing social support resources for families at risk of disruption through out-of-home placement. The project was implemented during the time period April 1987 through September 1988 in conjunction with Homebuilders, an intensive family preservation program located in Federal Way, Washington. The project was funded through a generous grant from the Edna McConnell Clark Foundation. The objectives of the project were to (a) identify assessment and intervention techniques to build, mobilize, and sustain social support resources in order to assist families in their parenting efforts; (b) identify practice approaches to bridge the gap between formal and informal sources of helping; (c) identify multiple ways in which professional activities can be linked to informal helping; (d) develop and pilot test a training module on social support for family preservation services workers.

Design of the Project

From its inception, the Family Support Project was designed to address a number of obstacles common to conducting research in agency settings. These include:

— Distance often perceived between the academic world and the world of clinical practice.
— Separateness of findings from research and clinical practice.
— Researcher's focus on the "average" client versus the practitioner's concern for the needs of the individual client and how best to meet those needs.
— Lack of clarity and consensus on the objectives of research that often exists between academics and practitioners (Wells & Whittaker, 1989).

First, the project sought to *involve practitioners actively and meaningfully in all phases of the project*. This meant that clinical judgment, practice wisdom, and the subjective evaluations of practitioners were viewed as valid and important pieces of information, and that this information informed the research questions and design. In order to involve practitioners and insure a means to link each Homebuilder therapist with the project, the Social Support Development Team was formed.

The team consisted of a representative from each of the four Washington State Homebuilder programs along with Homebuilder's director of training, and the university-based project researchers. The team met regularly and was responsible for setting priorities, directing the flow of research activities, making decisions on training needs and case consultation, reviewing materials, and serving as liaison with other staff. The team also played a key role in maintaining the interest and involvement of clinical staff. They carried out major portions of the training, case consultations, and presentations to professional conferences which were to come at later stages of the project.

The second way in which the project addressed obstacles to agency-based research was in its selection of *research and development methodology* (R&D). The emphasis of R&D methodology is on the design, development, field testing, and diffusion of new practice technology (Thomas,

1978, 1984; Rothman, 1989). Most findings of behavioral science research are descriptive in nature and lack clear specification regarding how they might be applicable to practice; they fail to tell the practitioner what to do in a given situation.

R&D methodology offers several advantages to child and family practitioners (Whittaker & Pecora, 1981). First of all, it is product-oriented. R&D projects create a specific solution, strategy, or answer to a specific problem. The primary research question is "how to" rather than "why." One Homebuilder aptly expressed this point: "We could find new ways to do things rather than being evaluated on what we've already done."

R&D efforts are also useful in generating a more testable body of technology for rigorous field experiments. This is particularly important in the area of practice with social networks. Much of the current state of knowledge regarding social support does not easily convert to concrete practice principles. Few guidelines exist to aid practitioners in planning and implementing social support interventions (Whittaker & Garbarino, 1983). Some of the specific areas for developmental testing of social support interventions include (a) the nature, intensity, and treatment integrity of the support intervention, (b) the skills, knowledge, and activities required by workers, (c) professional education and training appropriate to implementation of social support interventions, (d) the types of outcome changes, and (e) the organizational and service delivery requirements (Tracy & Whittaker, 1987). The Family Support Project examined these areas in relation to social network practice within brief and intensive family preservation services.

The third and final way in which barriers to agency-based practice were handled was in the adoption of an *individualized approach to assessment and intervention.* It was assumed from the outset that no one strategy would address the social support needs of all families. Due to the variety of family lifestyles and circumstances, the project team decided that its task was to provide family preservation workers with a framework for conceptualizing social support and tools for assessing support needs and implementing interventions as appropriate. The objective, consistent with the agency mission, was to help practitioners individualize social support interventions so as to enhance the overriding goal of placement prevention.

Project Activities

The objectives of the Family Support Project were accomplished through a variety of activities carried out in four major phases: Training, Assessment, Intervention, and Dissemination.

Training and Clinical Seminars

A variety of training sessions and clinical seminars were conducted with Homebuilders staff for the dual purposes of sharing information and contributing to the formulation of new social support assessment and intervention techniques. For example, in the early phases of the project, practitioners were asked to describe ways in which they currently gathered information about families' social networks and how they incorporated that information in case planning. This brainstorming session was helpful in generating realistic and relevant assessment formats. At a later stage of the project, Homebuilders were asked to identify social and communication skills they considered key to accessing and maintaining supportive relationships. These discussions yielded rich information for the development of intervention guidelines.

Development and Use
of Assessment Formats

A major product of the Family Support Project was the development of the Social Network Map (Tracy & Whittaker, in press). The Social Network Map facilitates collection of information on the total size and composition of an individual's network as well as the nature and quality of relationships within the network, as experienced by the individual. Administration involves first listing network members. Once the composition of the network has been visually displayed, a series of questions is asked regarding the nature of network relationships. These questions cover the types of support available (concrete, emotional, and informational), the extent to which network members are critical of the individual, the direction of help, the closeness of relationships, frequency of contact, and length of relationships.

Using the Social Network Map enabled families more clearly to understand their social resources. The map also provided workers with specific information about the family's social network and the degree to which the family felt (or did not feel) supported by that network. The map was used with 50 families seen by the agency during the time period September to December 1987. The information gathered about the families' social networks challenged some earlier assumptions and was valuable in informing the development of interventions. Findings from this phase of the project have been fully reported elsewhere (Whittaker, Tracy, & Marckworth, 1989; Tracy, in press); some of the main practice implications are reviewed below.

1. It is important to assess both structural and functional aspects of social networks. Structural measures, such as social network size, were

poor indicators of social support. Some people with very small social networks appeared to be receiving the types of support they needed. Other people with large social networks were receiving very little support from network members. Increasing network size alone, then, may do little to enhance social support.

2. Network composition does appear to be a relevant factor to assess. On the average, 40% of all network members were either household members or extended family. The category of friends constituted 22% of the network. However, both the number and proportions of friends in the network were associated with perceived social support. On the average, friends were the most frequently reported sources of concrete assistance and emotional support. Helping clients to build friendships and teaching skills in developing friendships may be promising interventions.

3. It is important to assess both positive and negative aspects of social networks. Social networks can extract costs, notwithstanding the availability of social support. The majority of respondents had one or more people in their network who were almost always critical of them. The proportion of critical network members was negatively related to emotional support. The findings suggest that interventions to decrease aversive interactions may be needed in conjunction with those designated to increase socially supportive behaviors.

4. Reciprocity appears to play a prominent role in informal helping relationships. Reciprocity was positively related to some types of support, particularly concrete support. Interventions to teach reciprocal social skills might be an effective way to enhance social support.

Development of Social Network Interventions

Weekly case consultation sessions were conducted with each Homebuilder team in order to develop and evaluate the impact of various social network intervention strategies. The goal of case consultation was to track the development, planning, and implementation of social support interventions with individual families. This consultation supplemented regularly provided case supervision and was limited to the development of social support interventions.

When a case was brought up for consultation, the first step was to review the results of the Social Network Map. Based on that information, the most appropriate social support goal was discussed and implementation strategies were designed. Over a period of time (from one to several weeks, depending on the family), what worked and what did not work were reviewed. In this way, program staff increased their knowledge about various interventions. Their ability to individualize interventions also increased. Several case summaries were then prepared and incorporated in staff training on social support.

In general, two types of social support goals were common. One type of goal was structural in nature, that is, to create or supplement the social network. The second type of goal was to improve or enhance the functioning of relationships within the network. Examples of family situations and related goals discussed in case consultation include:

- An isolated mother who exhibited poor social skills. The social support goal was to increase the size of her social network and the frequency of social contacts.
- Teenage parents experiencing violent marital conflicts. The social support goal was to increase the number of mutual social network members.
- A family living on a small Indian reservation. The social support goal involved teaching parenting skills to network members as well as to the parents.
- A 10-year-old boy with a developmental disability who was seen as unmanageable in his special education class. The social support goal was to teach the parents ways of establishing productive relationships with school personnel.

Dissemination Activities

The final phase of the project was the development of a training module on social support. This four-hour social support workshop covers rationales for and definitions of social support, social support assessment, and types of social support interventions. Experiential and skills building exercises are included along with case examples, bibliography, and handouts. Since the project's completion, the training module has been incorporated as part of the agency's on-going in-service training program. It is also used in training staff of other family preservation programs.

In addition to the training module, the Family Support Project produced a number of "research capsules" as a means of disseminating research-based information in short, easy-to-read formats. The research capsules were disseminated widely to other universities, social service agencies, and state/county public social service divisions. The research capsules supplemented more traditional dissemination efforts, such as presentations at professional conferences and papers submitted for publication.

Project Impact on Agency Services

A final component of the Family Support Project was to conduct a process evaluation of the project's impact on the agency. Some of the impacts to be considered included (a) staff knowledge and attitudes about social support, (b) assessment and intervention techniques, (c) case consultation and supervision, and (d) pre-service and in-service training.

In order to assess the project's impact, several major activities were carried out, including staff surveys and interviews, training evaluations, and an organizational impact survey conducted with all management staff. Based on this information, the project was considered successful in the following:

1. Providing an easy, clinically relevant tool (Social Network Map) for assessing social networks and social support resources, and which practitioners continued to use even after the project's completion.
2. Developing systematic assessment formats and intervention guidelines for social support interventions.
3. Involving staff in clinically relevant and meaningful ways.
4. Developing a training module on social support for family preservation workers.

Based on the experiences of the Family Support Project, the following recommendations can be made to other placement prevention programs:

1. Assessments of client's social networks and sources of social support are helpful in understanding the total family situation. An understanding of social support helps in evaluating the family's social environment, their resources for change, and the obstacles that might prevent change from occurring. Social support resources can often play a direct role in preventing the need for placement and in maintaining changes achieved through family preservation services.

2. It is important not to make assumptions about the social networks of at-risk families. Families may report a seemingly adequate number of people in their social network but not get the types of support they need, they may not perceive the network as supportive, or they may not have the skills needed to maintain supportive relationships with network members. In addition, the variety of ways in which social support is experienced by different families needs to be recognized.

3. Social support interventions need to be individualized to meet family needs. Some families are extremely isolated and will require new network resources. For other families, interventions to foster more supportive relationships with existing network members will be indicated.

4. Successful incorporation of social support interventions in family

preservation programs appears to require support and knowledge from all levels of the organization. Future projects on social support development would benefit from actively including and educating supervisory and management-level staff.

5. As a result of the Family Support Project, a more specific research agenda can be proposed. This includes testing of larger numbers of interventions, inclusion of a wider variety of outcome measures, and testing various packages of interventions. In addition, training models to teach skills for developing and maintaining social support networks need to be developed and tested.

THE SOCIAL NETWORKS PROJECT

The *Social Networks Project* at Boysville of Michigan involves two IFPS programs: one operating on the Homebuilders model ("Families First") and one operating from an eco-structural base. One of the objectives of our present effort is to learn more about the similarities and differences of network-based interventions in intensive family preservation programs operating from different theoretical assumptions. Several of the goals of this project share similarities with those of the Family Support Project as described above. The goals are:

1. To adapt social support assessment procedures and methods developed with Homebuilders for use in Boysville in-home programs.
2. To develop and test different social network interventions to improve informal community supports for youth and families in inner-city Detroit.
3. To conduct a tracking study to monitor changing patterns of social supports for high-risk families.
4. To develop and implement specialized clinical training packages on social network interventions.

In addition to a number of common goals, the Social Networks Project shares a number of structural features with its predecessor project. A Social Networks Project Team has been convened and has begun meeting regularly, in person and via telephone case conference calls, to review social support needs of families and to plan interventions. The team is made up of in-home workers, clinical supervisors, and program managers. In addition, representatives from the research and clinical training departments are included. The team has begun collecting data on social network characteristics and social support needs by implementing routine use of the Social Network Map at intake and at case closing with referred families. Initial training on social support assessment developed in the Homebuilders project has been provided to all team members.

There are a number of characteristics of the Boysville program, however, which make it a unique practice laboratory. First, Boysville provides a full continuum of care to troubled youth and their families, including in-home preventive services, residential, group home, and foster family-based treatment, as well as aftercare services. While the Social Networks Project is focusing its initial efforts with in-home program staff, the potential for expansion of social network interventions across a variety of services and the full range of the continuum is considerable. It will be possible to collect data on social support and related network characteristics across the continuum and compare and contrast social support needs and resources of families served in different programs.

Second, there is diversity even within Boysville in-home program models. Several in home programs called "Families First" have received training from Behavioral Sciences Institute and are following the Home-builders model. Other in-home programs, referred to as "Ecostructural" are based on family systems theory and work with families on a longer-term basis (up to 6 months). The theoretical orientations of these models are quite distinct, but the client populations they serve are very similar to each other. The differences in theoretical models afford an opportunity to examine differential applications of social network interventions across models. For example, in what ways will assessment of social supports facilitate understanding of family boundaries? In what ways might engagement/joining with the family be accomplished more easily through involvement of social network members? To what extent are social and communication skills training approaches consistent with social network interventions?

A third feature of the Social Networks Project is its explicit focus on the development of coordinated management information systems in relation to social network and social support data collection. Boysville of Michigan currently utilizes a comprehensive management information system developed by Grasso and Epstein (1987; 1989) for all routinely gathered data on children and families. Information about children and families and about the services they receive is collected at regular intervals during intervention and at set follow-up points after intervention has been completed. This information is "fed back" to all levels of the organization— direct line staff, family workers, supervisors, and program managers. The management information system allows for information about one family to be shared with their individual family worker — for example, the results of a stress and coping inventory. The system is also capable of providing group information to a supervisor or program manager about the children or families seen by one program or unit at any given point in time.

The Social Networks Project will be working toward the integration of social network and social support assessment information with the existing management information system. Feedback mechanisms will be developed to enable both workers and families to evaluate the social network information collected. In addition, procedures for describing and reporting social support needs and resources for groups of families served by individual in-home programs will be developed. These feedback mechanisms are viewed as essential in the development of interventions and in tracking social support needs across time and programs.

Finally, the client population served by Boysville as well as the inner-city settings in which services are delivered make for an interesting point of comparison with the Family Support Project. The large number of minority families working with Boysville staff offers an opportunity to examine cultural issues around social support. In particular, the role of the extended family, church, and community organizations will be of special interest. The social support strengths as well as the social support needs of minority families will be examined. Specialized training modules will be developed to enable staff to appreciate better and be sensitive to cultural expressions of social support. Another clinical feature is the presence of substance abuse. The role of social networks as supports for negative or dysfunctional behaviors is an important consideration. In a similar manner, the potential usefulness of social networks as supports in the recovery process needs further exploration. For this reason, specialized interventions will be employed using social network resources with substance abusing families.

IMPLICATIONS FOR FUTURE RESEARCH ON NETWORK INTERVENTIONS WITH HIGH-RISK FAMILIES

Based on our experiences to date, the following recommendations can be made with respect to network assessment with high-risk families.

First, we have found that systematic assessments of clients' social networks and sources of social support are helpful in understanding the total family situation. Regardless of the method selected to assess social support, the process of gathering the information and considering this information in relation to the family's needs may influence the success of the overall intervention. A critical task for the field is the development of valid and reliable measures for the *rapid assessment* of social support and related network characteristics and processes. We found, for example, in our original project that while there had been a veritable explosion of measurement technology in the last several years, relatively few instruments were clinically useful in a very brief in-home intervention with low-income families, many of whom were in crisis at the point of intake. A related challenge involves the modification of assessment technology for use in *routine agency data collection* at multiple time points such as intake, termination, and follow-up. Can we identify patterns of support/ conflict, for example, that can be used initially as measures of risk and acuity and then monitor them over time as the social equivalent of physiological "vital signs?"

Second, we have learned that it is important not to make assumptions about the social networks of at-risk families. Families may report a seemingly adequate number of people in their social network but not the types of support they need, or they may not perceive the network to be supportive, or may not have the needed skills to maintain supportive relationships with network members. The notion of social networks as a source of stress as well as support needs to be anticipated. In addition, the variety of ways in which social support is experienced by different families needs to be recognized. We are particularly mindful of the need to develop culturally sensitive methods of assessment that attend to actual and preferred patterns of support in particular minority communities. We must constantly remind therapists, clinical supervisors (and ourselves) of the following broad and commonly accepted generalization from network research: "More does not necessarily mean better."

Third, we are convinced that the form of social network intervention requires careful consideration and must be individualized to meet each family's needs. For example, not all social support interventions will involve increasing the size of the social network or linking the client with new resources. For some families, interventions with existing social network members will be more appropriate. Interventions may focus on skills training, which, while essential to maintaining socially supportive relationships, may not be substantially different from skills training that is ordinarily provided to reach other goals. For example, assertiveness skills may be needed to insure reciprocity in an existing relationship. Our future agenda includes adaptation of a number of known network interventions (such as network facilitation, use of natural helpers, and development of links with self-help and mutual aid) specifically tailored to intensive family preservation services. Our experience to date, particularly in Detroit, strongly suggests augmenting any network interventions to anticipate the pervasive abuse by clients of "crack" cocaine and other substances.

Fourth, and not surprisingly, we have encountered many barriers to the incorporation of network-based intervention in intensive in-home family-based services. The time-limited, crisis-focused nature of these interventions makes meaningful identification of network resources and network-based interventions a real challenge. We have encountered resistance from therapists of different theoretical persuasions and find we need to emphasize differing rationales to encourage a practice form which includes the client's wider social network. For example, more behaviorally oriented practitioners have been influenced by the potential for social support facilitation to help with maintenance and generalization of treatment gains, while more structurally oriented practitioners have appreciated the value of network assessment as a tool to aid in understanding family boundaries. Other barriers include non-facilitative internal agency structures, cultural ignorance, and problems in identifying work with collaterals as a "billable service."

Fifth, and finally, we are convinced of the utility of applied intervention research in agency settings. The models proposed by Grasso and Epstein (1987;1989), and Rothman and others (1989) involves practitioners, may be adapted to different problems, achieves maximum staff involvement, and allows for planned variation. This is particularly useful in an agency like Boysville, where the presence of a practitioner-oriented management information system allows for the design, implementation, continuous monitoring, and formative evaluation of novel network interventions as a prelude to more rigorous quasi-experimental designs.

REFERENCES

Bryce, M. & Lloyd, J.C. (Eds.). (1981). *Treating families in the home: An alternative to placement*. Springfield, IL: Charles C. Thomas.

Dumas, J.I. & Wahler, R.G. (1983). Predictors of treatment outcome in parent training: Mother insularity and socio-economic disadvantage. *Behavioral Assessment*, 5, 301-313.

Gaudin, J.M., Wodarski, J.S., Arkinson, M.K., & Avery, L.S. (1988). *Outcomes of social network interventions with neglectful families*. Unpublished manuscript.

Grasso, A. & Epstein, I. (1987). Management by measurement: organizational dilemmas and opportunities. *Administration in Social Work*, 89-100.

Grasso, A. & Epstein, I. (1989). The Boysville experience: integrating practice decision making, program evaluation and management information. *Computers in Human Services*, 85-95.

Hutchinson, J. (1983). *Family-centered social services: A model for child welfare agencies*. Iowa City: University of Iowa, National Resource Center for Family Based Services.

Kinney, J., Haapala, D., Booth, C., & Leavitt, S. (1988). The Homebuilders Model. In J.K. Whittaker, J. Kinney, E.M. Tracy, & C. Booth (Eds.), *Improving practice technology for work with high risk families: Lessons from the "Homebuilders" Social Work Education Project* (Center for Social Welfare Research Monograph No. 6, pp. 37-67). Seattle, WA: University of Washington, School of Social Work.

Lindblad-Goldberg, M. & Dukes, J.L. (1985). Social support in black, low-income, single-parent families: Normative and dysfunctional patterns. *American Journal of Orthopsychiatry*, 55(1), 42-58.

Lindblad-Goldberg, M., Dukes, J.L., & Lasley, J.H. (1988). Stress in black, low-income, single-parent families: Normative and dysfunctional patterns. *American Journal of Orthopsychiatry*, 58(1), 104-120.

Lloyd, J.C. & Bryce, M.E. (1984). *Placement prevention and family reunification: A handbook for the family-centered service practitioner*. Iowa City: University of Iowa, National Resource Center for Family Based Services.

Pecora, P.J., Fraser, M.W., Haapala, D., & Bartlome, I.A. (1987). *Defining family preservation services: Three intensive home-based treatment programs*. Salt Lake City: University of Utah.

Rothman, J. (1989). *Creating tools for intervention: The convergence of research methodologies*. Unpublished manuscript, UCLA School of Social Welfare, Center for Child and Family Policy Studies.

Thomas, E.J. (1978). Generating innovation in social work: The paradigm of developmental research. *Journal of Social Service Research*, 2(1), 95-116.

Thomas, E.J. (1984). *Designing interventions for the helping professions*. Beverly Hills, CA: Sage.

Tracy, E.M. (in press). Identifying social support resources of at-risk families. *Social Work*.

Tracy, E.M. & Whittaker, J.K. (1987). The evidence base for social support interventions in child and family practice: Emerging issues for research and practice. *Children and Youth Services Review*, 9, 249-270.

Tracy, E.M. & Whittaker, J.K. (in press). The Social Network Map: Assessing social support in clinical social work practice. *Families in Society*.

Wells, K. & Whittaker, J.K. (1989). Integrating research and agency based practice: approaches, problems and possibilities. In E. A. Balcerzak (Ed.), *Group care of children: Transitions towards the year 2000*. Washington, D.C.: Child Welfare League of America.

Whittaker, J.K. & Garbarino, J. (1983). *Social support networks: Informal helping in the human services*. New York: Aldine.

Whittaker, J.K., Kinney, J., Tracy, E. M., & Booth, C. (Eds.). (1990). *Reaching high risk families: Intensive family preservation in human services*. NY: Aldine de Gruyter.

Whittaker, J.K. & Pecora, P. (1981). The social "R&D" paradigm in child and youth services. *Children and Youth Services Review, 3*, 305-317.

Whittaker, J.K. & Pecora, P. (1984). A research agenda for residential care. In T. Philpot (Ed.), *Group care practice: The challenge of the next decade* (pp. 71-87). Surrey, UK: Business International Press, for *Community Care*.

Whittaker, J.K., Tracy, E.M., & Marckworth, M. (1989). *The family support project: Identifying informal support resources for high risk families*. Seattle, WA: University of Washington, School of Social Work.

The Black Church
and Family Support Programs

Harriette McAdoo
Vanella Crawford

SUMMARY. The churches in the African American community
have traditionally played many important supportive roles to families in many areas. Churches today are becoming more involved in
the provision of services to the community members in response to
many of the changes that are occurring in families, in employment,
and in areas of increased poverty. Churches play important supportive roles by caring for children after school. Project SPIRIT is a
program in which instructions are given in homework assistance,
cultural continuity, African American history, and self esteem.
These programs provide social support to all family members.

There have been many changes that American families and individuals
have been forced to make in the past few years. There are many serious
problems now facing the African American community. All of these
changes have caused individual and familial stresses.

Most African Americans are involved in stable families with working
parents (McAdoo, 1989a). This is despite the stereotyped view that is
portrayed about families in the media and in the social science literature. It
is important that concern for those who most need help should not cloud
the presentation of all African American families. The top one-fifth of
black families is enjoying an upper-middle and middle class lifestyle. The
middle three-fifths are in working class lifestyles (Sawhill, 1988). The
focus of this paper is the bottom fifth who are in desperate poverty.

The actual count of those who are in the most desperate conditions
represents only 6% of blacks. This small percentage, however, represents
70% of those who are in the most desperate situations (Population Reference Bureau, 1989). It is the group that has caused the most concern for
those who work in human services.

Poverty is increasingly becoming a condition of persons of color. Of those of color, the youth and young children are the groups who are impacted the most. Their futures are most cloudy and they are increasingly becoming more isolated from those who are in the mainstream of American life.

Despite six years of economic growth, one in every five children lives in a home in which the income is below the government's official poverty line. In African families, the figure is twice as high as in all American families, that is, two in five were poor in 1988; the poverty line was $9,435 for a family of three (Rich, 1989).

Parents face the loss of economic viability in work environments that are undergoing structural changes. Poverty is more apparent in families without father's income and presence. More and more families are finding themselves in this situation. One-third of the working population will be minority (McAdoo, 1989b). The structural changes in the workplace are making it more difficult for adults to maintain marital family units. The limited futures have become apparent to youth and they have become disenfranchised. The results are unemployment, too early pregnancies, and involvement in the drug culture.

As the situation for many blacks has continued to deteriorate, it has become obvious that an immensely talented heritage existed. Historically families have had many means of coping with adversity; strong family patterns, extended kin help systems, and strong involvement in churches. The patterns of coping with difficulty could be called upon now to replicate the supports that had been given in the past. Extended family help, social supportive networks from relatives and friends, and involvement in their religion was one of the bulwarks that allowed blacks to maintain their tenuous conditions (Hill, 1978). It allowed some to be able to be upwardly mobile in the past (McAdoo, 1989a).

CHURCH'S INVOLVEMENT IN SOCIAL ISSUES

The involvement of African Americans in their religious institutions has been one of the special strengths of the family (Hill, 1978). The black church has served an integral part of the underground railroad, and was the only place where children could receive both secular and religious education, both during and after the period of enslavement.

Churches later became the welfare department, insurance provider, hospice, and respite for the sick, the tired, and those who were in need. When the past is recalled, one can see that the churches have been a strong, powerful, and responsible source of family support.

Over the past few years the public has become more aware of the African American church's involvement in social issues. It is a reaffirmation of the roles that churches have always had. Only now more attention has been given to it by the news media. As problems have intensified in the black communities, the churches have increasingly become active. There has become a crisis of growing impoverishment in the black family and everyone has heard the cry.

Black churches have found themselves assaulted by many of the same problems that families have faced (New York Times, 5/23/88). Many have become financially strapped, as members find themselves in precarious positions. Churches have moved to try to repair the branches in family life and the disarray that many of the communities have found themselves in. The churches have realized that they have to go beyond praying and feeding and clothing people and start getting at the problems that are destroying the black community.

HISTORICAL ASPECTS
OF THE AFRICAN AMERICAN CHURCHES

America has always been a country in which churches have played a large part. The churches within the African American community have played special roles and therefore have special significance. More than any other contemporary influence, the churches are balanced upon centuries of customs in which religious practices and leadership have played important roles within the communities. The African American church plays many functions, besides religious ones. It provides calm for the soul, and provides refuge in time of need (McAdoo, 1989b).

The African continuity is clearly shown in the religious practices and customs (Herskovits, 1930). Even if Africans were not allowed to bring actual religious practices to America, they certainly did bring with them their religious memories and their temperament (Pipes, 1951). As Park (1919) said, the tradition may be American, but the temperament was African. The church of today therefore bases itself upon the sole surviving social institution of the African fatherland, that accounts for its extraordinary growth and vitality (DuBois, 1903).

The civil, judicial, and eventually the human rights enjoyed today were borne of the struggle that emerged from the African American church in America. Prior to the late 1700s, and during the 1800s, some southern states continued to outlaw the establishment of meeting houses for the purpose of worship.

The black church proved to be a necessary and essential catalyst for change and a conduit of cultural, social, and spiritual connectedness. The enslavers feared African insurrections and they continued to try to keep control of periods of worship. But worship and spirituality continued cleverly out of sight of the rage of white control (Lincoln, 1984).

They became separate denominations because of racism. Yet they went on to develop schools and colleges, political leaders, and millions of people to sustain (Lincoln, 1964). The church played many roles: social service center, political academy, financial institution, and champion of freedom.

Churches of all sizes engaged in social service outreach programs, from 250 to churches with over 10,000 members. The churches tended to be old, from many denominations, and had memberships that crossed income levels. The wealth of church members did not make a difference in the programs, but rather the generosity of the members (Billingsley, 1989). It reaches out to serve important functions for the community. It serves all social classes, often within the same structure.

The contemporary church survives in many variations, from the historically black Protestant denominations, to the black divisions of white denominations, to the Black Muslims. All are making different responses to the same problems that have impacted the black communities.

ROLE OF CHURCH AS SUPPORT OF MENTAL HEALTH

Churches are a valuable family resource that is important to those who are facing crises. However, the church provides help beyond that of crisis management. The churches have always provided support and help that contribute to good mental health.

Many of the "family" functions that churches provide is in the large number of role models that are provided for youth. The elderly make up a significant part of black denominations. They are able to receive respect and caring that provide a sense of family as they grow older (Boyd-Franklin, 1989).

The churches have been a center for the affirmation of the psychological strivings for a sense of self-esteem. The churches are preservers of the heritage and an agent for social change (Billingsley, 1989). They are unique institutions that relate to opportunities for self-esteem, self-development, leadership, and relaxation.

It is in the provision of religious education and youth programs that the church is a particularly unique service to the community. But the real contributions to promoting mental health go beyond the actual value of the service itself. It provides many with the opportunity for service and gives the church membership opportunities for leadership and opportunities to achieve status.

The church is the only institution in the black community that is owned, controlled, managed, supported, and patronized by African Americans. This fact alone is a source of positive self enhancement. The pastor is relatively free from outside competition (Mays and Nicholson, 1933). He is also free from outside control. Therefore, the pastors are able to be role models for the youth and older adults. Adults who are able to play positive role models are often missing in many of their lives.

Volunteers lead many of the programs. Women play a serious role in maintaining the programs, but usually not as ministers (Billingsley, 1989). Women have been historically relegated to playing self-positive roles. These programs of volunteers have played an important job in providing family support. Women of color have particularly benefited. The high unemployment levels the women face and the structural family changes, in which more than half are raising their children alone, have put them under unusual stress (McAdoo, 1989). Women and men are provided certain positions of authority and leadership that are absent outside of the church.

Many churches have been forced to overcome a traditional reluctance and have had to grapple with the issues of sexuality, conception, and drugs. This is an area in which it is difficult and a delicate matter to persuade churches to overcome their reluctance to confront drugs and sex. Churches have become very sophisticated about making their facilities available to programs that are run by other agencies that can respond to the sensitive issues of sex and drugs of the community. The theological conflict is still there, but the needs have being met (Lewin, 1988). Churches have had to decide how their theology would allow them to respond to sensitive issues. Churches have had traditions of being against premarital sex and drug and alcohol use, and sometimes birth control. To address the issues has meant an acknowledgment that "sinning" has been going on. They were uncomfortable with issues of sexuality and drug use. Many churches have not addressed these issues (New York Times, 1988). There have been road blocks that have prevented confrontation with these family issues.

These issues are unresolved in most churches, but they are beginning to be addressed as African American churches have started many community programs to reduce teenage pregnancy, to keep children in school, to provide adolescent boys with role models, and to find adoptive homes for black infants.

CONGRESS OF NATIONAL BLACK CHURCHES
AND PROJECT SPIRIT: A PROGRAM
OF FAMILY SUPPORT

The Congress of National Black Churches (CNBC) is an organization of six of the predominantly African American denominations. It is a voluntary, nonprofit religious organization that was designed to promote charity and fellowship among the members of their congregations. The denominations that are included are African Methodist Episcopal, Christian Methodist Episcopal, Church of God in Christ, National Baptist Convention of America, Inc., National Missionary Baptist Convention of America, and the Progressive National Baptist Convention, Inc.

All of these denominations have come together to provide services and programs that would not be possible for one denomination or congregation to handle alone. They have begun to provide family support to members and the community at large that is now having an important impact on many of the problems that are now present in the communities.

The programs of Project SPIRIT are offered to the wider community in churches in Oakland, Atlanta, Indianapolis, and Washington, DC. There are three parts of the programs. The first program is a parent education program that involves parents drawn from the community. The second program is pastoral counseling education programs for seminarians and in-service training programs for pastors and practicing clergy. The third and largest program is the after-school tutorial, coping skills development, and ethnic education programs for young children.

Project SPIRIT was funded initially by the Carnegie Foundation and the Lilly Endowment. This program has been conducted by church volunteers from the church families. Project SPIRIT includes an after-school program for 6 to 12 year old children. Each program provides after-school programs of tutorials, instruction, life skills, and counseling for elementary children.

They are picked up after school and taken to the centers. They have a snack, a prayer, the welcoming circle, and then 45 minutes is spent on their homework. They then have two hours for living skills, African American history, and coping skills. Most children do not have parents at home waiting for them. They are provided with a secure place to be, while their parents are at work. Some parents are unemployed, but children are still brought to a secure place where they receive the benefits of caring that are often missing in their homes. The time after school, before adults are present, is a period of time in which drug and sexual exploration are high.

Knowing that their children are safe and busy gives the parents a sense of peace.

The key to the effectiveness of Project SPIRIT is the emphasis on volunteers and their strong staff retention, staff development, and inspiration. Most of the volunteers are retired teachers and social workers. They are dedicated people who believe that children are valuable. There are several teachers who are employed in the public schools, who work full-time and then go to a church and work for three additional hours every day. They state that they do this because they have the opportunity to really teach and work with the children in a way that is impossible in the regular school. An emphasis in the program is that all children are talented and all have talents that can be developed.

There is a vibrancy and vitality that comes from a "living curriculum." A general curriculum is offered to all churches and the staff is brought to one site for intensive training and instruction. But volunteers are free to develop segments of the curriculum as they respond to the problems within the churches and communities. The living part of the curriculum comes into play as the staff creates segments of the program to incorporate their individual community and staff.

One anecdote very clearly serves as an example of the level of dedication and concern among the volunteers. In one of the sites, a retired educator had been serving as the church facilitator for one of the five churches in Oakland. He developed a cardiac condition and required surgery. As he gradually succumbed to the anesthesia, he began to mumble to his doctor about the care of his children. He kept on talking about his children. The doctor realized that the man's children were not young and was curious about the children. He asked the man's wife, who explained that he was worrying about the youngsters for whom he was in charge of at the church.

PARENTS OF CHILDREN IN PROJECT SPIRIT

Families of the programs were clearly facing the two problems that are concerns of those who are under the greatest stress, poverty incomes and parenting alone. Half of the parents were married and half were mothers who were parenting without a husband. Fifty-five percent of the families were clearly at or below the $14,000 poverty level for a family of four (*Washington Post* 9/1/88, A1). Thirty-three percent were clearly below the poverty level, for they earned from zero dollars to $9,599. Another 22 percent were at or below the poverty level for they earned from $9,600-

$14,599. They were typical of African American families who are under greatest stress.

To get an indication of the difficulties that the parents were facing, a measurement of the levels of stress was made. The parents were asked to indicate how much stress they faced with their daily life. The levels of stress that they perceived in their lives were very strong and wide ranging. The four highest ranked stressors were: (1) their work; (2) parenting concerns; (3) their health and safety; and (4) their finances. Each of these areas are an important dimension in their lives as they attempt to combine the demands of work, parenting, making ends meet when they are under financial stress.

Parents in these situations are in need of support from whatever source that they can find it. They are particularly stressed and in need of help from the churches and their programs.

PARENTS' EVALUATION OF THE BENEFITS OF PROJECT SPIRIT

An evaluation was done on all of the participants in Project SPIRIT during the first full year of the program. Both formative and summative evaluation approaches were used. The results were supportive of the positive view that parents and children had of that experience.

The parents were referred to Project SPIRIT by a number of channels. The important point was that the churches had reached beyond their own congregations and had recruited people from around the community. The participation in the programs had beneficial effects. Parents felt that the behavior of their children had improved (70%), as children went through the year. In addition they felt that the programs had resulted in higher grades for their children (75%). There were no differences between the parents of girls and boys, for all parents were positive in their evaluations (McAdoo and Crawford, 1989).

The parents indicated that they liked all aspects of the program: home work assistance, pride in their racial group, the religious stories, and the group activities that they experienced. The one portion of the after-school program that parents were very positive about was that the children were given assistance with their homework. In light of the long hours that the parents worked, and the limited time that they had to spend with their children, this is well expected. Without the help that was given by the volunteers to the children, many of the children would have had little help with their homework.

In addition to the help with school work, the next important areas that the parents liked about the program were the positive view that the children were given of the history of African Americans in America, and the knowledge that they gained about the contributions of members of their racial group. Parents then indicated that they felt that the children gained in self-pride and self-esteem. The parents indicated that they would like the programs to remain the same for the next year. They only wished that the program were open year-round. These are areas of strong support that are positive for the mental health functioning of all of the members of the family.

THE EFFECT OF PROJECT SPIRIT ON CHILDREN

The children are presented with experiences that are designed to let the children know about their own ethnic group. A respect for diversity was an important ingredient of the programs. The welcoming circle is adapted from circles in African cultures. The children are able to stress that they are persons of worth and that they know the families in which they were born. This was felt to be an element that was missing in their regular schools. It is not a part of the regular TV programming. Black children do look at TV more than non-blacks and are therefore more exposed to negative images and stereotypes.

It is therefore important that they learn the history and contributions of persons from their own group. It is anticipated that their self-esteems will be enhanced by the use of this part of the curriculum. The curriculum is designed to enhance the self perception, confidence, and competence of the children and their families.

The children had positive self-esteems that became even higher as the year went on. There was one aspect about self-esteem that was bothersome. Although the self-esteems remained high for all of the children, the younger children had significantly higher self esteems than those who were older, in the higher grades. The older children appear to have lost some of their optimism that was present in the younger children. The longer children are in the family situations in which they were growing up, the more at risk they were for becoming discouraged and overwhelmed by the situations in which they found themselves. It is important that all of the resources that are available within the communities be brought to bear, in order to prevent the assaults against their self-esteems that is so common today.

The children of Project SPIRIT have various stories of a personal nature that weave themselves into the phenomena of the curriculum. One youngster, who was in the first grade, had become despondent with school and her progress. This child's single parent, hearing about Project SPIRIT enrolled her child in the program. The mother reported that by the end of the school year that her child was happy with school and herself, and that she was now reading at the third grade level. Many different stories are told by volunteers and parents across the country.

CONCLUSION

As African American children and families continue to struggle against the vestiges of enslavement, be it spiritual, cultural, social, economic, or educational, they will need to have supportive institutions that are working for them. Projects, including Project SPIRIT and other family based efforts, are examples of effective, supportive church based programs that will move members of the community towards removing vestige of enslavement that have persisted to the present time. Such programmatic initiative recognizes that the challenges to liberation persist. The support that is provided to families by Project SPIRIT, and all of the other supportive programs of the churches, are attempts to address the many needs of families who live in African American communities. It will be the collective efforts of many programs of this type that attempt to address many of the serious problems that face the African American and the American community as a whole.

REFERENCES

Billingsley, A. (1989, May). *The Black church as a social service institution.* Paper presented at A National Symposium of Grant Makers.

Boyd-Franklin, N. (1989). *Black Families in Therapy: A Multisystems Approach.* New York: Guilford Press.

DuBois, W. E. B. (1903). *Souls of Black Folk.* Chicago: McGlurg.

Frazier, E. F. (1939). *The Negro Family in the United States.* Chicago: University of Chicago Press.

Herskovits, M. (1930). The negro in the new world. *American Anthropologist, 32* (November).

Hill, R. (1978). *The Strengths of Black Families.* New York: Emeroon-Hall.

Johnson, J. W. (1932). *God's Trombone, Seven Negro Sermons in Verse.* New York: Viking.

Lewin, T. Black churches: a new mission on family. *The New York Times,* August 24, 1988 A1.

Lincoln, C. E. (1984). *Race, Religion, and the Continuing American Dilemma.* New York: Hill and Wang.

Mays, B. and Nicholson, J. (1933, reprinted in 1969). *The Negro's Church*. New York: Arno Press and The New York Times.

McAdoo, H (1989b). Cultural Issues Affecting Labor Force Participation. *Investing in People: a Strategy to Address Americans Workforce Crisis*. 2 Washington, D.C.: Department of Labor 1313-1347.

McAdoo, H (1989). *Black families*: New York: Sage Publications.

McAdoo, H. and Crawford, V. (1989). Project SPIRIT Evaluation Report. Washington, D.C. The Congress of National Black Churches, Inc.

New York Times (1988). Editorial: Black churches, endangered children. May 23, A21.

New York Times (1988). Editorial: Black churches new mission on family. August 23, A23.

Park, R. (1919). The conflict and fusion of cultures with special reference to the negro. *Journal of Negro History* 4(2 April).

Pipes, W. (1951). *Say Amen, Brother!* New York: William-Frederick Press (2nd edition, forthcoming, Detroit: Wayne State University Press, 1990).

Population Reference Bureau. (1989) *America in the 21st Century: A Demographic Overview.* Washington, DC.

Rich, S. (1989). Despite U.S. prosperity, one in five youths in poverty. *The Washington Post*. November 23, A25.

Sawhill, I. (1988). Poverty in the U.S.: why is it so persistent? *Journal of Economic Literature*, 24, 1073-1119.

Woodson, C. (1921). *The History of the Negro Church*. Washington, DC. Associated Publishers.

Preventing Adoption Disruption

Richard P. Barth
Marianne Berry

SUMMARY. Older child adoptions are increasingly common. Older children who are adopted were previously abused or abandoned and have typically learned a range of behavior which make family formation challenging. When adoptions of older children are successful, these children and their families receive a wide range of benefits. When adoption disruption occurs and children are returned to agencies, children and parents often experience great hardship. Adoption disruptions are relatively rare and occur in about 11% of adoptions. Risk factors that increase the likelihood of disruption and services that counter those risk factors must be understood if disruption is to be prevented. Ecologically-based services and intensive in-home adoption preservation services are needed. Adoptive families who have received these services, rather than conventional counseling, have fared well.

Children deserve willing and able families to love and protect them. Adoption is a legally sanctioned procedure for providing a family when the family into which a child is born is unable or unwilling to parent. Adoption is not only a program for children. In its intent, adoption benefits are equally shared by parent(s). Adoption creates or expands a new family by bestowing the rights and responsibilities of parenting from the child's birth parent(s), or from social service agencies who have guardianship of children, to new parent(s).

The conventional wisdom is that about 3% of children are adopted, but no precise figure is calculable. Older child adoptions have increased in proportion to other forms of adoptions in the last decade and will continue to do so. However, not all older child adoptions succeed — the difficulties

---

The authors wish to thank Sharon Ikami for preparation of this manuscript. Support was provided by Office of Human Development Services/ACYF Grant #90-PD10075.

205

of creating a new family are at times too great. Efforts to strengthen older child adoptions, the focus of this chapter, have implications for allied efforts to preserve other family relationships.

Adoptions are grouped into four categories: independent, intercountry, step-parent, and relinquishment or agency. Independent adoptions occur when the parent(s) place the child directly with the adoptive family of their choice without an agency serving as an intermediary. Nationally, about 25,000 children are adopted independent of agencies each year. Intercountry adoptions involve the adoption of foreign-born children by adoptive families; almost 10,000 foreign-born children are adopted in the United States in 1985-86 (Immigration and Naturalization Services, 1987). Step-parent adoptions concern the adoption of the children of one's spouse. Older child adoptions (age 3 to 18) are those which follow the voluntary or involuntary legal severance of parental rights to the child and are overseen by a public or private agency.

Older children placed for adoption are children who have been abused or neglected and freed from their parents' custody after efforts to return them home failed. Legislation in 1980 (PL 96-272) mandated the preference of adoption when foster children could not be returned home. There are roughly 15,000 adoptions of such older children (usually defined as children aged three or older) each year (Maximus, 1984). As reports of child abuse add to the numbers of older children who will be removed and freed from abusive homes, and as infant adoptions decrease, older child adoptions will grow in number.

Problems of children adopted when older are more common than those for adopted infants. Older children are adopted after considerable time in the child welfare system and have varied histories that always include abuse or neglect, and often include parental problems of substance abuse or mental illness, and other unfortunate environmental and economic conditions. These conditions affect the child's behavior and understanding of family life and have an impact on his or her adjustment to adoption. Numerous studies (Boyne, Denby, Kettenring, & Wheeler, 1984; Groze, 1985; Nelson, 1985; Zwimpher, 1983) inform us that these older adopted children may display dramatic and problematic behavior.

Because of these difficulties, older child adoptions are more likely than infant and step-parent adoptions to be shortlived. Nonetheless, about 89% of older child adoptions are successful; that is, only about 11% of these adoptions "disrupt"; in these cases, the child is returned by the adoptive family to the agency (Barth et al., 1988; Partridge, Hornby, & McDonald, 1986; USRE, 1985). However, adoptions can be termed "successful" to varying degrees. The adoptive families of older children may expend enormous amounts of patience, energy, and time endeavoring to stay together.

Given conventional adoption services, about 1,500 of the 14,400 adoptive older child placements each year will disrupt. For youth adopted as adolescents, the disruption rate approaches 25% and for some sub-groups, the rate is higher yet (Berry & Barth, in press). At least 2,000 of these children will be at risk of disruption but many of their families will find an alternative to disruption. In most such situations, families turn to informal support systems to seek assistance. In some cases, they will call on the agency to assist them in preventing disruption. Families that recover from the brink of disruption rarely credited conventional social services and referral to psychotherapy as a significant contributor to the stability of their adoption (Barth, 1988). Conventional child welfare services to prevent disruption also seem to have minimal success. Although all family formation includes some (usually worthwhile) risk of dissolution, the personal and financial costs of disruption to the child, family, and children's services agency call (subject to costs) for additional knowledge and reformed practice to prevent unnecessary disruptions.

RISK FACTORS

Risk factors can guide decision making and services, although they should not be used to preclude adoptive placements. Our recent study (Barth & Berry, 1988) examined characteristics of older children, adoptive families, and services involved in 926 older child adoptions. The adoptive placements in the sample included children aged three and older at the time of placement. This provided a sample of 1156 children. The status of their adoption was verified by the agencies as (a) still intact, or stable (n = 831); (b) no longer intact, or disrupted (n = 95); and (c) outcome unknown (n = 230).

Having a previous adoptive placement (and subsequent disruption), being older, having a greater number of child problems, not being adopted by foster parents, and having college educated adoptive mothers were significantly associated with disruption as shown in Table 1. The following discussion explains these risk factors.

Prior disruptions have a strong relationship to subsequent disruptions, although this relationship does not hold for children over 12, or for placements with siblings together. This relationship was true for both boys and girls and single and two-parent adoptions, regardless of subsidies.

Age is a strong associate of disruption and was expected. Older children

208   *FAMILIES AS NURTURING SYSTEMS*

Table 1.

Characteristics of Disrupted (n=94) and Stable (n=832) Groups

	Disrupt	Non-Disrupt	χ^2 or t
Child			
Age of child	9.29	6.93	-6.67***
Gender of child[a]	male (63%)	male (52%)	3.56*
Child's ethnicity[a]	white (62%)	white (63%)	8.61
Parental rights termination[a]	no (60%)	no (55%)	.56
Months in foster care	34	35	.64
No. of children's problems	.89	.59	-3.31***
Previous adoptive placement	no (75%)	no (95%)	56.11***
Child's wait (days)	642	621	-0.27
Placement			
Foster-parent adoption[a]	no	yes	24.77***
Sibling placement[a]	no (70%)	no (66%)	.64
Single parent placement[a]	no (86%)	no (85%)	.02
Financial resources per child	$14,160	$13,290	-0.62
Annual family income	$30,132	$26,728	-1.91
Mother's education[a]	college grad	h.s. grad	18.34**
Mother working[a]	split	not	1.98
Parent's wait (days)	377	365	-0.29
No. of other children in home	2.00	1.90	-0.51
Age of adoptive mother	36	38	1.72
Age of adoptive father	39	40	1.28
Match Between Birth and Adoptive Parents			
Same education[a]	no (82%)	no(79%)	.34
Same race[a]	same (82%)	same (81%)	.03
Same religion[a]	no (76%)	no (73%)	.13
Same county placement[a]	same (86%)	same (91%)	1.64
Subsidy			
Received subsidy[a]	yes (59%)	yes (53%)	1.40
Monthly subsidy	$119	$125	0.37

[a]Modal values given
*p < .05
**p < .01
***p < .001

have consistently been more likely to require replacement in foster care and adoption. The relationship between age and disruption is very clearly seen by examining disruption rates per 3-year age group. Between ages 3 and 5, 5% of cases disrupted, between ages 6 and 8 the rate was 10%, between 9 and 11 the rate was 17.1%, between ages 12 and 14 the rate of disruption was 22%, and between ages 15 and 18, 26% of adoptions disrupted.

Age also interacted with other associates of disruption. Children under 12 who have had a previous adoptive placement are far more likely to disrupt than are their peers without such a history. After the age of 12, however, the association weakens. The presence of multiple child problems is significantly associated with disruption for 6 to 8 year olds and, to a lesser extent, 12 to 14 year olds. Among children ages 3 to 11, children who are adopted by foster parents are significantly less likely to disrupt. The significant differences are attenuated for children 12 years old or older.

The number and type of child problems significantly differentiated disruptions from non-disruptions. Disruptions were significantly more likely among children with emotional problems (16% vs. 8%), behavioral problems (21% vs. 9%) and mental retardation (23% vs 10%), but not more likely among children with a physical disability or a medical condition.

Previous findings that sibling placements are more likely to disrupt (e.g., Kadushin & Seidl, 1971) were not confirmed, except for sibling placements for children older than 15 which tended to disrupt more than single-child placements. The data do, however, support previous findings that sibling placements into homes with other children are significantly more likely to disrupt for one or both children (28 of 268: 10.4%) than sibling placements into homes with no other children (Boneh, 1979; Seidl, 1971). In our study, *none* of the 47 children placed in sibling groups into childless homes disrupted. A strong and counterintuitive finding—albeit on a small sub-sample—was that sibling groups in our study (n = 8) with a previous adoptive placement did *not* subsequently disrupt. Social workers apparently made good judgments about which sibling groups could succeed together; the data cannot inform us, however, about outcomes for siblings who were separated after an earlier disruption and placed into different homes.

Single parent adoptions were no more prone to disruption than two-parent adoptions but had several unique characteristics. Single parents were significantly more likely to adopt older children—only 25% of the children adopted by single parents were younger than nine years of age— and more likely to adopt boys than were couples. Single parents less commonly adopted siblings or adopted foster children than did couples. There were no differences on the previous adoptive status of the child. Single and two-parent adoptions had the same likelihood of having a disruption regardless of the age, gender, and race of the child, sibling placements, subsidy or no subsidy, and previous adoptive placements.

Higher disruption rates were associated with higher mother's education.

The disruption rate among those having some college or a college degree was almost double that of mothers with a high school diploma or less. Among new parent adoptions, parents with college degrees had a disruption rate of 26%, followed by parents with some college (19%), high school graduates (11%), and parents with less than a high school diploma (0%). College educated parents were somewhat less likely than less educated parents to have children with special needs or problems placed with them. College educated parents experienced a sharply higher disruption rate with children aged 3 to 9 (11% vs. 4%), but not for children 10 and older. The higher disruption rate for college educated parents is lessened in placements of children with prior adoptive placements and among adoptions by nonwhite parents. In foster parent adoptions, education of foster parents was not related to disruption. Foster parent adoptions occurred, however, far less frequently among more highly educated parents.

From the larger sample, a second sample of 120 families with especially high-risk placements were drawn for interviews in order to gather more explicit data on the child's behavior and on services. Social workers and family members in this sample were contacted regarding their adoption. Parents in 85 families filled out the Achenbach Child Behavior Checklist (CBC) concerning the child's behavior during the first six-months of the adoption (the remaining families could not be contacted). The subsample of 85 cases with child behavior data was composed of 28 disruptions (33%) and 57 nondisruptions (67%). This overrepresents disruptions in the general population of older child adoptive placements by more than 2 times. There were slightly more boys than girls, with an age range of 3 to 15 at placement, and a mean age of 8 years. The majority of children in this sample were White (77%), with smaller numbers of Black (11%) and Latino (7%) children. About half of the children were adopted by their foster parents (48%).

Most children adopted when older have a history of some type of abuse or neglect. Of the children in this sample, adoptive parents indicated that 82% had been neglected, 63% had been physically abused, and 33% had been sexually abused before the placement. The majority (69%) had a history of multiple homes. According to the adoptive parents, these children currently had significant conditions or problems: emotional or behavioral problems (86%), a learning disability (58%), a developmental disability (41%), or a physical handicap or medical condition (31%).

Among the sample of all older adoptive children with completed CBC's, the most common behavior problems were: cannot concentrate, demands attention, acts too young for his/her age, impulsive, stubborn, temper tantrums, poor school work, and does not feel guilty after misbe-having. In fact, this sample of older adopted children had high scores on many behavioral dimensions. A full 76% had at least one "clinical" score — that is, the T-score was greater than 70 — in some dimension. The average scores on many behavior dimensions were near the clinical range (see Table 2). Many of the boys were in the clinical range on aggressive, immature, delinquent, obsessive/compulsive, and hyperactive. Many of the girls were in the clinical range on social withdrawal, depressed, and hyperactive.

Children in disruptions had significantly higher external behavior scores than did children in intact adoptions (72 vs. 64), while there was no difference on internal behavior scores. The subdimensions of aggression and delinquency also distinguished children who disrupted from those who did not. The child's age at placement was significantly associated with his or her delinquency and hyperactivity scores.

The behavior problems that significantly differentiated disrupting chil-

Table 2.
T-Scores of Disrupting and Non-Disrupting Children (n=85)

Dimension	Total (n=85)	Disrupt (n=28)	Non-Disrupt (n=57)	t
Hyperactive	75.42	76.54	74.67	0.59
Withdrawn	69.58	73.50	68.53	0.86
Delinquent	69.28	73.15	67.26	2.29**
Aggressive	68.20	73.18	65.75	2.68**
Depressed	66.81	66.76	66.83	0.03
Schizoid/anxious	64.78	63.82	65.25	0.71
Somatic complaints	61.11	60.79	61.26	0.27
Summary	68.26	70.57	67.12	1.17
External	66.55	71.79	63.98	2.62**
Internal	65.57	64.50	66.11	0.62

**p < .05

dren from those in stable adoptions are shown in Table 3. The top five items distinguishing children in disruptions were: threatening people, cruelty or meanness to others, getting into fights, arguing, and disobedience at school. Most of these items indicate troubles with interpersonal relations. Children that disrupted were significantly more likely to display these behaviors, whereas "feels he has to be perfect," was less likely among children in disruptions.

The child's history of sexual abuse in particular is related to several behavior dimension scores. A history of sexual abuse was associated with high externalizing behavior and clinically aggressive and delinquent behavior. Children with learning and/or developmental disabilities scored highly on the somatic complaints and hyperactive dimensions.

Services

Perhaps the best adoption outcome is to make and sustain a very high-risk placement. Better information about the child's pre-adoptive experience, adequate adoption subsidies, and more experienced social workers are associated with lower than expected disruptions. Provision of subsidies was associated with adoptions that were predicted to disrupt but did not. Among adolescents, there is an outright and positive relationship between subsidies and adoption stability (Berry & Barth, in press). Perhaps the worst outcome of an adoption is to have a low-risk placement that disrupts. The lack of adequate information about the child, having a change in social workers, and the lack of a subsidy are associated with low risk placements that disrupted (Barth & Berry, 1988).

In sum, the risk of disruption is linked with the child's age, prior disruptions, behavioral problems (especially cruelty, fighting, disobedience, and vandalism), and non-foster parent adoptions. Also linked to disruption are higher education of parents, higher expectations on the part of adoptive parents, and pre-placement information about the child that was scanty or too favorable.

Knowledge of risk factors informs the pursuit of strategies to prevent adoption disruption. Whereas the goal of many prevention programs is to reduce the risk of untoward outcomes by avoiding risky situations (e.g., Barth, Middleton, & Wagman, 1989), the goal of older child adoptions is to encourage informed and reasonable risk taking on the part of adoptive families. Further, service providers must enhance family and community mechanisms that protect against disruption. To take advantage of the lower risk of placing younger children, disruption prevention activities begin with the earliest possible decision that a child is available for adop-

Table 3.

Percent of Children (n=85) for Whom Behavior Item Indicated "Very Often True" or "Sometimes True," Distinguishing Disruptions and Non-Disruptions

| Item | Disrupt (n=28) | | Non-Disrupt (n=57) | | χ^2 |
	Often	Sometimes	Often	Sometimes	
Threatens people	14%	32%	9%	4%	15.30*
Cruelty, meanness to others	36	39	12	21	13.62*
Gets in many fights	39	32	14	16	13.48*
Argues a lot	57	29	25	25	12.23*
Disobedient at school	46	25	14	33	10.83*
Hangs out with bad friends	21	36	11	12	10.10*
Disobedient at home	46	36	16	44	10.00*
Physically attacks people	25	32	9	14	9.94*
Destroys others' belongings	32	29	12	18	8.00*
Feels he has to be perfect	14	4	23	25	7.99*
Swearing, obscene language	18	29	7	11	7.94*
Vandalism	11	11	5	0	7.45*
Trouble sleeping	21	0	5	7	6.78*
Lying, cheating	43	36	32	19	6.33*
Prefers younger children	32	39	35	16	6.33*

*p < .01

213

tion and yield a placement with all deliberate speed. The homestudy must consider child and family risk factors and enhance the social and informational support available to the family. After placement, formal and informal supportive services must be continued and may need to include in-home adoption preservation services that work to address the behavior problems of children that otherwise may lead to disruption.

PRACTICES AND PROGRAMS
TO PREVENT DISRUPTION

The last two decades have witnessed the emergence of adopting handicapped children, of adoption by foster parents, open adoption (in which contact with birth parents continues), and post-legal adoption services. The field continues to pursue new initiatives to create and preserve adoptions of children with special needs. These initiatives include pre-placement activities that better prepare the family; post-placement services that ease the adjustment to new family life; and post-legalization services that support adoptions across the life span.

Pre-Placement Activities

Speedy efforts to place children while they are young and more able to fit into an adoptive family's home represent the starting point for preventing later problems in adoption. Efforts to more quickly terminate parental rights when reunification with birth parent(s) is improbable and to move children into foster placement-adopt situations are critical to preventing disruption. Many states require an evidentiary hearing in family or juvenile court to determine that the child should be freed for adoption, and then require a separate civil court hearing to terminate parental rights. This is virtually triple jeopardy for children. The first jeopardy is that the family court will return them to a situation which is least likely to promote their well-being and allow them to grow unharmed. This is the jeopardy which we condone in public policies that are overly protective of parental rights. If they avoid that jeopardy, the second jeopardy is that the civil court — in its inexperience in these manners — will, after much delay, overturn the family court decision. The third jeopardy is that the child will grow without a plan, without the right to join a family, and without the freedom of permanence. The hearings should remain separate to protect parents' rights, but both be conducted in juvenile court to protect the child's right to a swift and informed hearing.

Preventing disruptions begins with the "homestudy" (or evaluation of the family and home environment) and selection and matching of adoptive families and children. In traditional homestudies, adoption workers attempt to ask questions of parents to determine their suitability for adoption and the likelihood of success and happiness while parenting older children. This approach may rely too heavily on the wisdom of the interviewers and allows for too many false expectations about older child adoption by parents.

Couples or individuals that meet with others in a like situation can more effectively challenge a potential adoptive parent's false expectations. The benefits of support groups to ease family formation is well known (e.g., McGuire & Gottlieb, 1979). Barbara Tremitiere (1979) described the earliest group model for parents adopting older children. The nine session format includes: (1) informing the 5 to 7 couples or single applicants of the purpose of the group and what will follow; (2) exposure to panels of adoptive parents who present the challenges (and threats) of adoptive parenting; (3) clarification of family and individual values about adoption; (4) visits with a family that has adopted a child with characteristics similar to the child of interest to the adoptive parent(s); and (5) completing the writing of the homestudy which is a joint effort by the applicant and social worker. A more recent version of group preparation is the "Model Approach to Partnership in Parenting" or MAPP (Child Welfare Institute, 1986). MAPP prepares participants to become adoptive or foster parents — the parents have the greatest say in determining that choice.

The group approach to pre-placement endeavors provides opportunities for ongoing support. Adoptive families who begin the process in such multi-family groups often maintain contact with one or more families — many times well beyond their time of contact with their social worker. Many agencies still do not use such a model despite the evidence that it strengthens high risk placements (Barth & Berry, 1988).

Post-placement Services

While matching of compatible children and families has been identified as important to adoption success, the assurance of proper matching before placement is not the sole requirement for a successful placement. Agency support after placement is also essential. Any placement will have challenges. The goals are to be close enough to the family to remain aware of problems and to guide the family to resources to aid in their resolution.

Both the child and the parents have needs in post-placement services. The agency should maintain close contact with the family during the first three months to reassure the child of continuity with his past and to enable the family to explore uncertainties without feeling lost (Fitzgerald, Murcer, & Murcer, 1982). The intent is to catch problems early in the placement before they escalate into unsalvageable disasters. Yet, the evidence is increasingly clear that three months is far too brief a time; in our research the mean time to disruption was 18 months (Barth & Berry, 1988). Mechanisms must be established in agencies to provide more lasting services and especially services for high risk-placements throughout the adolescent years. This is not simply a call for *more* post-legalization *counseling* services. These may be useful, but are not specifically pitched at preserving placements on the verge of disruption. They tend to serve adoptees placed as infants — not older child adoptees — and help them with reconciling their adoptions and making decisions about searching for birth parents, and other concerns of adopted children when they *become* adolescents. Families that adopt older children may need more continuous consultation regarding the management of conditions that existed before adolescence and before the adoption.

Agencies are beginning to facilitate support groups of adoptive families for parents and children. Support groups probably operate best when started during the homestudy, but successful versions have also been developed after placement to support high-risk placements. There were 250 parent support groups for adoptive parents in 1980 (Meezan, 1980). Adoptive Families of America (AFA: formerly OURS, Inc.), is the largest of those and is a non-profit organization of over 9,000 families and professionals "recognizing a need to share information, support one another and keep the children in contact with one another." AFA provides adoption information, a 'helpline,' resource materials, a bimonthly magazine, and donations and support to children in need of permanency. Parents and children find it helpful to meet and talk with people in similar circumstances.

Many post-placement services involve fostering a support system for adoptive families. Besides parent groups, agencies offer individual and family counseling, retreats, "help lines," reading lists and materials, and video information (Spencer, 1985). The North American Post-Legal Adoption Committee considers post-legal services as a logical extension of pre-placement services, that should be offered "at whatever point in their lives these [needs] may arise (Spencer, 1985; p. 5)." They argue that post-placement services should be available, for a (sliding) fee, for the rest of an adoptive family's lives. The call for more available and continuous post-placement services is coming from many quarters, although existing evidence is unclear about the type, timing, and effectiveness of such services for older child adoptions.

A program that pairs experienced adoptive parents with those new to adoption was developed by the North American Council on Adoptable Children (NACAC). The Buddy System is a cooperative effort between adoption agencies and adoptive parents (Boersdorfer, Kaser, & Tremitiere, 1986). Bringing these families together provides opportunities for pre-adoptive families to learn what to expect in their own adoption, enables them to develop lasting supportive relationships, and helps the more experienced (but still in progress) adoptive families to benefit from the review of their adoptive accomplishments. Buddies are often drawn from an adoptive parent organization; families known to the adoption unit can be solicited for participation as buddies. Foster parents can also make good buddies and can be recruited through their association (which are more numerous than adoptive parent organizations). Buddies are assigned according to the type of adoption anticipated. For instance, a family planning to adopt a sibling group of three children might be assigned to another family that adopted a large sibling group and fost-adopt parents would be paired. Ideally, the buddy will participate in parts of the parent participation and home study process since this is a time when families are deciding what kinds of children they want to and can parent. Supportive post-placement activities include occasional phone calls, cards, invitations for a cook-out, sharing books and articles, and referrals to other resources, and explaining the many mysteries of the agency. Another strategy for providing support to adoptive families is via an adoption warmline staffed by other adoptive families. The model is designed to help families reach out to needed resources without calling the social worker who they may perceive as a threat to their placement.

The development of community resources knowledgeable about adoption can help make the promise of treatment for an adopted child more than just a prayer. Community-based mental health and educational service providers can be invited to participate in the group homestudy process and during agency adoption training. Part of that training should involve participation in in-house reviews of each disruption. Adoption workers and the therapists to whom social workers refer adoptive families need greater understanding and commitment to working with educational systems — particularly special education. Numerous families in our study identified obtaining an appropriate public or private special or regular education program as a turning point away from a disruption. Typical post-placement services that are limited to office or kitchen counseling and fail to fully explore the child's broader world suggests that many social workers do not recognize or know how to respond to the importance of schools in the lives of parents and children. Collaborative training with educators, school social workers, and school psychologists would benefit adopted children.

Adoptive and foster parent associations are beginning to develop respite care arrangements as another important post-placement service. Families agree that they would be willing to provide care for a child in their home for a time — some families designate three weeks and some designate three hours. Arrangements are made for reimbursement of meals and other expenses. (For children in foster-adopt programs, agency guidelines about the use of respite must be clarified to keep within foster parent obligations to the agency.)

Post-Legalization Services

Post-legalization services are those focused on helping families after the first year of placement when the placement is legally finalized. A recent committee on post-legal services (North American Post-Legal Adoption Committee, 1984) offered this list of methods for the provision of post-legal services: (1) individual and family counseling, (2) intermediary in legal matters, (3) workshops on topics such as transracial and intercountry adoption, (4) support groups, (5) classes, (6) retreats, (7) social events, (8) intermediary in "adoption triad" matters, such as specifics of visitation, (9) professional consultation, (10) information, (11) films and other materials for distribution, and (12) research on evaluation of services as well as other post-legal concerns. Searching for birth families is another key component in those agencies which do provide post-legal services. While laudatory and helpful to facilitate adjustment to adoption, this is only a small part of the spectrum of services needed by families in crisis.

There is a clamor for the development of post-placement and post-legalization services that meet the demands of supporting older child adoptions. The clarion call is for something far more than mandatory visits soon after the adoption. While this principle is sound, a few concerns arise. First, post-adoption services should not be staffed at the expense of recruitment and home study efforts. Dollars spent on conventional post-placement services are probably not as valuable to agencies and families as dollars spent on recruitment. Second, whereas referral to services is often useful, social workers involved with the family should be primarily available to assess the situation and coordinate post-placement services from other providers. Families are less likely to request timely assistance from the agency when they lose contact with the worker who did their home study (Barth & Berry, 1988). The homestudy is a poignant process that builds strong bonds between the worker and family. The organization of services should facilitate a continuous relationship between the family and social worker. In addition, to appropriately study and orient families, adoption workers need to know about the legal delays and challenges that await families.

Intensive Adoption Preservation Services

The adjustment to older child adoptions is often difficult. At times, the future of the adoption is in doubt. With so much riding on the outcome of such an adoption crisis, reliance on conventional social casework counseling or office-based psychotherapy is unwise and often unsuccessful. Intensive in-home adoption preservation services may be needed. Over the last decade, such exemplary services have emerged in most of our states but have been primarily reserved for preventing entrance into the child welfare or mental health systems. Programs like Homebuilders (in Washington and New York) have had remarkable success in preventing the placement of children who are at "imminent risk." The contributors to the success are not fully understood, but intensive home-based family preservation services involve a crisis time-limited orientation, use of social and cognitive methods of intervention, intensive work that occurs in the home and linkage to other resources (see Whittaker & Tracy, this volume).

Adoption agencies have generally not called on these services to help preserve adoptive placements. Recently, however, Medina Children's Services, the Seattle-based agency specializing in adoption of older and special needs children, and the Behavioral Sciences Institute (the organizational sponsor of Homebuilders) have begun collaborating to develop and evaluate intensive adoption preservation services and provide training in its use. As in all Homebuilders interventions, each full-time therapist in the project has a caseload of two families, the intervention consists of four weeks of in-home therapy, and the therapist sees the family as often as needed — typically, three to five sessions of 2 hours or more. To date, 89% of adoptive families who were experiencing an adoption crisis and were at-risk of a disruption have been helped to maintain the placements. Project Impact in Boston has also successfully used the Homebuilder's model with adoptive families and now includes a briefer and more intensive (12 hours per day for three days) in-home service.

Few adoptive families now have the benefit of intensive home-based, family preservation services which have a striking success rate at preventing family breakdown. For families in crisis, such brief interventions reduce the likelihood of alienation that can occur during out-of-home care. The specific presenting problems that precipitated disruptions are those that signal the break-down of other families such as assault, running away, and noncompliance of latency and teenage children (Barth & Berry, 1988). Whereas such intensive services are costly, they can be favorably weighed against the lifelong benefits that follow adoption.

CONCLUSIONS

Adoption is cost effective. The cost of conventional adoption services to agencies is $46,000 less than the cost of foster care for the average 8-year-old who is adopted out of foster care (Barth & Berry, 1988). Implementation of intensive adoption preservation services would save an additional $13 million per year, nationally (Barth & Berry, 1988). This ignores the additional incalculable family benefits to the children whose placements last.

Given that adoptions provide a nearly total environmental intervention, the value of each dollar spent to make or maintain a placement may comprise one of government's greatest returns. The risks of wounding the spirit and hopes of young people are only a few of the costs of disrupted adoptions or the decision not to try to place a child for adoption. These children are also kept from obtaining a substantial personal dowry from permanent membership in a family. Adoptive families can have a great and lasting influence on children. The success of intensive pre-school educational programs like the Perry Preschool Program and Headstart, is in much part attributable to enhanced family involvement (Berreuta-Clement, Schweinhart, Barnett, Epstein, & Weikart, 1984). Older child adoption exceeds those programs on that account and, when they last, may also have greater benefits to children. Agencies incur considerable expense when they fail to make or maintain adoptive placements. Since intensive interventions seem to be effective in preventing disruptions, agencies should see that they nurture family preservation services for use by families at risk of breaking up at every point in their child serving system. A growing number of child welfare agencies have standing arrangements to provide intensive in-home services to families just entering the child welfare system but have no mechanism for using them to prevent the disruption of existing adoptions. This should be remedied in every agency.

Some adoptions do disrupt despite the best services. The effects of disrupted adoptions on children and parents is currently unknown. Further, the success of adoptions cannot be evaluated only on the basis of place-ment stability. While this provides a basis for estimating the quality of the adoption, other indicators of success in child welfare include protection from reabuse, achievement of developmental outcomes, and child satis-faction. The outcomes of adoptions, whether disrupted or not, must be compared to long-term foster care, guardianship, or residential care on these criteria. Fortunately, the evidence suggests that adoptions do have advantages over other permanency planning options and appear worth the calculated risk that they might disrupt (Barth & Berry, 1987).

Once placements are made, adoptive families typically receive fewer services than do birth families with a lesser chance of providing adequate developmental resources to a special needs child (Barth & Berry, 1987). Adoptive families are given equivalent statutory rights to birth families, but not equivalent assistance. Wider use of intensive adoption preserva-tion services would correct this imbalance. Services to adoptive families who are in trouble must go beyond counseling about adoption and include the broad array of educational, social, recreational and financial services warranted in a community-centered intervention to rescue the dream of a forever family.

REFERENCES

Barth, R. P. (1988). Older child adoption and disruption. *Public Welfare, 46*(1), 23-29.

Barth, R. P. & Berry, M. (1987). Outcomes of child welfare services since per-manency planning. *Social Services Review, 61*, 71-90.

Barth, R. P. & Berry, M. (1988). *Adoption and disruption: Risks, rates, and responses*. New York: Aldine.

Barth, R. P., Middleton, K., & Wagman, E. (1989). A skill building approach to preventing teenage pregnancy. *Theory into practice, 28*, 183-190.

Bass, C. (1975). Matchmaker-matchmaker: Older child adoption failures. *Child Welfare, 54*, 505-512.

Belkin, L. (1988). Adoptive parents ask states for help with abused young. *New York Times*, Monday, August 22, 1988.

Berrueta-Clement, J. R., Schweinhart, L. J., Barnett, W. S., Epstein, A. S. & Weikart, D. P. (1984). *Changed lives: The effects of the Perry preschool pro-gram on youths through age 19*. (Monographs of the High/Scope Educational Research Foundation, No. 8). Ypsilanti, MI: High/Scope Press.

Berry, M. & Barth, R. P. (in press). Adopting adolescents. *Child Welfare*.

Boersdorfer, R. K., Kaser, J. S., & Tremitiere, W. C. (1986). *Guide to local TEAM programs*. York, PA: Tressler-Lutheran Services Associates.

Boneh, C. (1979). Disruptions in adoptive placements: A research study. Massa-chusetts Dept. of Public Welfare (unpublished manuscript).

Boyne, J., Denby, L, Kettenring, J.R., & Wheeler, W. (1984). *The shadow of success: A statistical analysis of outcomes of adoptions of hard-to-place children.* New Jersey: Spaulding for Children.

Child Welfare Institute. (1986). *Manual for Model Approaches to Partnerships in Parenting.* Athens, GA: Author.

Feigelman, W., & Silverman, A.R. (1983). *Chosen children: New patterns of adoptive relationships.* New York: Praeger.

Fitzgerald, J., Murcer, B., & Murcer, B. (1982). *Building new families through adoption and fostering.* Oxford: Basil Blackwell.

Groze, V. (1985). Special needs adoption. *Children and Youth Services Review, 8,* 363-373.

Immigration and Naturalization Service, Statistical Analysis Branch. (1987). *Statistical year books.* Washington, D.C.: U.S. Government Printing Office.

Kadushin, A., & Seidl, F.W. (1971). Adoption failure: A social work postmortem. *Social Work, 16,* 32-38.

Maximus, Inc. (1984). *Child welfare statistical fact book: 1984: Substitute care and adoption.* Washington, D.C.: Office of Human Development Series.

McGuire, J. C. & Gottlieb, B. H. (1979). Social support groups among new parents: An experimental study in primary prevention. *Journal of Clinical Child Psychology, 8,* 111-116.

Meezan, W. (1980). *Adoption services in the states.* U.S. Department of Health and Human Services. Washington, D.C.: Author.

Nelson, K.A. (1985). *On the frontier of adoption.* New York: Child Welfare League of America.

North American Council on Post-Legal Adoption Committee. (1984). *Model statement on post-legal adoption services.* St. Paul, MN: Author.

Organization for United Response, Inc. (1987). Brochure. Minneapolis, MN: Author.

Partridge, S., Hornby, H., & McDonald, T. (1986). *Legacies of loss/Visions of gain: An inside look at adoption disruption.* Portland, Maine: University of Southern Maine, Center for Research and Advanced Study.

Post-Adoption Center for Education and Research. (1986). *Newsletter.* Walnut Creek, CA: Author.

Spencer, M. (1985). Meeting the need for comprehensive post-legal adoption services. *Permanency Report, 3*(4), 5.

Tremitiere, B. (1979). Adoption of children with special needs: The client-centered approach. *Child Welfare, 58,* 681-685.

Urban Systems Research and Engineering, Inc. (1985). *Evaluation of state activities with regard to adoption disruption.* Washington, D.C.: Author.

Zwimpher, D. M. (1983). Indicators of adoption breakdown. *Social Casework, 64,* 169-177.

How Fathers Respond When Their Youth Leave and Return Home

Robert A. Lewis
Stephen F. Duncan

SUMMARY. Few social scientists have examined the impact that adult children's leaving and returning home have upon fathers and their family relationships. In a sample of 325 fathers in Indiana and Michigan, 41% reported some stress as negative/disturbed reactions about a child's leaving home. These reactions were much greater than some earlier studies have shown. Overall, (as explained by the A-B-C-X Model of Stress) the fathers' definition of their situation was the factor most related to the fathers' negative feelings about their child's leaving home, to their related psychosomatic complaints and their lower sense of well-being. It was not related, however, to fathers' satisfaction with their family life. Implications of these findings are discussed.

Untimely leaving home and returning home can be traumatic for some young adults and their parents. Mental health therapists, psychiatric social workers, counselors, and family life educators often counsel families with problems directly or indirectly related to leaving home and returning home. Therapists, however, are concerned, usually, with the negative impact of family stress due to the untimely leaving or returning upon the young adult first and secondly, the impacts upon the mother (Bane, 1976; Barber, 1981; Bart, 1971; Boss, 1987). Not as often has the family professional or interventionist been concerned about possible, negative impacts upon the father (Boss & Greenberg, 1984; Burr, 1973; Campbell, Con-

Appreciation is expressed to the Cooperative State Research Services for administration of, and the United States Department of Agriculture for its financial support of, this longitudinal study, the Agricultural Experiment Station Regional Research Project, NC-164, STRESS, COPING AND ADAPTATION IN THE MIDDLE YEARS OF THE FAMILY LIFE CYCLE.

verse & Rogers, 1976). This neglect of the impact upon fathers has been due in part to the general devaluing of fatherhood in our society (Clemens & Axelson, 1985) and to the general neglect of fathers by researchers (Deutscher, 1964).

STRESSES FROM LEAVING HOME

While the majority of mothers and fathers do not appear to suffer much from the transition to the "empty nest" (Edgar & Maas, 1984; Glenn, 1975; Barber, 1981; Boss & Greenberg, 1984; Hawkins, 1978; Bart, 1971; Hill, 1958; Boss, 1987) there seems to be a minority, but perhaps an important minority, of both fathers and mothers (about 22-24%) who report continuing feelings of unhappiness especially when their last child leaves the home (Lewis, 1985; Boss & Greenberg, 1984).

For mothers, the impact appears more negative when they have been overinvolved or overprotective of the child (Bane, 1976; Lewis, 1986) or when the last child's leaving was related to "poor timing," e.g., the "off-time," sudden departure of a child for military service (Lewis, 1985).

On the other hand, the impact of the emptying nest is more disturbing for fathers who are more nurturing, have fewer children, are older and/or retired, and have lower quality marriages, i.e., they feel more neglected by their wives, receive less understanding from them, are more lonely and less enthusiastic about the wives' companionship and have less empathic wives (Boss & Greenberg, 1984).

STRESSES FROM RETURNING HOME

Leaving home is not the only family event which may result in stress for middle aged parents. The unexpected returning home of an adolescent or young adult (the "fledgling adult") who was thought to have permanently left home also appears to produce stress in some families (Lewis & Roberts, 1979; Lowenthal & Chiriboga, 1974). Families, therefore, may experience stress due to changes in family structure either by the loss of a member or by the addition of a member, especially when it is sudden and unexpected.

According to a 1983 study by the U.S. Census Bureau, there is a growing tendency for young adults to either remain with or return to the homes of their parents. The number of young adults aged 18-34 living with their parents between 1970 and 1983 has "skyrocketed by 84.8 percent." These adult children remain at home for various reasons. Bane (1976) suggests that the major reason for young adults remaining in the homes of their parents is economic, i.e., the low incomes of these older children. Although very few studies have been done on the "fledgling adult," Murray (1973) has reported from national data that one-fifth of fathers, aged 58-63, who had at least one child still living at home, reported themselves "not too happy" with the situation. As Clemens and Axelson (1985) conclude from the little available evidence, "a considerable number of these (parental) marriages experience some form of adversity leading to a lessening of life satisfaction" (p. 263).

THE PROBLEM

Only a few studies have investigated the impact upon fathers of adult children leaving home (Lewis, 1985; Edgar & Maas, 1984; Boss & Greenberg, 1984; Hawkins, 1978; Neugarten, 1970; Hill, 1958). Even fewer studies have investigated the impact upon fathers and fathers' relationships of adult children returning home (Lewis, Freneau, & Roberts, 1979; Murray, 1973; Lowenthal & Chiriboga, 1972). The purpose of this study was to develop some base-line data on fathers in "normal families," i.e., non-clinical families where adult children are leaving home and returning home. The ultimate purpose was to estimate the degree of negative and positive impacts of leaving and returning upon the fathers through a study suggested by the A-B-C-X Model of Family Stress (Norem, 1984).

A MODEL OF STRESS AND FAMILIES

Several explanations or theories exist in the family stress literature, e.g., Boss' (1987) explanation of family boundary ambiguity; Burr's (1973) synthesis of family stress research; McCubbin's (1983) double A-B-C-X Model and Hill's (1958) original A-B-C-X Model. Some of these theories could be used to help explain why children's leaving home may be experienced as stress by some fathers and not by others. One of these theoretical explanations or models of stress in families is that proposed by Burr (1973); it is based upon the A-B-C-X Model of Hill (1958). In sum, this model posits three important antecedents of crisis: "A" (the stressor or change-producing event in family life); "B" (the family's resources used to cope with or to counter stress); and "C" (the family's subjective definition of the severity of the stressor).

This model holds that the three antecedents (A, B, and C) interact with each other to produce "X" (the amount of family crisis). The second and third antecedents, i.e., "B," the resources for countering stress, and

"C," the family's definition of the stressor event, exist within a family and are modified by a family's structures and values. The stressor event may lie either inside or outside a family. In the two situations of an adolescent's leaving or returning home, the stressor events ("A") are the child's leaving and/or returning home. The father's resources for coping with that event are "B," while "C" is the father's definition of the severity or seriousness of that event. The interaction of these factors should account for "X," the amount of family crisis which is perceived by the father as reflected in his feelings about the event and his satisfactions with his life, his health, and his family relationships. (See Figure 1.)

Our study first tested the impact of the events themselves (the leaving and returning) on the dependent variables. Secondly, we assessed the added impact of the fathers' reported distress, i.e., their definitions of the situation caused by the stressors, and their resources for coping with the stressors upon the dependent variables, e.g., upon the fathers' satisfaction with their family life, upon their personal well-being, upon their feelings about the event, and upon the extent of psychosomatic complaints of the father.

METHODS

The Sample

Data for the present study were collected by mailed questionnaires from a two-state, stratified random sampling of 325 fathers living in Indiana and Michigan. Fathers were included only if there was at least one child living at home and if the mother (their wife) was between 35-64 years of age in 1983, that is, they were a launching family.

These fathers ranged in age from 24 to 76, with an average age of 50.4. On the average they had spent 14 years in formal schooling. They were predominantly white, Protestant, had a median income of $35,000 to $39,999, were employed full-time, and had relatively large families (mean = 3.6 children). Most of these fathers lived in urban or rural/nonfarm areas.

Measures and Descriptive Findings

Independent Measures

The stressor events of children leaving and returning home ("A") as in Figure 1, were measured by asking fathers the following questions: (1) "Have any of your children left home in the last two years?" and (2)

Figure 1.

The A-B-C-X Model of Family Stress Applied to Fathers Whose Young Adult Children Are Leaving and Returning Home

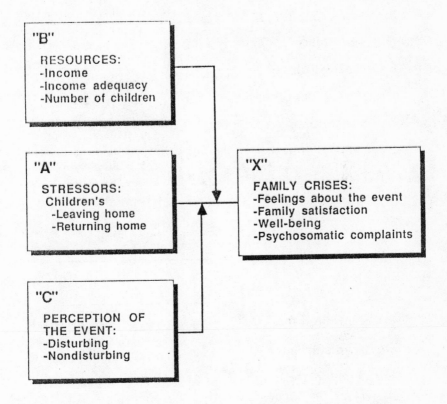

"B"

RESOURCES:
-Income
-Income adequacy
-Number of children

"A"

STRESSORS:
Children's
-Leaving home
-Returning home

"X"

FAMILY CRISES:
-Feelings about the event
-Family satisfaction
-Well-being
-Psychosomatic complaints

"C"

PERCEPTION OF
THE EVENT:
-Disturbing
-Nondisturbing

(Modified and adapted from Burr, 1973: 203.)

"Have any of your children returned home to live with you in the last two years?" Of the 325 fathers, 108 reported having a child leave, while only 36 fathers indicated that a child had returned home again. The perception of the events ("C") was assessed by asking the fathers to indicate how disturbing these events were to them, with possible responses ranging from "not at all" to "extremely disturbing."

As shown in Table 1, relatively few of the fathers (only 12%) reported

Table 1.
Father's Perception of Child's Leaving Home

Response	Frequency	Percent
Not disturbing	31	31
Slightly disturbing	28	28
Moderately disturbing	29	29
Quite disturbing	7	7
Extremely disturbing	5	5
Total	100	100

Father's Perception of Child's Returning Home

Response	Frequency	Percent
Not disturbing	9	36
Slightly disturbing	8	32
Moderately disturbing	3	12
Quite disturbing	5	20
Extremely disturbing	0	0
Total	25	100

that their child's leaving home was either a "quite disturbing" or "extremely disturbing" event.

It is interesting that relatively few of the fathers reported that their child's leaving home was either a "quite disturbing" or "extremely disturbing" event. However, more than twice as many (29%) described the event as "moderately disturbing," while 28% reported the event as "slightly disturbing." On the other hand, nearly a third of the fathers (31%) reported that the child's leaving was "not disturbing."

In light of the fact that very few of these children were the "last child to leave" the home (thereby creating the "empty nest"), we interpret these findings as supporting earlier studies about fathers whose last child had left home. That is, we would suspect that these fathers' reactions would have been even more disturbing, if most or all were *last* children leaving the home.

In contrast, of those fathers experiencing a child's *returning* home, 36% were not disturbed, 44% were slightly or moderately disturbed, and more (25%) were "quite disturbed." Perhaps returning home, especially for some "wrong" reasons, is just as stressful to some fathers as children's leaving home.

Dependent Measures

Overall evaluations of fathers' well-being was assessed by the Index of Well-Being (IWB) developed by Campbell, Converse, and Rogers (1976). The alpha value for the present study was .95. Fathers' satisfaction with family life was assessed by the Kansas Family Life Satisfaction Scale, or KFLSS (Schumm et al., 1986). The alpha value for the current study was .86. Frequency of psychosomatic complaints was assessed using an index of various health conditions which could be exacerbated under conditions of increased stress, e.g., having trouble sleeping, weight problems, headaches, or being depressed. Possible responses ranged from "never" to "almost always."

Finally, the fathers' overall personal feelings about their adult child's leaving home was assessed by asking: "Overall, how do you feel about your adolescent leaving home? Potential responses ranged from "very bad" to "very good." As shown in Table 2, only 9% of the fathers chose the "very bad" response, while 26% indicated "neutral" and 65% reported "good" or "very good" reactions. Measurements on the fathers' feelings about adult children's returning home, unfortunately, were not included in the questionnaire.

Table 2.

Fathers' Overall Feelings About Adolescent Leaving Home

Response	Frequency	Percent
Very bad	1	1
Not good	7	8
Neutral	24	26
Good	32	35
Very good	27	30
Total	91	100

TESTING THE A-B-C-X STRESS MODEL

Our primary interest in this study was to assess whether the events of adult children's leaving and returning home, by themselves, affected the fathers' overall well-being, their family life satisfaction, the frequency of reported psychosomatic complaints and their personal feelings about the child's leaving. Given the A-B-C-X Model's emphasis upon the significance of perceptions, neither leaving nor returning had any statistically significant influence on any of our dependent variables.

Perceptions of the Event

A different picture emerged, however, when we considered how the events were perceived by the fathers. From Pearson product-moment correlations, we ascertained that the fathers' perceptions of their child's leaving home *was* significantly related to: the fathers' feelings about the leaving ($-.42$, $p < .001$); the frequency of psychosomatic complaints (.20, $p < .05$), and subjective well-being ($-.17$, $p < .05$), but not to their satisfaction with family life. (In contrast, none of the family resources ("B"), e.g., family income, age of the father, number of children, etc., nor the perception of distress upon the adult child's returning home was related to any of the dependent variables.)

In summary, our findings generally supported the A-B-C-X Model of family stress which suggests that it is the *perception* of the stressor event which determines if a family event will be experienced as stressful. For those fathers who reported one or more adult children having left home within the last two years the stressor events by themselves were not significantly related to any indicators of fathers' stress. On the other hand, if the child's leaving home was interpreted or defined by fathers as "distressing," then the stressor event was significantly related to many negative outcomes for the fathers but not for their family relationships.

CONCLUSIONS

In summary, this study is only one of a few which has examined the impact that adult children's leaving home has upon fathers and their family relationships. As also found in earlier studies, the majority of our fathers in Indiana and Michigan did not have bad feelings over the leaving home of a child. Forty-one percent, however, did report some negative reactions, even though these children were not the last child to leave the home. We believe that the fathers' negativity would have been even greater, if all of these children were the "last to leave the nest."

After describing the fathers' feelings about the events, we tested the impact of the events (the leaving and returning) themselves upon our sample of 325 fathers in Indiana and Michigan. Then we assessed the impact of the fathers' definition of the situation, i.e., their perceptions as to how disturbing the stressors were, upon the dependent variables. Lastly, we checked the importance of some family resources as potential buffers which might check negative impacts.

Overall, we discovered that the fathers' definition of their situation seemed to be the most critical factor in the model, i.e., it was most correlated with the fathers' negative feelings, the number of their psychosomatic complaints, and their lower sense of well-being. In sum, the measures of fathers' stress were worse where they defined their young adult's leaving as disturbing. These findings generally supported Hill's A-B-C-X Model of family stress in which it is assumed that stressors are experienced as stresses only where family members define stressors as stressful (disturbing).

IMPLICATIONS

The findings of this study have some implications in terms of practice and policy for those family interventionists who work with fathers in counseling and similar situations.

For example, case workers, family counselors, mental health practitioners, and family life educators and the fathers in the middle years with whom they work may not be able to do much about the actual events of their young adults' leaving and returning home. To prevent grown children from leaving home in this society which stresses adequate independence between generations would be dysfunctional for both the child and the parents.

However, since the *perception* of the normative event of leaving home appears to be the crucial issue for fathers in this study, one area of prevention would be for the male client and the family professional to focus on reframing or positively enhancing the father's definition of the situation.

If fathers define their perceptions of situations as real, they are apt to be real in their consequences. For example, if fathers believe that children's leaving home is a negative experience, it probably will be; and in comparison, if they define the leaving home as positive for their marriage, there is a greater chance that the outcome of that event will be positive.

For example, the fathers' voiced perception that "my child is leaving forever and I'll never be able to associate with him/her in the same way ever again" could be reframed with the help of the professional to reflect and develop more positive dimensions. Examples overheard in counseling sessions are as follows: "We'll be able to relate to each other more like friends than just an adult-child and myself (as his/her middle-aged father)" and "my young adult child will be able to grow in many important ways, which may not be as probable, while still living in 'the nest.'"

A second mode of intervention would be to help these fathers better understand the nature of developmental transitions within individuals and families and therefore better prepare for their future relationships through "anticipatory socialization." For example, there are interventions and pamphlets such as "How to Get Ready to be a Father at a Distance" which help maintain family ties, while the adult children are away in college.

The senior year in high school is a "teachable moment," a particularly good time for fathers to discuss their child's upcoming developmental transitions which will be triggered by their leaving home. Such dialogues between fathers and their children could form a valuable part of a family life education curriculum both at school and in the home.

In all, the leaving of children from their home appears to have a significant, negative impact upon a significant minority of fathers. Meaningful intervention with these and similar fathers, however, may be a potent way to prevent stress for the fathers and other family members as well as promoting overall family health.

REFERENCES

Bane, M.J. (1976). *Here to stay: American families in the Twentieth Century*. New York: Basic Books.

Barber, C.E. (1981). Parental responses to the empty-nest transition. *Journal of Home Economics*, 73, 32-33.

Bart, P.B. (1971). Depression in middle-aged women. In V. Gornick & B.K. Moran (Eds.), *Women in sexist society*. New York: Basic Books.

Boss, P. (1987). Family stress: Perception and context. In M.B. Sussman & S. Steinmetz (Eds.), *Handbook on marriage and the family*. New York: Plenum.

Boss, P. & Greenberg, J. (1984). Family boundary ambiguity: A new variable in family stress theory. *Family Process*, 23(4).

Burr, W. (1973). *Theory construction and the sociology of the family*. New York: Wiley & Sons.

Campbell, A., Converse, P.E., & Rogers, W.L. (1976). *The quality of American life*. New York: Russell Sage Foundation.

Clemens, A.W. & Axelson, L.J. (1985). The not-so-empty-nest: The return of the fledgling adult. *Family Relations*, 34, 259-264.

Deutscher, I. (1964). Socialization for post-parental life. In A.M. Rose (Ed.), *Human behavior and social processes*. Boston: Houghton Mifflin.

Edgar, E. & Maas, F. (1984). Adolescent competence, leaving home, and changing family patterns. *Proceedings of the 20th International CFR Seminar on Social Change and Family Policies*. Melbourne, Australia, August.

Glenn, N. (1975). Psychological well-being in the postparental stage: Some evidence from national surveys. *Journal of Marriage and the Family*, 37, 105-110.

Hawkins, E. (1978). Effects of empty nest transition on self-report of psychological and physical well-being. *Journal of Marriage and the Family*, 40(3), 549-556.

Hill, R. (1958). Generic features of families under stress. *Social Casework*, 49, 139-150.

Lewis, R.A. (1985). Men's changing roles in marriage and the family. In R.A. Lewis & M.B. Sussman (Eds.), *Men's changing roles in the family*. New York: The Haworth Press.

Lewis, R.A. (1986). What men get out of marriage and parenthood. In R.A. Lewis & R.E. Salt (Eds.), *Men in families*. Beverly Hills: Sage Publications.

Lewis, R.A. & Roberts, C.L. (1979). Postparental fathers in distress. *Psychiatric Opinion*, Nov./Dec.

Lowenthal, M.F. & Chiriboga, D. (1972). Transition to the empty nest: Crisis, challenge, or relief. *Archives of General Psychiatry, 26*, 8-14.

McCubbin, H.I. & Patterson, J.M. (1983). The family stress process: The double ABCX model of adjustment and adaptation. In H.I. McCubbin, M.B. Sussman, & J.M. Patterson (Eds.), *Social stress and the family*. NY: Haworth Press.

Murray, J. (1973). Family structure in the pre-retirement years. *Social Security Bulletin, 36*, 25-45.

Neugarten, B. (1970). Adaptation and the life cycle. *Journal of Geriatric Psychiatry, 4*, 71-87.

Norem, R. (1984, October). *Opportunities, organization, and outcomes of consortium research: 1,000 families and stress*. Paper presented at the Theory Construction Workshop of the National Council on Family Relations, San Francisco.

Roberts, C.L. & Lewis, R.A. (1981). The empty nest syndrome. In J.G. Howells (Eds.), *Modern perspectives in the psychiatry of middle age*. New York: Brunner/Mazel.

Rose, A.M. (1955). Factors associated with the life-satisfaction of middle-class, middle-aged persons. *Journal of Marriage and the Family, 17*, 15-19.

Saunders, L.E. (1974). Empathy, communication, and the definition of life satisfaction in the postparental period. *Family Perspective, 8*, 21-35.

Schumm, W.R., McCollum, E.E., Bugaighis, M.A., Jurich, A.P., & Bollman, S.R. (1986). Characteristics of the Kansas family life satisfaction scale in a regional sample. *Psychological Reports, 58*(4), 975-980.

Spence, D.L. & Lonner, T.D. (1971). Career set: A resource through transitions and crisis. *International Journal of Aging and Human Development, 9*, 51-65.

Young C. (1983). Leaving home and returning home: A demographic study of young adults in Australia. *Proceedings: Family Formation, Structure, Values, 1*. Australian Family Research Conference, November.

The Oldest Old:
Caregiving or Social Support?

Sally Bould

SUMMARY. Thus far the literature has failed to distinguish adequately between caregiving and social support. Since caregiving is generally conceptualized as burdensome and social support as positive this distinction is especially critical for many of the oldest old who are likely to have a need for help, but the help needed could be delivered in the context of social support. Caregiving implies dependence but social support implies interdependence. Interdependence permits the elder self-determination allowing her/him to remain in charge of her/his own life. A careful examination of the needs and resources of the oldest old indicates that they are at high risk for anxious adult children assuming premature caregiving roles. Intervention strategies should aim to prevent caregiving by encouraging families to strengthen social support networks in general and helping networks in particular. This would promote interdependence. Community supports should be designed to enhance and supplement helping networks.

INTRODUCTION

Among the oldest old, over half (54%) require the help of another person in at least one activity of daily living; almost half (45%) of those who need help are institutionalized.[1] For community-dwelling oldest old, the need for help can range from 24 hour-a-day care to one-hour-a-week help with shopping or bathing. While the presence of a caregiver can be critical in preventing or postponing institutionalization for those who need exten-

This work is built upon the author's research presented in *Eighty-five Plus: The Oldest Old* (Bould, Sanborn and Reif, 1989). The author is most indebted to Beverly Sanborn for their endless discussions on interdependence. Helpful comments were offered by colleagues Joseph Lucca and Anne Mooney. A special thanks is extended to Donald Unger for his careful editorial attention and critical suggestions.

235

sive help, caregiving may not always be necessary or even appropriate for those who need help with a bath or transportation. This paper will focus on distinguishing the need for help from the need for a caregiver. This is an important distinction for all of the elderly, but especially the oldest old.

The line between caregiving and helping has been a grey area. Greater specification of this line is critical in the prevention of premature caregiving. The most important indicator of this line is the identification of who, in fact, takes the responsibility for seeing that the necessary help is provided. If that responsibility is retained by the elder then caregiving is not involved; when the responsibility for providing needed help is assumed by another person, then that person becomes a caregiver. The elder will be dependent on the caregiver's taking responsibility for providing help. Caregiving can thus be understood in terms of dependence. When elders are not dependent they do not have caregivers, although they may need help. Families and elders need to evaluate the role of helper as an alternative to the role of caregiver whenever possible. By only providing help, families could postpone the assumptions of responsibility and dependence implicit in the caregiver-care recipient roles.[2]

The alternative to premature caregiving and dependence for the oldest old, however, is not autonomy and independence. It is rather self-determination within a context of interdependence. Interdependence allows for self-determination because the individual can still negotiate the terms of the help given. The elder remains in charge of his or her own life. The goal is to avoid premature caregiving in cases where all that is necessary is help. An understanding of the importance of this goal was reached as a result of intensive interviews and the analysis of national data for the oldest old which are presented in *Eighty-five Plus* (Bould, Sanborn and Reif, 1989).

Among the elderly, the oldest old are at greatest risk of being thrust prematurely into dependency and the care-recipient role. There are a number of reasons for this. First, those eighty-five and over are often perceived as frail and they may look frail. Second, even the oldest old person in good health often needs help in tasks related to physical agility — such as shopping, lifting and household chores — and visual acuity — such as driving or money management. Third, they are least likely to have incomes sufficient to pay for the help they need. Fourth, at this age they are less likely to have a spouse with whom to develop an interdependent life style. And last, many of their age peers may no longer be available to help (Bould *et al.* 1989). The above factors make the oldest old vulnerable to anxious and well meaning adult children who may rush into the caregiving role and/or precipitate a premature move into the adult child's home rather than explore alternative means of providing help within the context of interdependence.

INTER-GENERATIONAL RELATIONS

The relationship where the risk of premature caregiving is greatest is that between elderly parent and adult child. Critical to understanding this relationship is Mutran and Reitzes' conclusion that "the combination of increased longevity, the absence of well-established role models, and uncertainty about responsibilities and obligations of adult child and elderly parent make the intergenerational family role especially problematic" (1984, p. 117). An increase in the need for help can precipitate a premature move into a caregiving-care receiving relationship. The death of a spouse or living companion can lead anxious adult children or other family members to consider taking over the responsibility for their elderly relative's care.

Mrs. White, at age 79, was at risk of premature caregiving upon the death of Mr. White. Mrs. White was physically exhausted from the heavy caregiving demands of her husband during the last eight years of his life. Furthermore, Mrs. White was legally blind. "Can mother take care of herself?," was a critical question especially for the daughter who lived nearby. After a short stay in her daughter's home, however, Mrs. White recovered her energy and was prepared to resume an interdependent life style engaging friends and family for the help she needed. Fortunately, Mrs. White understands reciprocity and interdependence; she also has a friend next door who can drive. Her approach to needing help is to "keep it even." When Mrs. White and her friend go out for a meal, her friend drives and she pays the tip. With her daughter who lives nearby she has built up an interdependent life style and stored credit over many years, especially in helping her daughter with child care.

Mrs. Brown at 90 is frail, has some pain and moves slowly with a cane. Her eyesight is poor and she needs help with household chores. Although childless, she is part of a close family network. For 10 years she lived with her sister with whom she shared housekeeping chores. When her sister died last year everyone in the family was anticipating that she would become dependent and perhaps even move in with her sister's daughter because she was unable to cope.

But the loss of her sister did not render Mrs. Brown dependent, nor did it make her depressed. Instead of despairing, she preferred to remember all the good times in her sister's long life of 93 years. She forcefully convinced her concerned relatives that she was not going to become dependent. Indeed, she had built up an inter-dependent life-style not only with her sister but with others as well. She has two close friends and two nieces with whom she has built up helping networks. Although she receives more help than she gives, a balance is achieved by her hospitality. Entirely on her own, she provides heavenly meals and amusing company. Guests are not allowed to do anything. Even though she is concerned about "not getting around as good as she used to," her supercoping capacity and interpersonal skills will protect her from becoming dependent. If her health becomes worse, she does have moderate economic resources with which to continue to repay any help needed, even if the food is carry-out and the cleaning up is done by paid help. (Bould *et al.* 1989)

Both Mrs. Brown and Mrs. White had sufficient resources—friends, family and money—so that they could, with help, still manage their own life in spite of changing circumstances. Well-meaning relatives kept to helper roles. The danger is not, as was often hypothesized in the past (Shanas, 1979), that the adult child would abandon their needy parent. Rather, problems are most likely when the adult child is overwhelmed by a sense of responsibility and unnecessarily appropriates the responsibility which should rightfully remain with the elderly parent. Unfortunately this can happen at the prompting of health care professionals who lack adequate training in the care of the very old. When Mrs. White, now 85, arrived in the emergency room confused and fearing a heart attack, the young doctor on duty told Mrs. White's daughter that her mother would have to live with her or be placed in a nursing home. The doctor's failure to adequately diagnose Mrs. White was rectified by her daughter's careful supervision. Mrs. White's confusion was the result of too many tranquilizers which she began taking when her daughter was in the hospital for a hysterectomy. Mrs. White stopped taking the tranquilizers and again resumed her interdependent life style in her own home; caregiving and/or institutionalization was avoided.

Mrs. White has been fortunate in that her daughter sustains a basic belief in her mother's ability to remain in charge of her own life. In similar situations, Cicirelli (1989) has identified certain personality characteristics of adult daughters which could lead to a paternalistic intervention and premature caregiving. This intervention is justified by a belief that the "daughter knows best." Daughters in his sample of 46 mother-daughter pairs were more likely to believe in paternalism when they held negative attitudes about the elderly and had low levels of education. Higher levels of education and more positive attitudes towards the elderly may reduce the risk of paternalism in the future.

Authoritarian personality characteristics of the mother may also precipitate caregiving activities. Elders may demand that their adult children take charge when there is no health problem. The interpersonal relationships could involve a passive elder who now wants to die or an elder who requires that her child takes over the responsibility while continually criticizing what is done. Mrs. Young at 89 is an example of the latter type. She is fully recovered from a hip fracture she suffered two years ago, but she still demands that her son and daughter do everything for her, including shopping, cleaning and cooking. Although they have acceded to their assigned role as caregivers they have refused to get her the amount of nonprescription drugs she wants. For these drugs she walks to the drug store by herself. Clearly she is able to manage physically but not emotionally. She has been unable to negotiate relationships of interdependence with her children, friends or neighbors. She is now dependent on her two children as caregivers.[3]

CAREGIVING OR HELPING

An understanding of self-determination within the context of interdependence can be reached by a careful analysis of the marital dyad. Here, caregiving can be clearly distinguished from helping. If one spouse provides assistance in shopping, transportation and money management, it does not mean that the other spouse is dependent because physical health limits his/her ability to do these tasks. In marital relationships, as in other close relationships, physical disability may require that the division of labor be renegotiated. But dependence would not be assumed if one spouse can no longer do the shopping and now requires the other spouse to perform this task. An examination of married couples where one spouse is disabled should make clear that needing help with a specific task and providing assistance with that task do not, in themselves, make a caregiver-care-receiver dyad. The give and take between the spouses or even a redivision of labor can sustain interdependence.

Married couples are assumed to be interdependent, not independent. The context of interdependence allows for the accommodation of a disabled individual without escalating the relationship to one of dependence and caregiving. It is only when one spouse is no longer able to function in an interdependent arrangement that the other spouse must move into the caregiver role. Therefore, a caregiver is necessary only when the division of labor can not be further renegotiated because the care recipient is too impaired to sustain interdependence.

Spouses who were nominated as caregivers in the National Long Term Care Demonstration Survey[4] provided very high levels of care. The spouse caregivers averaged 2.5 daily assists with getting out of a bed or chair and 2.2 daily assists with toileting. Sixty percent of the spouses provided this level of help (Christianson and Stephens, 1986). This type of help suggests that the care-recipient is dependent upon the caregiver in a relationship which is very different from marital interdependence. It would appear that for married couples the distinction between interdependence and dependence is clear. When one becomes a caregiver the other is unavoidably dependent.

Another situation in which the identification of a "caregiver" is likely to reflect a dependent situation is when the care-recipient lives in the home of the non-spouse caregiver. An elder's move into a daughter's home is most likely prompted by a high level of physical and/or mental disability. Such a change in living arrangements usually reflects the caregiver-care recipient relationship. It is noteworthy that in the National Long Term Care Demonstration Survey persons nominated as non-spouse caregivers provided a level of care equivalent to spouse caregivers *only* when the care-recipient lived with the caregiver.[5]

The situation of the identified "caregivers" who did not live with the care-recipient was very different from that of the spouse or live-in caregivers. These caregivers provided only one fifth of the hours of other caregivers (spouses or live-in caregivers) in personal care and medical care. The average non-live-in "caregiver" did not provide daily help with getting out of a chair or bed or toileting (Christianson and Stephens, 1986). It is the contention of this paper that many of these situations where the caregiver does not live with the care-recipient could more accurately be described in terms of social support and helping networks. In others, the dependence implicit in the care-recipient's role could be avoided by renegotiating the terms of reciprocity so that the elder has an opportunity to provide assistance in return.

Of course, in the continuum of needing help, there is a point at which the adult child must assume responsibility for their disabled elderly parent if the parent is to remain in the community. The elder, then, becomes dependent due to "a loss of self-determination that results from requiring the help of others but being unable to negotiate the terms of the help received" (Bould *et al.* 1989, p. 4). Indeed most of the persons targeted as care recipients in the National Long Term Care Demonstration Survey exhibit a high level of need which would inevitably result in their dependence on a caregiver who assumes responsibility for their care. But others might be helped by a combination of social support and formal services. For example, an elder meeting the criterion for inclusion in this study could require help with taking a bath, help with shopping and household chores. With adequate community resources—a nurse's aid to give the bath—and economic resources to hire domestic help to clean the house, all the adult child would need to do is provide help with shopping. This level of assistance could be repaid by the elder reciprocating in areas where she is capable—for example taking telephone messages for the adult child through the mechanism of call forwarding. The elders in this sample represent moderate to high levels of need—"at least two categories of service affected by functional disabilities or impairments for six months" (Applebaum 1988, p. 54). Yet, for some of the 43% of the sample where the care-recipient does not live with the designated "caregiver," a caregiver-care-recipient relationship may not be necessary. Helping networks could take care of the elders' needs in the context of interdependence. If this possibility exists with the moderate level of need in this survey, then lower levels of need, such as help with transportation only, should be approached even more cautiously.

Premature caregiving and dependence can also be due to some combination of limited economic resources, a physical impairment, and the lack of suitable and affordable housing. These factors can result in the elder becoming dependent on the adult child for a place to live. Self-determination is usually lost because the elder can no longer negotiate the terms of the help received and must accept the household space which the adult child or other relative offers. The elder is beholden to the adult child in ways which can not be repaid; the possibility of exchange is lost. One quarter of the oldest old in the community live in the household of an adult child or other relative (Bould *et al.* 1989, p. 13).

While living arrangements are often indicative of dependence this is not always the case. The situation where the adult child moves into the parent's household may be one of interdependence in that the elder is "providing a home" for the adult child (Noelker and Ehrlich, 1989). Among the oldest old 9.4% live in their own household with a relative (Bould *et al.* 1989, p. 36). It is important, therefore, not to assume dependence based on living arrangements. Even when the elder lives in the adult child's home, it is necessary to examine the relationship between the elder and the helper/householder in order to see if the relationship could be characterized as one of interdependence, as in the case of Mrs. Davis.

> Mrs. Davis, at 84, does not worry about needing more help in the future. "I know my family will care for me like they always have," she says. She now needs help with transportation and heavy housework and also needs to be reminded to take her medication for high blood pressure. These things are easy for her daughter and granddaughters to provide, since they have shared a household for 24 years. During that time, Mrs. Davis has taken the major responsibility for household management and child care while her daughter worked. She still does light housework, gardening, sewing, and shopping as long as transportation is provided. She feels secure and does not fear requiring more help in the future. (Bould *et al.* 1989, pp. 88-89)

THE CAREGIVING LITERATURE

The literature currently fails to provide an adequate or even consistent definition of the concept of caregiving (Walker and Pratt, 1989). Raveis, Siegel and Sudit (1988-89, p. 51) in their review of caregiving studies highlight the problems of definition which include self-report and nomination by the care-recipient as well as the establishment of empirical criteria. In a recent analysis of parents and adult children (Blum, Kelly and Gatz, 1989) one third of the adult children who did not see themselves as caregivers were classified as caregivers by the empirical criteria. These adult children would probably be more accurately described as providing social support (i.e., visiting and helping with shopping) for their elderly parent in poor health. In this same sample one third of the adult children called themselves caregivers when they did not meet the empirical criteria; this group may contain premature caregivers. In a review of caregiving studies from 1978 to 1988, Walker and Pratt (1989) find that in 61.3% of the studies the care recipient was demented or significantly disabled. This leaves almost 40% where the relationship might be better understood in terms of social support rather than caregiving.[6]

The problem with most caregiving studies of elders with a range of physical and mental limitations is that there is little or no examination of the dyadic relationship (Kahana and Young, 1990). Studies often examine only what the care recipient gets but not what he/she gives or has given. Also, data are often presented in such a way that providing housing is not taken into account, yet living arrangements may be a critical dimension of the reciprocity or dependency established (Montgomery, Kosloski, and Borgatta, 1988-89). A divorced daughter who moves into her mother's home in order to provide more assistance may feel that reciprocity and interdependency is sustained. An elderly parent's move into an adult child's home usually, but not always indicates dependency. In the study by Blum *et al.* (1989) discussed above, when the elderly parent lived in the child's home the child always saw him/herself as a caregiver.

The recent work on caregivers who are employed (Scharlach and Boyd, 1989) illustrates the problem of the broad use of the term caregiver. Here, a caregiver was one who provided special assistance to a person age 60 and over. The most common forms of assistance were companionship (58%) and transportation (56%). Only 8% provided personal care with activities of daily living such as bathing, toileting and dressing (p. 384). While the study showed that this involvement could interfere with work it also suggests that much of the assistance given could be better conceptualized as social support. As is common in such studies, no questions were asked concerning the symmetry of the relationship or forms of possible reciprocity.

AN ALTERNATIVE TO PREMATURE CAREGIVING

Interdependence is the alternative to premature caregiving for the elder who requires help with activities of daily living. Help can be exchanged in such a way that the elder can sustain reciprocal give and take. This is particularly important for the oldest old who are most likely to need help but are still able to provide assistance in return. Engaging in reciprocity can provide the elders with the help required while leaving them in charge of their own life. The elder's self-determination is thereby preserved, dependence and caregiving are avoided.[7]

Interdependence can be understood under a conceptualization of social support, both given *and* received. In contrast to the concept of caregiving, social support consists "of interpersonal transactions that express positive affect, affirmation, and aid" (Kahn, Wethington and Ingersoll-Dayton, 1987, p. 146). In fact, much of what is now labeled "caregiving" for the elderly, could be more appropriately termed social support. For example, the emotional and financial support provided by parents to their daughter in her thirties is appropriately labeled social support but the same flow of emotional and financial support to a parent in their eighties is often termed "caregiving."

Within the context of a life course perspective and the Sociology of Age (Riley, Foner and Waring, 1988) any definition of social support or caregiving would be more appropriate if it were applicable across all ages.

Activities which constitute caregiving for middle aged adults could be the same as those for the elderly. A flow of support from parent to an adult child can be similar to a flow of support from the adult child to the parent. To assume that social support is "caregiving" when the recipient is an elderly parent but social support when the recipient is an adult child is to overlook the fact that the elderly parent may be only in need of social support and the adult child may in fact, be in need of caregiving. A personal or health crisis could leave the adult child unable to manage his/her own affairs and require that the elderly parent step in and take over responsibility.

In contrast to younger ages, the elderly are most frequently in need of social support in the form of aid defined as "instrumental or assisting transactions in which information, money or direct effort are provided to another person" (Kahn *et al.* 1987, p. 146). Requiring assistance with money management or help with transportation does not mean, however, that the elder can not reciprocate in return. In fact, for financial support the net flow of support is consistently from the elderly parent to the adult child throughout the life course (Cheal, 1983). It is hypothesized here, however, that in terms of reciprocity, aid must be balanced by aid; other forms of social support such as emotional support, can not fully reciprocate for help with transportation. Therefore, while elders can and do provide emotional support to their adult children, they also need opportunities to provide social support in terms of aid, since they are very likely to need aid in return.

As Kahn *et al.* (1987) point out, the degree of reciprocity and symmetry is an important element in understanding a relationship involving social support. For the elderly who need help, the importance of reciprocity and symmetry requires the analysis of aid *given* and *received*. In both the concepts of social support and caregiving, however, the analysis is often unidirectional. Social support has most often been the study of the respondent's self-report of *receiving* aid, while caregiving is often studied in terms of how much aid the caregiver *provides*. In order to adequately distinguish social support from caregiving it is necessary to examine the extent to which help is given and received within the dyad. Furthermore, as Wellman and Hall's (1986) analysis suggests, it is important to go beyond the dyad to the network itself which is more than the sum of individual dyads. Where aid is a critical element of social support these networks will be termed helping networks.

In the case of parents and children, moreover, it is not only the current reciprocity in terms of help given and received, but also the past history. The dyad is most likely to operate on the basis of a deferred exchange strategy (Sahlins, 1965). That is, parents have opportunities to "store credits" while they are in good health. As in the case of Mrs. Davis, noted above, her long history of helping her daughter's family will sustain reciprocity during the years ahead when her health may limit her ability to give aid. Clearly her extensive help when the grandchildren were young means that her current need for assistance with shopping and taking medication can be acknowledged in terms of a deferred exchange strategy. This sustains reciprocity and interdependence in spite of the fact that Mrs. Davis lives in her daughter's home. Even within the context of parent-child relationships, however, immediate repayment, or even token repayment may be very important as in the case of Mrs. Evans. Mrs. Evans, an elderly women in her 80's, reciprocates for help with transportation by giving gifts and invitations to lunch. She also pays her grandson for his help with the yard work. Just recently he refused to accept her money; she became very angry and told him, "I'm not a charity case. I can pay people for their help" (Bould et al. 1989, p. 92). Having the extra cash to pay for help and to give gifts enhances even a disabled elder's ability to reciprocate. For this reason the ability to give gifts may be especially important for the oldest old (Tobis et al., 1986).

A careful examination of the relationship between the elder and the helper is necessary in order to ascertain if the elder is in fact dependent on the helper as a caregiver. If the elder has retained self-determination and responsibility, the relationship would better be analyzed in terms of social support. This is important not only conceptually but also because social support is commonly conceptualized as positive (Berkman, 1989); caregiving is viewed as involving negative "burden" characteristics for both the caregiver and care-recipient (Zarit, 1989; Kahana and Young, 1990). Caregiving is essentially different from that of social support in that the care-recipient is dependent on the caregiver; she is no longer involved in an interdependent network of give and take. The caregiver, furthermore, must take on the responsibility of providing for the needs of the care recipient. This definition of caregiving is equally applicable to the parent caring for minor children and disabled adult children as well as the adult child caring for a disabled elderly parent.

AVOIDING DEPENDENCE

The concepts of caregiving and dependence may be avoided if the situation is handled within the framework of social support in general, and helping networks in particular. The most common example would be the dyad of an elderly mother and her daughter who do not live together. Prior to the onset of disability in the elderly parent, the relationship may have been one of independence, or may have involved reciprocal emotional support. A sudden need for help with transportation may make the elderly parent feel herself to be a burden and the daughter may slip into the role of caregiver. But this escalation may be unnecessary as well as undesirable.

Alternative solutions such as identifying other transportation resources should be explored, thereby allowing the new need to be met outside of the relationship. If this is not possible then the goal should be to restructure the relationship so that both parties are now contributing direct effort to aid the other. This means that the two parties need to seek out ways in which the elderly mother can reciprocate within the constraints of her restrictions. This approach would increase the interdependence of the pair rather than catapulting the elderly person into a dependent relationship. Thus, caregiving can be postponed and self-determination preserved.

A strong note of caution, however, is in order. If the prior relationship has not been one of closeness between the elder and the adult child, the evolution of reciprocal helping between the pair may be a difficult one. Feelings of closeness are related to helping the elderly parent; Mutran and Reitzes (1984) hypothesize that it is the closeness which enables help to be given without a sense of dependency developing. Without closeness it may be difficult to develop interdependence when the elder begins to need assistance. In the situation of the independent elder without family closeness, community services such as specialized transportation would be necessary to sustain independence and postpone the need for family assistance.

Community services can be critical in preserving interdependence as well as independence. The availability of extensive community health and hospital services enables elderly persons to sustain high rates of living alone (Krivo and Muchler, 1989). Similarly, suitable housing is critical in sustaining interdependence (Schwenger, 1989). Housing and community services can postpone or prevent dependency and, thus, caregiving. This does not mean that families do not help, but rather that their help, when necessary, can be integrated in a social support helping network rather than a caregiving network. For instance, the availability of extensive health and social services provided in the National Long-Term Care Demonstration did not result in a lessening of family effort (Christianson, 1988). What is needed is a partnership approach (Cantor, 1989).

Some types of assistance are better delivered by the formal service system rather than nonspouse helpers. Of particular note here is help with taking a bath. For adult children, helping their parent bathe can be an activity that unnecessarily propels the dyad into a caregiver/care-recipient relationship. The level of implied intimacy/dependence is often too great to be handled within the context of interdependent reciprocity. Here, the availability of a public health nurse's aid to help with the bath can be essential in order to sustain independence or interdependence and avoid dependence.

If the relationship had already been one where high levels of aid were exchanged, then it will be easier to rearrange such assistance to accommodate a specific need for assistance, as well as the specific abilities of the elder. The prior interdependent relationship on the basis of choice would have prepared the way for an interdependent relationship on the basis of necessity. While there may be certain kinds of assistance, such as giving a bath, which may risk straining the interdependent relationship, many tasks can be rearranged in order to meet the norms of reciprocity.

The avoidance of dependence and the postponement of caregiving for each dyad requires a specific analysis of each case: (a) what is possible given the prior relationship; (b) other potential helpers; (c) the disability of the elder; (d) the availability of community social services; and (e) the financial resources of the elder. The last item, the financial resources of the elder, is clearly a critical element in the package since elderly parents with greater financial resources receive less help from their children (Mutran and Reitzes, 1984) presumably because they can purchase help. Nevertheless, those most in need of help—the oldest old—are least likely to have adequate economic resources.

Of course there are a number of situations in which the disability itself creates a level of dependence in spite of the prior relationship or alternative resources. Thus, in the case of Alzheimer's disease, a caregiver is required. The key factor here is that the Alzheimer's victim, even with community services and sufficient financial resources, can not manage his or her own care. The responsibility for managing must be assumed by a caregiver who, in nearly all cases, lives with the patient. A person with Alzheimer's but without a live-in family caregiver will soon end up institutionalized. With Alzheimer's the relationship is unambiguously one of caregiver and care-recipient. Furthermore the dyad is critical and merits the emphasis given. A large caregiving network is rarely involved. Unlike care for lucid elders, care for the Alzheimer's victim is usually restricted to household members (Birkel and Jones, 1989).

CONCLUSION

The analysis of the situation of the elderly needing help, and the practice of helping elderly in need should be carried out within a perspective of interdependence and social support rather than the dominant perspective of caregiving and dependence. Caregiving for dependent elders is often necessary, but only a minority of the oldest old—that group of elderly most in need of help—requires this level of care. With increasing numbers of oldest old who are likely to need help, it is important to reorient research and practice in ways that promote an understanding of the relationship in terms of interpersonal interaction and reciprocity rather than the unilateral provision of aid and assistance. In the context of interdependence the elder can be viewed as an actor who has the capacity for self-determination in negotiating the terms of any help needed as long as potential helping networks are available. Social support with an emphasis on balancing reciprocal helping relationships within the network should be the dominant mode of analysis even for the oldest old. Caregiving should be reserved for when the physical and/or mental disabilities of the elders prevent them from taking responsibility for managing their own care. This is the point at which responsibility for their care must be assumed by a family member or an institution.

Research and practice in analyzing the help given or needed by the elderly should be informed by the perspective of social supports which emphasizes symmetry and reciprocity. Needing help should not mean unavoidable dependence. Alternative ways of providing help, both through the formal system and through family and friends should be explored. Perhaps what is required is a reevaluation of our culture's emphasis on independence. Noting that the days of the log cabin are long gone, Erikson, Erikson and Kivnick (1986) suggest that interdependence is not only adaptive for old age, but may be necessary for survival itself. Their advise is "trust in interdependence. Give and accept help when it is needed . . . When frailty takes over, dependence is appropriate and one has no choice but to trust in the compassion of others . . . " (p. 333). Their advise is supported by recent research on elderly widows (O'Bryant, 1989) which found that, contrary to the original hypothesis, being self-sufficient was related neither to happiness nor to life satisfaction. With increasing numbers of elderly who are at risk of needing help, alternatives to self sufficiency which preserve self-determination need to be explored both in the public and private spheres.

NOTES

1. Activities of daily living include shopping, performing household chores, preparing meals, managing money, walking, going outside, bathing, dressing, using the toilet, getting in or out of a bed or chair, and eating. See table 3.1 Bould *et al.* (1989, p. 54).

2. When the elder is placed in the nursing home the primary responsibility for

providing the help needed is transferred from the caregiver to the nursing home. This transforms the caregiving role; it also produces burdens and stresses (Brody, Dempsey and Pruchno, 1989).

3. This pattern has been identified by Joseph Lucca of the University of Delaware, among some of his elderly patients needing physical therapy. Dr. Lucca arranged for the interview with Mrs. Young's daughter. This situation may also be the result of traditional ethnic expectations with regard to the roles of adult children and widowed mothers. See also Kahana and Young (1990).

4. The caregiver data were collected from family members named by elder members of a special subsample. Almost 2000 primary caregivers were interviewed between November 1982-May 1983. This is part of the larger Channeling Demonstration involving experimental and control groups at 10 sites around the country. See Christianson and Stephens 1986, pp. 1-3.

5. Non-spouse live-in caregivers, like spouse caregivers, provided help with getting out of a chair or bed an average of 2.5 times a day and help with toileting an average of 2.2 times a day, and provided 3.0 hours a day in medical and personal care compared with 3.1 hours for spouses (Christianson and Stephens, 1986).

6. Walker and Pratt (1989) review 10 years of articles published in the Gerontologist and the Journal of Gerontology. What was underrepresented in the literature is the lesser level of needs which might be better characterized under "social support."

7. There has been an attempt to coin the term "consultative autonomy" to describe a situation which approximates my use of "self-determination in the context of interdependence" (See Cicirelli, 1989; and Pratt, Jones, Shin and Walker, 1989).

8. There is a great variability in the availability of community resources in the United States. Some communities provide specialized transportation, visiting nurses, and case management; other communities provide no services except those covered by nationwide Medicare program (Bould *et al.* 1989, p. 155ff).

REFERENCES

Applebaum, R.A. (1988). The evaluation of the National Long Term Care Demonstration: 3 Recruitment and characteristics of channeling clients. *Health Service Research, 23*(1), 51-66.

Berkman, L. (1989, October). *Psycho-social influences and aging in E.P.E.S.E. studies.* Paper presented at a conference on Aging, Health Behaviors, and Health Outcomes at the Pennsylvania State University Gerontology Center; University Park, PA.

Birkel, R. C. & Jones, C. J. (1989). A comparison of the caregiving networks of dependent elderly individuals who are lucid and those who are demented. *The Gerontologist, 29*(1), 114-119.

Blum, M., Kelly, M., and Gatz, M. (1989, November). *Empirically defined caregivers versus self-defined caregivers for aging parents*. Paper presented at the annual meeting of the Gerontological Society of America, Minneapolis.

Bould, S., Sanborn, B. and Reif, L. (1989). *Eighty-Five Plus: The Oldest Old*. Belmont, CA: Wadsworth Publishing Co.

Brody, E., Dempsey, N., and Pruchno, R. (1989, November). *Sons and daughters of institutionalized aged: mental health effects*. Paper presented at the annual meeting of the Gerontological Society of America, Minneapolis.

Cantor, M. H. (1989). Social Care: Family and community support systems. *ANNALS*, 503 (May): 99-112.

Cheal, D.J. (1983). Intergenerational family transfers. *Journal of Marriage and the Family*, (November); 805-812.

Christianson, J. B. (1988). "The evaluation of the National Long Term Care Demonstration: 6. The effect of channeling on informal caregiving." *Health Services Research*, 23(1), 99-117.

Christianson, J.B. and Stephens, S.A. (1986). *Informal Care to the Impaired Elderly: Report of the National Long Term Care Demonstration Survey of Informal Caregivers*. Princeton, New Jersey: Mathematica Policy Research, Inc.

Cicirelli, V. (1989, November). *Relationship of personality characteristics to belief in paternalism in parent caregiving situations*. Paper presented at the annual meeting of the Gerontological Society of America, Minneapolis.

Erikson, E.H., Erikson, J.M. & Kivnick, H. (1986). *Vital Involvement in Old Age*. New York: W.W. Norton.

Kahana, E. & Young, R. (1990). Clarifying the caregiver paradigm: Challenges for the future. In D.E. Biegel and A. Blum (Eds.) *Aging and Caregiving*, forthcoming. Newbury Park, CA: Sage Publications.

Kahn, R.L., Wethington, E., and Ingersoll-Dayton, B. (1987). Social support and social networks. In R.P. Abeles, (Ed.) *Life-Span Perspectives and Social Psychology*; pp. 139-165. Hillsdale, New Jersey: Lawrence Erlbaum Assocs.

Krivo, L. and Mutchler, J.E. (1989). Elderly persons living alone: The effect of community context on living arrangements. *Journal of Gerontology: Social Sciences*, 44(2), S54-S62.

Montgomery, R.J.V., Kosloski, K. and Borgatta, E. (1988-89). The influences of cognitive impairment on service use and caregiver response. *The Journal of Applied Social Sciences*, 13(1), 142-169.

Mutran, E. and Reitzes, D.C. (1984). Intergenerational support activities and well-being among the elderly. *American Sociological Review*, 49, 117-130.

Noelker, L. S. and Ehrlich, P. (1989, November). *Forming shared households for caregiving*. Paper presented at the annual meeting of the Gerontological Society of America, Minneapolis.

O'Bryant, S.L. (1989, June). *Older widows and independent lifestyles*. Paper Presented at the XIV Meeting of the World Congress of Gerontology. Acapulco, Mexico.

Pratt, C.C., Jones, L.L., Shin, H. and Walker, A.J. (1989). Autonomy and decision making between single older women and their caregiving daughters. *The Gerontologist,* 29(6), 792-797.

Raveis, V. H., Siegel, K. and Sudit, M. (1988-89). Psychological impact of caregiving on the careprovider. *The Journal of Applied Social Sciences, 13*(1), 40-79.

Riley, M.W., Foner, A. and Waring J. (1988). Sociology of age. In N.J. Smelser, (Ed.) *Handbook of Sociology*; pp. 243-290. Newbury Park, CA: Sage Publications.

Sahlins, M.D. (1965). On the sociology of primitive exchange. In M. Banton (Ed.) *The Relevance of Models for Social Anthropology*, pp. 139-227. London: Travistock.

Scharlach, A.E. and Boyd, S.L. (1989). Caregiving and employment: Results of an employee survey. *The Gerontologist, 29*(3), 382-387.

Schwenger, C.W. (1989, June). *Housing and institutionalization of the elderly.* Paper presented at the XIV meeting of the World Congress of Gerontology, Acapulco, Mexico.

Shanas, E. (1979). Social myth as hypothesis: The case of the family relation of old people. *The Gerontologist, 19*(1), 3-9.

Thuras, P.D. (1989, November). *Relationship quality and care expectation: Older mothers and their daughters.* Paper presented at the annual meeting of the Gerontological Society of America, Minneapolis.

Tobis, J.S., Reinsch, S., Rubel, A., Ashurst, J., Friis, R., and Fallavollita, B. (1986, November). *A profile of the robust very old.* Paper presented at the annual meeting of the Gerontological Society of America, Chicago.

Walker, A.J. and Pratt, C.C. (1989, November). *Sampling bias in family caregiving studies: A research note.* Paper presented at the annual meeting of the Gerontological Society of America, Minneapolis.

Wellman, B. and Hall, A. (1986). Social networks and social support: Implications for later life. In V.W. Marshall (Ed.), *Later Life: The Social Psychology of Aging*, pp. 191-231. Beverly Hills, CA: Sage Publications.

Zarit, S.H. (1989). Do we need another "stress and caregiving" study? *The Gerontologist, 29*(2), 147-148.